THE WINONA LETTERS
BOOK THREE

RICHARD N. WILLIAMSON

THE WINONA LETTERS • BOOK THREE
IN THE *LETTERS FROM THE RECTOR* SERIES

THE COLLECTED WORKS ✦ VOLUME IV

ISBN (paper) 9781940306124
ISBN (Kindle) 9781940306131
ISBN (ePub) 9781940306148
ISBN (PDF) 9781940306155

For more information,
or for additional titles, contact:

Marcel Editions
An Imprint of the St. Marcel Initiative
www.stmarcelinitiative.com
c/o BRN Associates, Inc.
9051 Watson Rd., Suite 279
St. Louis, MO 63126
(855) 289-9226

Marcel
EDITIONS
A St MARCEL INITIATIVE IMPRINT
Jesu Christo Regi æterno milito
—MARCELLUS CENTURIO, A.D. 298

St. Louis, Missouri ❧ 2019

CONTENTS

Can Cardinal Ratzinger be Trusted?

C AN CARDINAL RATZINGER be trusted? Conservative Catholics tend to think so. "Nice" Traditional Catholics wish to think so. "Nasty" Traditionalists think not. Who is right?

The question arose in agonising form in 1988 when Archbishop Lefebvre was negotiating, principally with the Cardinal, to obtain bishops for Catholic Tradition. Conservatives blamed him then (and still do) for not, finally, trusting Rome. Ten years later Conservatives found themselves facing the same question when the Cardinal appealed to them to trust Rome in the matter of the liturgy. Do they now follow through on their own policy of trust?

The occasion was the Conservative Catholics' gathering in Rome last October to celebrate the 10th anniversary of the Pope's Motu Proprio *Ecclesia Dei* of July 1988, condemning Archbishop Lefebvre but apparently favoring the pre-Vatican II liturgy. Here is a fair summary of the speech, quoted in full in the December issue of *Inside the Vatican*, in which the Cardinal appealed for the Conservatives' trust:

Richard N. Williamson

- Despite the positive fruits of *"Ecclesia Dei,"* said the Cardinal, there is amongst Conciliar Catholics much distrust of you Conservative (*Ecclesia Dei*) Catholics, because of your attachment to the old liturgy. This need not be, if only both sides will abide by the letter (as opposed to the so-called "spirit") of the Second Vatican Council.

- For on the one hand, the Cardinal went on, the text of the Council's Constitution on the Liturgy does not promote the wild excesses of the so-called "creative" liturgists who, by pushing the text too far in one direction only, have in the name of community worship virtually emptied out the priesthood, sacrifice, all mystery and sacredness. Quite to the contrary that text never forbade the Tridentine Mass, it does not mention Mass facing the people, it encourages Latin. In fact when a celebration of the New Mass is faithful to Pope Paul VI's Missal, it is closer to the Old Mass than it is to any of the wild new liturgies.

- On the other hand the same text, following the admirable Liturgical Movement which led up to the Council's Constitution, does call for more active participation of the people in the liturgy, as opposed to the excessively private and individual following of Mass which had become the norm for Mass-goers before the Council.

- Therefore, concluded the Cardinal, a new Liturgical Movement to restore a truly liturgical unity-in-diversity of Conciliarists and Conservatives is not something that you Conservatives must distrust. Quote: "Dear friends, I would like to encourage you not to lose patience – to keep trusting . . . "

Thus Cardinal Ratzinger seems to be suggesting that Rome is pondering another liturgical reform which would give us a Mass neither wildly new nor completely old, and he seems to be asking lovers of the old liturgy to wait patiently for this reform of the reform, and to trust Rome meanwhile. Now the Cardinal seems to be a "nice" man, and few Cardinals in Rome say so many favorable things about the old liturgy as he does. Yet can Rome, even as represented by him, be trusted in the matter of the liturgy?

Alas, the answer must be no. Why?

Because while the Cardinal's heart may be open to the Tridentine Mass, his mind is blocked, and in a man of his caliber, the mind rules the heart. His sympathy with the old Mass is relatively superficial, his opposition to it is profound. All this is clear to see in the autobiographical memoirs for the first 50 years of his life, 1927–1957, which he published two years ago in a little book called *Milestones.* The matter is of interest to all Catholics, because it shows how crippled is even the seeming best of today's Romans when it comes to defending the Faith. Despite their apparent benevolence they cannot defend what they no longer understand.

Josef Ratzinger was born of humble but devout parents in 1927 in a deeply Catholic part of the world, South Germany, close to the Austrian frontier. Youngest of three children in a tranquil home, he grew up with a natural love of God, Church, family and homeland which never left him. He describes how he was also indelibly marked in childhood by the Traditional (then normal) Catholic liturgy, because the great Church ceremonies of the different seasons of the year impressed deep in his soul the sense of the Catholic mysteries.

Here is why the Cardinal has so little sympathy for the so-called "spirit of Vatican II" in the name of which the Church's liturgy has been turned into a wasteland.

Towards the end of *Milestones* are a few pages severely condemning the Novus Ordo Missal of 1969 as a "self-made," or artificial, liturgy, pages which Conservative Catholics love to quote and which many a Traditional Catholic could not have written better. No wonder the Cardinal seemed to receive Conservatives kindly in Rome last October! No wonder he might tempt Traditionalists out of their Traditional fortress!

Then where is the Cardinal's problem? Back to *Milestones*. After his happy childhood overshadowed by the rise of Nazism and the wartime years marked by its collapse, in 1945 he entered near Munich the reconstituted Major Seminary to begin his studies for the priesthood, where he says (p.42), "We wanted not only to do theology in the narrower sense, but to listen to the voices of man today" – here for the Catholic reader a red light begins to wink! For nobody may mind any brave young man wishing to grapple with horrors which have just nearly engulfed his world – but what Catholic can conceive of his Church's eternal theology as being somehow too narrow to embrace modern man?

So the young Ratzinger plunges with enthusiasm into the study of modern philosophers. "By contrast, I had difficulties in penetrating the thought of Thomas Aquinas, whose crystal-clear logic seemed to me too closed in on itself, too impersonal and ready-made." For, says Ratzinger, he and his fellow seminarians were presented with "a rigid neo-scholastic Thomism that was simply too far afield from my own questions . . . We, being young, were questioners above all." (p.44)

Now it is all very well pleading youth, but since when was the point of questions anything other than to find answers? Is searching better than finding? That is the modern mentality. Either Ratzinger's teachers did not appreciate the Catholic truth of St. Thomas, or Ratzinger did not appreciate his teachers. Whichever it be or both, this young philosophy student is missing out on truth. His brilliant mind is pursuing something else – its own satisfaction upon its own (modern) terms? What will he do when he comes to theology? The crucial Chapter VI tells.

To begin theological studies in 1947, he asks to go not to the diocesan seminary, but instead to the Munich University Theological Faculty "to become more fully familiar with the intellectual debates of our time" (p.47), so as to become later a professional theologian. But, again, are modern (university) questions really more valuable than the Church's (seminary) answers? Does this student have a sense of truth? The star teacher at the Faculty, whose "liberalism restricted by dogma" deeply appealed by its modern-ancient balance to the young Ratzinger (p.52), was a certain Professor Maier, whose "liberal-historical method" in approaching Scripture "opened up dimensions of the text that were no longer perceived by the all-too-predetermined dogmatic reading" (p.52)! In other words, history's relativising had more to give to our young theologian than dogma's absolutes? His mind is at sea!

For he is thinking with the mind not of the Catholic Church but of these humanly brilliant German thinkers, about whom he says, "German arrogance perhaps also contributed a little to our belief that we knew what was what better than 'those down there' (i.e., in Rome)" (p.58). Ratzinger and his teachers would submit to a decision of Rome, but basically they felt themselves superior. Chapter VI of *Milestones* abounds in quotations to illustrate the downfall of our pious young Bavarian – intellectual pride.

The pious heart is still there, but it is completely outweighed and outgunned for Ratzinger by the dazzling intellectualism of Germany's top modernists, all of whom he will meet and befriend when, after being ordained priest in 1951, he embarks in 1952 upon the academic career he has hoped for. For the next 25 years he is professing theology in Germany in one prestigious seminary or university after another. Let us take a look at how his mind is now working as he sets out to teach (p. 108, 109).

In 1953, to obtain his "Habilitation," or final qualification to profess theology, he describes how he prepared a thesis on the great medieval Doctor, St. Bonaventure. Here is Ratzinger's argument, in which he says he still believes (comments in brackets):

The word "revelation" can mean either the act of revealing or the content revealed [true]. Whereas we usually use the word to mean the content revealed [true], Bonaventure uses it to mean the act of revealing [maybe]. Therefore "revelation" means the act of revealing ["Therefore"? Who made Bonaventure dictator of meanings?]. But there is no act of revealing without someone to reveal to [true, but wait for it . . .] . Therefore Church Revelation [act or content??] always includes as an essential element the Church being revealed to. Therefore Revelation, Scripture and Tradition [now Ratzinger has definitely slidden back from act to content!] are all incomplete without the Church or persons being revealed to. Therefore whatever of religion comes to us from God must be no ready-made and finalized product or content such as Catholicism was always supposed to be, but it must incorporate the input of us modern men. In brief, in the old days God told men what was in the Catholic religion, but that religion fell dead. Now man tells God what is in the Catholic religion, and religion is again living!

From 1953 to 1988 to 1998 we can see that Cardinal Ratzinger's thinking has not changed. In 1988, in the name of "living Tradition," he did his honest best to stop Archbishop Lefebvre from going into "schism" with his "dead Tradition." In 1998 he did his honest best to keep Conservative Catholics loyal to Rome by trust in a new liturgical reform movement which will of course actively involve living modern man, because without that living input the liturgy, like Revelation and Tradition, will be dead. But the excessively private Tridentine Mass is too fixed and ready-made to allow for any such input. Therefore the Cardinal's Rome can be trusted not to preserve the Tridentine Mass.

Yet all the while the Cardinal in his heart genuinely appreciates the incomparable sacredness and mystery of the old liturgy (pp. 18–20, 146–149). Alas, that liturgy never took a hold of his head, so it cannot govern his thinking or action. Unless or until he changes his thinking, i.e., doctrine, the Tridentine Mass is bound to remain for him a sentimental sideline. In other words, prior to the Council Josef Ratzinger was a ring leader of Fiftiesists or Bing Crosby Catholics. Maybe his heart was "dreaming of a white Christmas," but his head was ready filled with the poison of man-centered Vatican II.

Your Eminence, if ideas did not matter, you might be a good Catholic, but since the virtue of faith is seated in the mind and not in the heart, then so long as your mind swings between Tradition and modernity you are, despite yourself, in your position as Guardian of the Faith, a terrible enemy of the Catholic Church.

We might wish to trust you, but we cannot.

Sincerely yours in Christ.

Clinton's Acquittal

W HEN THE UNITED States Senate voted last month to acquit President Clinton of crimes of which all the known evidence had until then made him guilty, it was a sign of the times, marking an extraordinary degradation in the public life of the leading nation of the Western world. However, rather than heap blame on the sign, let us consider the times. In what does the degradation consist? Who is mainly responsible? What is its purpose?

The degradation consists essentially in the fact that instead of good accusing evil, it is now as though evil accuses good. Instead of decent standards being accepted while the facts are in dispute, now the indecent facts are widely accepted while the standards are in dispute. In this sense, what the Senate did last month is merely the culmination (for the moment) of a process of overthrowing old values. This process has been going on for a long time but on this occasion it broke out in spectacular fashion. Again and again during the last six years, "decent" Americans must have said to themselves, "But the public can't stand for this! The people will react against that!" But the reaction never came. Again and again such Americans have had to lick their wounds. It is as if the old moral standards no longer applied. The people seemed to rejoice in their being blown away.

Here are two examples. Firstly, when President Nixon was nearly impeached in 1974, the New York Stock Exchange fell disastrously. When Clinton was really impeached in 1998, it hardly wavered. That represents a very different public attitude. Second symptom: when the private adultery of an old-breed American politician becomes public, it can still destroy his career, because he admits it is wrong. But no adultery of any new-breed politician can give leverage to a blackmailer because then it is virtually a badge of honor. We are, as Americans say, in a completely new ballgame.

The next question is, who is mainly responsible for this enormous change in morals, merely shown forth in politics? For an answer let us return to the recent decision of the Senate. Was the system responsible? For instance, some people would say that the whole episode was just typical of the United States. Well, it may be true that the Puritanism rooted in the American soul twists out of true all kinds of moral reactions here, but can it be said that the moral rot is markedly worse in the USA than in many other Western nations, especially those repudiating a Catholic past which the United States never enjoyed? Surely not.

Then maybe the systematic liberalism of the US Constitution was the problem in Clinton's acquittal? Now it is certain that the US Constitution is not the all-saving remedy that some patriots pretend it to be, but in this case the impeachment process that it contains would have worked well, had it been operated by men whose first concern was the truth. As Catholics have always known, Constitutions are only worth what is in the hearts and minds of the men operating them. "Madam, you have a Republic, if you can keep it," said Benjamin Franklin on emerging from the Convention that forged the US Constitution. This recent acquittal showed that today's Americans, by what they have in their hearts and minds, are fast losing their republic.

Then is systematic democracy the problem, which made the constitutionally appointed Senators bow under the pressure of the opinion polls? No doubt public opinion did put the Senators under pressure, but did it force them to acquit Clinton? Of course not. Many senators voted against acquittal. In conclusion, as Catholics should know, systems are not the problem, but people. What people were responsible for this acquittal?

It is interesting in this respect to compare the acquittal of Clinton with the release of Barabbas (Mt. 27: 15–23). When Pontius Pilate released this "notorious prisoner," there were three parties responsible. Pilate himself bore the official responsibility, because only he could give the order for Barabbas to be released. The "chief priests and ancients" bore the leading responsibility, because it is they who persuaded the crowd to cry out for the release of Barabbas, and to raise such a tumult as made Pilate give way. The crowd bore the ultimate responsibility, because when Pilate washed his hands in front of them to protest that he was innocent of the blood of "this just man," i.e., Jesus, the whole people answering said, "His blood be upon us and upon our children."

Official responsibility, leading responsibility, ultimate responsibility – which was the main responsibility? Surely not Pilate's, because he would obviously not have released Barabbas or condemned Jesus had he not been put under severe pressure by the crowd and its leaders. The responsibility of the conspiratorial chief priests and ancients (cf. Jn. 11: 47–53 for their conspiracy) in the release of Barabbas and death of Jesus is overwhelming. However, without the crowd, they were powerless to force Pilate's hand, and they could not force the crowd, therefore the main responsibility must be that of the crowd, which freely chose to follow those evil leaders.

For just as the most skilful horse rider can only work with the horse that he has beneath him, so the most skilful politician, be he democrat or aristocrat or king, can still only work with the people that he has beneath him. In the case of Barabbas' release, God punished both leaders and people, with the destruction of Jerusalem in 70 A.D., and then with that curse they had called down upon themselves, and from which only those blessed few escape who call down the Precious Blood as a laver of regeneration.

Now let us apply these principles to Clinton's acquittal. Official responsibility lies obviously with the Senate. Like Pilate, they did not want to handle the case but were forced to do so. Like Pilate, they might have preferred to judge in accordance with justice and truth, but they chose to yield to the cries of the opinion polls, and so they bear an inescapable responsibility for the sentence of acquittal.

However, leading responsibility lies with the media which mould public opinion in modern democracies, and with the money men who control those media. Why are the media so powerful? Because the liberals said to God, "We can do without you, all we need to run our affairs is an informed democracy," and the Lord God replied, "Alright, see where democracy by godless information gets you," and we have government by vile media, vile because moving all the time away from God. As for the money men controlling the media that agitate the crowd, they are the direct successors of the chief priests and ancients, and like them, their prime motive in this acquittal is to destroy Jesus. Here is one of their spokesmen, as quoted in the *Wanderer* of last Dec. 24: "We are in a culture war . . . a vote against impeachment of Clinton is not a vote for Clinton but a vote against fundamentalism and the pro-life movement. The anti-Clinton alliance is the forces of evil! – evil! – genuine evil!."

Nevertheless, even if the money men wield enormous power by their money and their media, still, like the chief priests and ancients, they could not exercise successful pressure on the Senators except through the people, and even with their media they could not force the people to support Clinton. Therefore the ultimate responsibility for Clinton's acquittal lay with the American people, who, when all is said and done, have the media and the leaders and the President that they deserve. The people want the President they now have because, like them, he defies the Ten Commandments, and he makes them feel good doing so.

That is why, to come to our third question, for leaders and for people the real purpose of the Clinton acquittal, as of the release of Barabbas, is to get rid of Jesus. The Clinton acquittal is a battle not only in a culture war but in a religious war. The people want to sin. They want money, materialism and all the pleasures money can buy. They want no restraints upon their sinful ways. This is what the money men and corrupt politicians give them. This is why they want power to the money men and to corrupt politicians. This is why Barabbas was released and Clinton was acquitted.

However, all is not lost, far from it. Even in Jerusalem's darkest hour under the "power of darkness" (Lk. 22: 53) when Our Lord was being betrayed and crucified, still there was a Veronica, a Simon of Cyrene, a Joseph of Arimathea, and an unwavering Mother of God. Amidst the crowd baying for the blood of Our Lord, still there will have been single souls or families not following the wicked crowd, but looking up to God, trusting God, and begging Him for the grace not to abandon Him. Nobody can force us to follow the movement of the crowd, to desire money, to expose ourselves to the media, to live sinfully. If only Catholics were Catholic and truly renounced the world and the flesh and the devil, the money men and the media would rapidly lose their power. The more we analyze their power, the more we see how dependent it is on sin, which depends on my free will and the lack of grace.

Then let me pray to recover or to re-enforce grace. Let me pray quietly and steadily, each day at least five, preferably fifteen, Mysteries of the Holy Rosary. Let me get to Mass as often as possible, and to Confession. Let me stop watching television, and read a minimum of newspapers. Let me read Catholic classics, pre-Council from TAN Publishers, post-Council from the Angelus Press. And let me trust in God, who even if He has to destroy Jerusalem, will make all work for good to those who love Him (Rom. 8: 28). We are in His hands.

Men, also make use of the Ignatian Exercises available here at the seminary, the first just after Easter, as per the enclosed flyer. And use the courses of Family Doctrine, and Literature. Catholic lives need Catholic minds, Catholic minds need Catholic truths.

Theological Study of the '88 Consecrations

To THIS DAY there must be many good Catholic souls longing to follow Archbishop Lefebvre or his SSPX, but who hesitate to do so because they feel he went against Catholic principles, especially when he made four bishops in Ecône, Switzerland, on June 30, 1988. Let such souls read a theological study of the consecrations that appeared three months ago in the Italian bi-weekly, *Si Si, No No*, and many may hesitate no longer. The article's first part proves that those Episcopal Consecrations were even a duty for the Archbishop, the second part proves that the Pope's explicit prohibition made no difference to that duty!

Not that the Archbishop himself did not know what he was doing. He explained himself clearly and often. Nor that Catholic souls following him then and since have not known what they were doing, because all along they have recognized the true Catholic bishop. "I am the good shepherd," says Our Lord, "and I know mine and mine know me" (Jn. 10: 14).

The problem is rather that since in the circumstances of the 1970's and 1980's the Archbishop had to break a number of the Church's normal rules in order to maintain the SSPX and in particular to consecrate four bishops, then it always looks as though he had the Catholic rule book against him. And this is what made – and makes – so many Catholics hesitate. At last, the article of "Hirpinus" in *Si Si, No No* has gone deep into those rule books and shown, in a way I think nobody has shown before, that the Archbishop's action was fully in conformity with the truest principles of Catholic theology and Canon Law.

It stands to reason. After all, how could the Archbishop's work have borne so much good fruit if it was out of line with Catholic principles? That makes no sense. Yet to this day enemies of his Society, even conservatives whose survival is one of his fruits, cast in the Society's teeth the Catholic rule book: "Where the Pope is, there the Church is," "Catholics must obey the Pope," "Obedience is a virtue," etc., etc. Let us with Hirpinus take a good look at the Catholic rules, however briefly.

The first major principle that comes into play is that while ordinary cases are dealt with by ordinary laws, cases out of the ordinary, or emergency cases, need to be dealt with by principles behind and above the ordinary laws. That is common sense. For instance, in front of the hospital there is normally no parking, but if I am rushing my wife to the emergency room, then I can park wherever there is a space.

Now if, as the Vatican claims, there is no emergency in the Catholic Church today, then of course there can be no appeal to higher principles. However, as Hirpinus points out, Popes Paul VI and John Paul II have themselves by moments admitted that there is a very serious problem in the post-Vatican II Church. Paul VI's references to the Church's "self-destruction" (Dec. 7, '68) and to the "smoke of Satan in the temple of God" (June 30, '72) are famous. Similarly in a speech quoted in the

Richard N. Williamson

L'Osservatore Romano of Feb. 7, '81, John Paul II referred to the "upset, confusion, perplexity, even delusion" of a "great part" of Christians. So Hirpinus' article is not for those who deny there is a post-conciliar emergency, rather it is for those who recognize the emergency, but fail to see how the Episcopal Consecrations were justified by that emergency.

The whole first part of the article examines then what are the duties and powers of a bishop in an emergency. Grave spiritual need is that of any soul whose Catholic faith or morals are threatened. Extreme spiritual need is that of any soul virtually unable to save itself, without help. Grave general or public spiritual need is where many souls are being threatened in their faith or morals, for instance where heresy is being spread in public. Today numberless Catholics are being threatened in their faith and morals by the public spread of neo-modernism, which is the reinvigorated "synthesis of all heresies." So today the Catholic Church is filled with grave general or public spiritual need.

Now wherever there is grave public spiritual need, the Catholic theologians teach that the situation is equivalent to that of extreme individual spiritual need, because for instance in a grave general need, many individuals will be in extreme need. So what a bishop or priest may or must do in an individual's extreme need, he may or must do in grave general need, like today's.

Now all legitimate pastors are bound in JUSTICE to help souls in a state of need, but if these pastors fail for whatever reason, then in CHARITY anyone else is bound to help who can, notably other bishops or priests. These latter will have no normal Church jurisdiction over souls coming under other pastors, but, by their ordination as bishops or priests charity includes for them a duty of state to help as they can. Now as the duty of charity binds under pain of mortal sin to help an individual neighbor in extreme need (especially spiritual), so it binds gravely to help a people in grave need (see above), even requiring if need be the sacrifice of life, reputation or property (Archbishop Lefebvre certainly sacrificed his reputation!).

If then today's neo-modernist errors and heresies are being put forward, or silently approved, or at least left unopposed, by the legitimate pastors themselves, Pope and bishops and priests, it follows that today's state of general need is without hope of relief from the legitimate pastors, in which case any other pastors are, by their ordination which empowers them to give spiritual relief, gravely bound in charity to help such needy souls as best they can (Just as, if a husband refuses to look after his family, the wife under him must supply as best she can, so if a Pope refuses to look after the Church, a bishop under him must supply as best he can).

And what gives such emergency pastors the right (or jurisdiction) to supply for the legitimate pastors? The grave need of many Catholics. The Church teaches that according as needy souls resort to emergency pastors, so these pastors receive from the Church emergency, or "supplied," jurisdiction. For as in a (genuine!) physical emergency all property belongs to all men, so in a spiritual emergency all episcopal and priestly powers are at the disposal of all souls. Divine and natural law then override normal Church law restricting jurisdiction, otherwise too many souls would be eternally lost. Jurisdiction is for souls, not souls for jurisdiction.

Now this principle of emergency rights, or "supplied jurisdiction," applies also to the case of a bishop consecrating bishops without the Pope's approval, because of grave public need. Certainly Christ instituted Peter as head of His Church, with the fullest possession of Church power to govern souls, towards eternal life. But that power, while wielded by Peter, is owned by Christ. It is to benefit souls, not its possessor. It is to save souls, not damn them. As for the machinery of Peter's control of the consecration of bishops, Christ left it flexible, so that Peter could, down the ages, tighten or loosen that machinery according as different historical circumstances would require for the good of the Church. Medieval popes tightened it, as did Pius XII because of a problem in China, but the Church has approved of Eusebius of Samosate consecrating bishops without the Pope's permission in the 4th century. Therefore if a Pope by his fallibility were to tighten that control to the grave harm of souls, the Church would supply jurisdiction for a bishop to take that consecration into his own hands, as did Archbishop Lefebvre. For the manner of Episcopal Consecrations is a matter not of divine law, but of human Church law, allowing for the exceptions possible in all human Church law.

Objection: but Eusebius of Samosate consecrated bishops without but not against, the Pope's express will. How could Archbishop Lefebvre go against the known and expressed "No" of the Pope? This question takes up the second part of Hirpinus' article. The answer flows from the principles laid out in the first part: however much the Pope said "No," he could not exonerate the Archbishop from his higher duty in charity to help souls in grave and general need.

Firstly, as to the subject, charity looks to the need, not to the cause of the need. When a road accident happens, helping the injured comes first, questions come later. Charity binds whoever can succor souls in grave need to do so, even if, especially if, legitimate Superiors are causing that need.

Secondly, as to the Superior, if he refuses to help souls in grave need, he has no power to bind others from doing so, any more than a husband refusing to provide for his children has power to bind his wife from doing so. The Pope is no exception to this rule, because while his authority is unlimited from below, it is limited from above by divine law, natural and positive, which binds gravely in charity whoever is able to succor souls in need, to do so. Archbishop Lefebvre was uniquely able, by being a bishop refusing neo-modernism, to succor souls wishing to remain Catholic.

Thirdly, as to the situation, it is natural to necessity to know no law, or, to place the subject in the impossibility of obeying the lower law, because the subject could only do so by disobeying a higher law. The Pope as Superior is no exception because even he comes under divine law. And if it is he who creates the necessity, as does JP2 by favoring neo-modernism, then it is the Superior himself who is making it impossible for his subject to obey him!

Notice however that whosoever disobeys in an emergency is disputing neither the authority nor its lawful exercise, but merely its unlawful exercise. He is not judging the lower law to be bad but merely inapplicable in the given emergency. Thus Archbishop Lefebvre contested the Pope's right to control Episcopal Consecrations not in general, but only in the particular emergency of the grave need of souls for the SSPX to survive his own imminent death. The Church's supreme law is the salvation of souls, to which the law of papal primacy must, if necessary, give way. The Catholic's supreme virtue is charity, not obedience.

Therefore as soon as the Archbishop had prudently established that divine law was entering into play, he was not only entitled but even bound to disregard the Pope's express prohibition. For when divine law came into play, the Archbishop had to consider not the Superior's will which may be what it may be, but his power, which is fixed by Catholic theology and law. These say that once the emergency is reasonably proved, the subject may and must act on his own authority without recourse to the Superior, because in an emergency the subject needs to obey firstly God makes who makes that recourse to the Superior irrelevant. Therefore, even if the Superior wanted to bind his subject against God, he could have no power to do so.

In conclusion, Archbishop Lefebvre was bound in charity to help souls, once they were in grave need with no hope of relief from their lawful superiors. He was bound by his episcopal powers to consecrate bishops to ensure for many needy souls the doctrine and sacraments owed to souls by the Church for their salvation. He was absolutely bound not to heed the Pope's "No," because by so doing he would have sinned gravely against the higher duty of charity. By consecrating bishops despite that "No," he neither denied the Pope's primacy nor in any real sense disobeyed the Pope's authority which cannot oppose divine law.

That is only the skeleton of Hirpinus' article. Its muscle consists in a mass of quotations from the most respected Catholic theologians, saints and lawyers. Of course! Catholic principles are in line with common sense, and Archbishop Lefebvre acted in line with both. Praise be to God! Make sure to read the complete article when it appears in English in *The Angelus*. Truth is mighty, and will prevail. Blessed are the souls who never took scandal from the Archbishop!

As for world events, our sins have deserved much tribulation. Pray mainly that souls be saved.

What is Happening in Yugoslavia?

WHAT IS GOING on in Yugoslavia? Why on earth has a coalition of NATO nations, with the USA in the lead, been reducing Serbia to rubble with week after week of relentless aerial bombardment? In defense of human rights? To defend a people, you smash their country to pieces? You have to believe the media to believe that!

Then what is going on? It is time to ask. Firstly, if the poltroons who command the Western "democracies" commit the ultimate folly of engaging a ground war in Serbia, then at latest when the bodybags begin coming home, "patriotism" will shut down minds, and clear thinking will become, if not impossible, at least unsayable.

Secondly, modern wars are never what they are made to seem, and Catholics must be careful how their "patriotism" gets engaged. For instance, many American Catholics, by embracing heart and soul the great liberal crusade of World War II, came out of the war with their Catholicism so wedded to liberalism that they fell easy prey to Fiftiesism and Vatican II, with the loss of

millions of their souls. "My country, right or wrong" is
not only foolish in this life, it is downright dangerous for
eternal life. "Patriotism is not enough," said Nurse Edith
Cavell (1865–1915).

Then what is happening in Yugoslavia? War is always
a consequence of sin, as the Apostle James (4: 1) tells
us, so we know that in one way or another the justice of
God is being wrought there upon sins of men in general (Medjugorje?). But who is sinning in particular? Of
course the liberals and their vile media are telling us
that the Americans are saints and the Serbians are devils. But when we recall that exactly the same liberals and
media, now screeching like hawks and waving the flag,
were, over Vietnam, screeching like doves (some doves!)
and burning the flag, we smell a rat. What is going on?

Any war, like any divorce, is a complicated and messy
affair, with the fault rarely being on one side only. Because of historical circumstances, Yugoslavia is a particularly complicated part of the world, riddled with tensions and bitterness and ancient hatreds. All the more
reason, one would have thought, for NATO not to get in
the middle of local conflicts! What on earth does it think
it is doing?

A wise commentator, not a Catholic but a nationalist, has a good part of the answer. Let us call him E.Z.
for easy reference. He tells how, from the beginning of
the Western nations' onslaught upon Serbia, he could
make no sense of what he was hearing and seeing of the
endless destruction, until several weeks later when the
NATO spokesman in Brussels, a Jamie Shea, explained:
What was at stake in Yugoslavia was the upholding of
multi-ethnic, multi-cultural, multi-religious societies
and thus of modern states, into the next century and the
new millennium.

Now it was clear, writes E.Z. The artificial and anti-natural "nations," constructed on the revolutionary

basis of the Secret Societies' "Liberty, Equality, Fraternity," must be preserved and upheld by guns and bombs. That is why the Serbian leader Milosevic was perfectly acceptable to the New World Order so long as his repression and crimes were serving to protect the artificial construct known as "Yugoslavia," but as soon as Milosevic realized from a visit to Kosovo in 1993 that the Muslim immigrants in Kosovo, which is historically sacred to Serbia, risked taking it over by their superior birth rate, so that he began defending the natural nation of Serbia for the Serbians, then he instantly became the new Hitler-of-the-day, like Saddam and Khadafi before him. Likewise, what US officials had branded as a "terrorist organization" changed overnight into Kosovo's "Liberation Army"!

Thus for E.Z., NATO here represents artificial internationalism waging ruthless war upon what still remains of natural nationalism. Why NATO? Because its recent expansion makes it for the internationalists a more suitable instrument of control than their other artificial pipe dream, the United Nations, which has failed them too often lately. Not enough of the little nations represented in the UN are yet sufficiently de-natured to be blind to the crushing threat hanging over all of them if NATO's murderous meddling in the internal affairs of Serbia is successful.

E.Z. adds various possible secondary motives for the onslaught in Yugoslavia. These are useful to understand the modern world. Amongst others are the need for war to prevent the world economy from falling into a depression (only World War II and not the New Deal pulled the USA out of the Great Depression of the 1930's); the need for industrialists to make billions of dollars from replacing the planes and missiles reducing Serbia to rubble, and for the international mega-corporations to make billions more out of rebuilding from the rubble;

the need for the military to test their high-tech hardware in action; the need maybe for masses of rubble to warn the Red Army in Russia of what could happen to them if they dare to rise up against the New World Order gangsters presently ruining their country; the need for the same gangsters to get control of what is known to be Kosovo's fabulous underground mineral wealth.

Howsoever it be with these secondary motives for the NATO onslaught, E.Z. is surely right as to the primary motive: the exemplary crushing of the last remains of nationalism by Judeo-masonry's New World Order internationalism. But there remain for a complete understanding of events in the Balkans (and in many other places) two major questions which must escape the best of nationalists: why must the New World Order smash natural nationalism, and how can it be succeeding in a purpose so unnatural? Only a Catholic can answer these questions because they involve Jesus Christ, King of the Nations such as only Catholics believe Him to be.

We must backtrack to the Middle Ages, the highpoint of Christendom, when Christian civilization was largely Catholic and when all Christians acknowledged Jesus Christ (at least in principle) as King of kings and Lord of lords (Apoc. 17: 14). At that time Christendom consisted of a family of nations, each with its distinct identity, yet all enjoying together Christian unity. By contrast nationalism preserves the identity (e.g., Serbia for the Serbians) but it destroys the unity (Serbia against Croatia against Bosnia, etc.), whereas internationalism restores a certain unity (League of Nations, United Nations) while dissolving identity (in multi-ethnic, multi-cultural, multi-religious constructs). How did Christendom achieve simultaneously both the nations' identity and their unity?

Because Our Divine Lord does for nations what He does for individuals. Just as, for an individual, "Whosoever will save his life, shall lose it: and whosoever shall lose his life for My sake and the gospel, shall save it" (Mk. 8: 35), so too for a nation. If (at least since Christ) a nation seeks its identity outside of Christ, it is heading for destruction or for loss of identity in liberalism, whereas if in pursuit of Christ it renounces any self-fulfillment it holds dear, not only will it discover its true identity in Christ, i.e., whatever God meant that nation to be, but it will simultaneously achieve automatic harmony and unity with all other nations likewise "losing" themselves in Christ. In other words Our Lord says to the nations what he says to persons, "Seek ye first the kingdom of God, and His justice, and all these things shall be added unto you" (Mt. 6: 33).

Thus within medieval Christendom, nations enjoyed, as never before or since, both particular identity and general unity. But this was only possible in Jesus Christ. As soon as the nations began to turn away from Him, then to preserve their identity they lost their unity – that was nationalism with its unprecedentedly terrible wars, like World War I. Or, if the nations still would not learn their lesson but persisted in their apostasy, then they recovered an artificial unity by trashing their national identity – that is internationalism with its United Nations, New World Order, etc.

Thus the breakdown of Christendom took place in two stages, by the Freemasons' famous "Solve et Coagula," or, "Break up and reassemble." In the first stage, nationalism broke up Christendom into nations by turning natural identity against (Christian) unity. In the second stage, internationalism reassembles the nations by turning (Judeo-masonic) unity against natural identity. NATO's onslaught in the Balkans is a clear example of this second stage in action, our Western "leaders" having long been controlled by Judeo-masonry.

Now we are in a position to answer the questions that must escape the nationalist. Why must the internationalists destroy the last vestiges of nationalism? Because Judeo-masonry, to make man into God, must make war on God and on the human nature that God made, and which can always lead back to God. But nationalism is natural, insofar as it respects and follows the God-given differences between races, continents and nations which are at least as real as the differences between all the brothers and sisters in one family. For just as God meant all these differences to complement one another in the harmony of a united family, so He obviously meant the different races and nations to look after one another in the completeness of the human family of mankind. Therefore internationalism must wipe out these national differences which tend to recreate a natural order, and it must smash to pieces any nationalist resistance, as in Serbia.

But how can internationalism succeed in such an unnatural enterprise? By appealing precisely to men's natural sense of the unity of mankind, and to a lingering nostalgia for the unity of Christendom. Neither unity is possible without Christ, as Napoleon and Hitler discovered when both strove to imitate Charlemagne, but the striving remains. And that is why the media's nonsensical rhetoric about "human rights" in Kosovo nevertheless deceives people. Men always have a sense of their natural unity to be appealed to, however artificial the appeal.

In conclusion, this war in the Balkans represents the outright enemies of God making war on, so to speak, His half-friends. Now it may seem better to be Christ's half-friend than his outright enemy, so nationalism may seem preferable to liberalism. But Our Lord Himself said that with Him there is no such thing as half-and-half friendship. We cannot serve two masters. With Him it is all or nothing. That is why nationalism without Christ is doomed to fail. That is why nationalist Serbia does not have the answer to NATO unless it seriously returns to Christ. That is why Christ is allowing in the modern world one worse horror after another to make us turn to Him. Either we seriously convert, or it will be a third World War, such as will make the first two pale in comparison. NATO may be playing games, but Our Lord is not! Not "Get the US out of the UN," but "United States, United States, convert to the Lord thy God!"

The world needs Christ, Christ needs priests, priests need seminaries. Dear friends, thank you for your grand support through the month of April.

What is Going Wrong With Our Children?

VER SINCE THE April 20 school shooting in Littleton, Colorado, anguished Americans have been asking themselves, "What has gone wrong with our children? What has gone wrong with our culture?" Dear Americans, you have no hope of finding the real answer until you ask, "What has gone wrong with our religion?"

The Colorado shooting was merely the latest and bloodiest in a series of shootings that have burst out in schools all over the United States in the last few years. This time 12 school children were killed, many more injured, and one adult teacher died. Then the two killers, apparently normal and good looking boys of 17 and 18 years of age from a wealthy white Denver suburb, having turned their school into a slaughter house filled with smoke and blood and corpses, turned their guns on themselves. What is the problem?

All the Liberals and liberal politicians have used Littleton to clamor for more gun control laws. Now every such advance in tyranny may well be deserved by a people rendering themselves otherwise ungovernable, but gun control remains the stupidest of solutions to Little-ton. Americans gained their Republic by guns, and they have kept their guns at home for over 200 years without their children serially killing one another. Obviously the problem is not the guns, but the mentality of whoever handles them. Where does the murderous mentality come from?

A less stupid but still relatively shallow solution is to blame the young minds' being formed to murder on the violence everywhere to be found in Hollywood films, television and computer games. True, these are filled with violence but they do not – yet – drive many people to actually killing. If so many suburbanites are presently wallowing in such fantasy violence, is it not because they have achieved their high degree of security and comfort only by eliminating from their Dilbertian existence so much of life and interest that they need the fantasy violence to even feel alive? Yet the more they are thus entertained, are they not the more deep down bored? Then rather than blame the killers on the videogames, would it not be truer to blame both killers and videogames on the nature of today's big city or suburban way of life which is so dissatisfying for human beings? We should be getting warmer, because instead of blaming things, we are beginning to situate the problem where all real human problems belong, in the sinful human heart. But what is sinful about suburban culture?

For a start, the public schools which generate a good deal of that culture. There was an admirable analysis in the June issue of *Summit Journal* as to how, if one wanted to produce school killers, the present curriculum in American public schools could hardly have been better designed! The author, Dr. David Noebel, knows what he is talking about. Over years he has built up a highly effective organization to counteract the public schools' godlessness, by teaching the anti-modern principles of

Protestant godliness to adolescents otherwise defenseless against the skilful perversion wrought upon their minds and hearts by these schools which, as far as education goes, have become organized treachery. Some instinct that this is so surely explains in part why the Littleton killers took out their rage on their school.

However, if school killers had healthy – truly healthy – homes, would even the betrayal they undergo at school inspire in them such murderous rage? Surely not. Surely in this respect the real evil of suburban or modern culture is what it has done to the family and to the home. For years – you readers should know – this Letter has here been trying to make the alarm bell ring off the wall. It has resorted to "shocking" language (dreams not dry), "shocking" people (Unabomber), "shocking" musicians (Pink Floyd), "shocking" condemnations (the "Sound of Music" is way out of tune) and "shocking" facts (children of either sex being commonly violated at home by their own fathers "But, mummy, you dress like that!"), in order to punch some reality into Catholic minds, where it belongs. (Bless you, dear readers, easily most of you have already signed up to continue being punched, despite the faintly sharp challenge to do so, written by me, only signed by Mrs. Mehren! She is innocent!)

Here is more of the same. In the last few days we learned (not in the confessional) of the case of a 15 year old girl here in small town Winona being repeatedly violated and finally impregnated by her drunken father, who to all appearances, sincerely! – claims he has no idea what he was doing! Mother worked the night shift, perhaps to avoid his drinking, so she too claims she has no idea what was going on! The girl, helped to flee to a foster home in a mid-size town nearby, took her 13 year old sister with her in the hope of continuing to protect her (all that these children have is one another!), only to discover there that the little sister shares her condition! America, WAKE UP! YOUR CHILDREN ARE SCREAMING!

I am sorry, readers, but if you want a Minnie Mouse religion, you should not be Catholics. The guardian of the foster home said (but how much longer will there be any sane adults to provide guardians?), "Imagine how much more of this there is in our mid-size town, let alone in the big cities!" Imagine also the rage in the heart of the older girl, who is convinced she let down her little sister! Now, in home dramas of this kind, or in the whole culture that generates them, is there not the proportionate explanation for the rage, for example, manifested to all the world on the website of the leader of the two Littleton killers . . . ? Over generations, but especially since the demonic 1960's, modern parents have lost the art of parenting, homes are no longer true homes, and there is a devastating coldness and emptiness in the hearts of the children, hardly any more children.

What ever happened to the family? The atom is tightly bound together by natural forces, but once it is split, those forces create a devastating explosion. Natural family bonds are enormously strong, but once they are pulled apart, they wreak untold havoc. So how were grand- (and great-grand-) parents pulled apart from grandchildren, when each has so much to give that is human that the other needs? How did parents largely lose the art of parenting (it can be regained), and begin treating their children like adults or babies, in any case not like children? How did husband and wife lose all sense of the difference between man and woman and of their complementary natures and needs?

Answer, the family was torn apart starting over one hundred years ago by the same false gods that had revolutionized society at large one hundred years before that: liberty, equality, human rights, democracy. If I am tied, I am not free, so freedom tears out all family ties. Equality wipes out complementarity. Democracy destroys all hierarchy or order, like children honoring parents while parents look after children, wife obeying husband while husband cherishes wife. Human rights block out human duties, especially towards God, and with no God, nothing so human as the family can go right for long. Thus the whole culture of our revolutionary society turns families into bunches of individuals merely living under the same roof. These non-homes are what makes the hearts of killers.

And where does this anti-natural worship of individualism come from, and how can it have such power? Christianity taught mankind the value of each man. Individualism run wild in modern Western society is that same Christianity without Christ. Its power came from the Catholic Church, its running wild came straight from the smashing of that Church, i.e., Protestantism. If, as Luther said, I need no supernatural society such as the Catholic Church to mediate between me and my God for my eternal needs, such as justification and salvation, why should I need any natural society for any of my lesser needs? I, who deal directly with God, stand on my own!

And thus between society and the individual, although designed by God for one another, be it the Communion of Saints in Heaven or the practice of justice and charity on earth, there is introduced an unnatural dialectic, a fatal opposition, emerging clearly into view in Shakespeare's famous play *Hamlet* (to which we shall return), and surfacing in blood in Littleton. So a decent Protestant with his decency and an upright use of Scripture (which is Catholic) can work a good way back towards the true and only possible solution (which is Catholic) of the modern world's artificial clash between society and individual, between rotten school and raging killer, but to any extent that he still shares in the false worship of individualism, Lutheranism or Liberalism, to that extent he can only help to perpetuate the clash.

Dr. Noebel, you have done sterling work in arming thousands of abandoned children against the devils of their miseducation. It only remains for you to clean out the father of most of these devils – Martin Luther.

Yet what chance does a Dr. Noebel have of discerning today what the Catholic Church truly teaches about Luther, when the Vatican itself is making a Joint Declaration with Lutherans to say they have come to an agreement, and is then issuing a Clarification of the Declaration to say it is not an agreement? What confusion! But that is the subject of another letter. Doctor, all I can say meanwhile is that the Catholic Church today is like Our Lord carrying His Cross. On that Way of the Cross, how difficult it would have been to recognize him as God, but true God he still was!

Patience, dear readers. Our Catholic Faith is our victory over all the problems around us, and it is our launching pad for an eternity of bliss.

Lay Spirituality

A LETTER WRITTEN to me a few weeks ago criticizing the present teaching of Society priests in general tempts me to reply, "Don't shoot the pianists, they're doing their best." However, on reflection, the criticism merits a longer reply because it involves no less than the spiritual life of the laity.

Our correspondent – let us then call him O. C. – complains that the Society priests are not currently teaching the laity (as opposed to the clergy) enough positive specifics of the spiritual life. The laity are taught all about sin and modern errors, but little that is practical, applicable to daily life, about mental prayer, the practice of virtue, the growth of charity and the life of grace in the soul, etc. It is, O.C. goes on, as though the Society priests believe that large parts of the spiritual life are not for the laity, when in point of fact the spirituality of certain layfolk down the centuries has surpassed that of the clergy.

O.C. gives a long list of advantages to layfolk of leading a life of prayer and virtue, and a corresponding list of disadvantages of not doing so (!). Society priests, he says, may be learned, but they teach theology rather than virtue, so that what O.C. knows about the spiritual life he has had to learn from books rather than sermons. Was not this ignorance of the spiritual life amongst the laity the cause of that lukewarmness which God punished by allowing Vatican II? So to save the Church, concludes O.C., "it is far more important to preach about what is right than what is wrong," because it is not the fighting of error but the sanctification of souls which is the primary purpose of the Church.

Now this complaint of O.C., fairly summarized above, can be answered on a personal level, or, more importantly, on a level of principles. Let us get the personal answer out of the way.

OC, are you married? If you are, do you give to your wife and family the attention, time and affection which it is your God-given duty of state to give them? If not, do you realize that any so-called "spiritual life" resting upon this inability or negligence must be more or less of a fraud? And if you do give them that love and leadership, do you have much time or attention still available for what you aspire to as a clergy-level spiritual life? And if you are married and are looking for spiritual instruction, have you availed yourself of the instruction most practically available to layfolk at the Society's Ignatian Retreats? If not, can you say you know all that the Society priests teach? If so, have you put into (persevering) practice what you learned from them? If so, do you need more? The exercises of St. Ignatius combine enormous spirituality with great practicality. They were designed by God for our distracted last half-millennium before the Antichrist.

On the other hand if you are not married but are widowed, do you think married men have the time to devote to "spirituality" that you have? And if you are not widowed but separated from your wife, was perchance your "spirituality" part cause of the separation, or at least not able to prevent it? And if you have never been married, have you any idea what St. Paul means when he says (I

Cor. 7: 32–34) that only unmarried men or women can give their undivided attention to pleasing God, that married folk are necessarily divided between pleasing God and pleasing their spouse?

Dear O.C., it is you who complain that the Society priests "discuss the topic of virtue only on a very abstract level," so it is not you who can rule out of court these eminently practical questions of reality. Alas, does not "spirituality" so-called often act as a way of escaping from these demands of reality? Spirituality for a family mother – or father – goes directly through the fulfilling of God-given family responsibilities. Any Catholic neglecting them is worse than a pagan, says St. Paul (I Tim. 5: 8), and one might add that his "spirituality" is a sham.

Unfortunately, what passes for "spirituality" can be a sham on a level much higher than merely personal. It can be the self-deluding refuge of Catholics soft on principles of Church doctrine, especially in modern times. For while I lose my grip on dogma, am I not liable to say all the more that I am being "spiritual," that I am lovingly concentrating more on what is right than on what is wrong, etc., etc.?

But why must "hateful" and "divisive" doctrine come first? Because God is for real, Heaven is for real, the Ten Commandments are for real and the devil is for real, so that if I really want to get to Heaven, then I must firstly learn how these realities are (which is doctrine), and secondly submit my mind and will to them (which is piety). How can there possibly be true piety (or "spirituality") in the will without there first being true doctrine in the mind? If Society priests are insisting on doctrine, they are at least putting first things first.

Ask the most rabid liberal how to build a bridge across a dangerous river, and even he will first go to look it up in the engineering manuals. But then ask him how he is building his bridge to Heaven, and suddenly there is no more question of reality, only of his sweet feelings of "spirituality." Such people are not truly centered on grace, charity, virtue and so forth. These realities are for such people mere words to dress up how good they feel about themselves. A hellfire-and-brimstone sermon giving them back the least sense of objective reality would be the greatest "grace" for them, and the truest act of "charity."

Truly, the last half-millennium has been a difficult time for the Catholic Church. From peasants rooted in God's real soil, the mass of men have become suburbanites dependent on men's artificial machines. Now God remains God, and reality remains reality, but the physical and mental world that most men live in has become more and more detached from both. That is why the peasant had a solid spirituality while he never even thought about it, whereas your average suburbanite today is more or less incapable of true spirituality, even if he thinks and talks about it all the time!

Thus when a great 20th century Dominican theologian, Fr. Garrigou-Lagrange, complains of so many Catholic spiritual writers writing as though the laity are incapable of the spiritual heights and must content themselves with "mere" devotions, of course he is right, in theory. Of course the Lord God – from whom all prayer-life comes – can lead any soul He chooses at any time He chooses to the heights of spiritual contemplation. But if, for instance, so many Jesuit writers abstained from pushing layfolk to those heights, surely it was out of that practicality for which their Order was famous, whereby they realized firstly that modern man has lost, in general, that sanity of the peasant which Dominicans tend to assume is still there, and secondly that modern man's pride will snatch up the ball of "high spirituality" and run with it any which way. How much safer, O.C., a humble devotion than a proud "spirituality"! Back to the humble Rosary of St. Dominic, designed to be the layman's breviary!

For indeed modern man took, with Vatican II and all that went with it in those 1960's, such another lurch downward as to leave high and dry even the mass of writings of the Jesuits, in a manner of speaking. For of course the Catholic Truth does not change, and the Saints remain Saints. But as I have walked through the seminary basement book display, with row upon row of admirable and admired Catholic books prior to Vatican II, how often have I thought to myself, "Gentlemen, you have lost it! You are writing out of a world which is gone!" For while reality has not changed, computer man's sense of it has changed utterly. That is why Vatican II took place. Poor Pope Paul VI absolutely wished to get the Church back in touch with modern man, which apparently he could not do without betraying Faith and Church.

Dear friends, we have a gigantic problem of which O. C. is touching the fringe: mankind as a whole has moved by the end of this 20th century so far away from God that even when man thinks he is trying by "spirituality" to go back to God, he is often still only seeking himself. God is real, but mankind is now so far removed from reality that only a miraculous conversion or a merciful chastisement can possibly bring men back to their senses. At that point we will all recover a true spirituality, grounded in the fear of God, without our even thinking about it. God, have mercy upon us; Christ, have mercy upon us; God, have mercy upon us!

Meanwhile, dear Catholics, learn Catholic doctrine and take part in any doctrinal courses locally available. Pray, especially by attending Mass whenever possible, the greatest prayer of all. Get to confession regularly, to live in the grace of God. Pray the Rosary, the next greatest prayer, by its humility. Get to the Ignatian Exercises, never out of-date and capable of teaching all the spirituality most layfolk will ever need. And if you think you need still more, go to any prudent priest who will be God's channel for any further wisdom God judges you need.

Above all, never forget that the will of God lies hour by hour in our duty of state. If "spirituality" could not come through duty of state, why would God appoint for all of us so many hours of duty compared with so few hours of "spirituality"? Poor modern man! His most radiant smile is reserved for when he is being photographed. He cannot believe he is doing anything significant unless it is being videotaped. The spirituality of the kitchen sink consists precisely in its not being videotaped!

Dear friends, I am dropping out of circulation for the month of August. Pray that I may have a Transcendentally Significant Vacation!

Letter of Bishop Thomas to the SSPX

I T IS NOT often that anybody high in the official Church undertakes to argue with the SSPX, but it is revealing when they do. Each time it reveals, contrary to pious hopes and dangerous illusions, just how far apart in their thinking are the Society and the mainstream Church. Let us look at the argument of a mainstream bishop who attempted earlier this year to meet the Society on its own ground – Catholic Tradition.

Bishop Jean-Charles Thomas of the Diocese of Versailles near Paris, was responding to a circular letter sent out by the Society's District in France to some 20,000 Novus Ordo priests (yet he would accuse the Society of being closed in on itself). Here is the substance of his response:

He begins by recognizing that everybody, priests or laity, is "deeply convinced" that the Second Vatican Council was a "turning point," or "change," in the Church. The only question is whether this change is "a betrayal of the Church," as the Society claims, or "a return to a greater fidelity to Tradition," as (he says) the mainstream churchmen claim. And the answer to that question depends upon one's scheme of reference.

The Society's scheme of reference is certain writings of Popes between 1850 and 1950, forming "a brief, limited and recent source" of Catholic Tradition, lasting only 100 years, by which source the Vatican II change stands condemned. On the contrary the official churchmen's scheme of reference is all of Scripture, Old and New Testaments, especially God's Revelation through Christ, continually being renewed by the Holy Ghost in "a living Tradition now 20 centuries old."

These two schemes of reference, says Bishop Thomas, generate two very different versions of Catholicism. On the basis of its one-century Tradition, the Society neglects Scripture, Church Fathers and early Councils. It involves few souls and only their personal salvation. It leaves out mankind and the salvation of the world, and it glorifies Pope and priests at the expense of Bishops and laity. On the contrary Vatican II's 20-century Tradition means "the Good News of Salvation being put before all mankind," i.e., it means reconnecting with Bible, Church Fathers and early Councils, and it involves all men without exception and the world's salvation, in the wake of all the Church's great Founders of Orders and in line with the Holy Ghost "renewing the face of the earth" to the end of time.

Bishop Thomas concludes that whereas the Society's Catholicism is narrow, shut in on itself, out of touch with today's world and condemnatory, Vatican II is wide open, apostolic, contemporary and salvatory, or, aiming to save men instead of condemn them. So he hails Vatican II ecumenism with its joyful prospect of uniting "the children of God, presently so divided!"

In brief, Bishop Thomas wishes to take the word "Tradition" away from the Traditionalists, on the grounds that it is Vatican II and not Archbishop Lefebvre or the

SSPX that is in line with the first 1800 years of Church teaching and history. Let us check this argument against the facts and against Catholic doctrine.

Firstly, as to the facts it is easy to dismiss both Bishop Thomas' caricature of the Society's Catholicism and his rosy picture of the Vatican II religion. For instance, was Archbishop Lefebvre "narrow" when for 15 years to build up the Society he travelled all over the world to visit, confirm, and ordain? Was he "shut in on himself" when from 1970 to 1988 he kept going down to Rome, without being heard, to plead for the Church? Was he "out of touch with today's world" when in 1988 he had 300 journalists falling over one another to get a view and report on his Episcopal Consecrations? And was he "condemnatory" when he thus exhausted his old age to save souls? As for the Society, his relatively young disciples may not be up to his level, but who can deny they are doing what they can to imitate his worldwide striving for the salvation of souls?

Measured likewise against the facts, Bishop Thomas' glamorous portrait of the Vatican II religion is simply unreal. That religion is putting in front of men not Christ's Salvation which requires penance, baptism and living to die in the state of grace, but an old error of Universal Salvation whereby everybody is saved, regardless of their religion or way of life (see the four volumes of Professor Dörmann's "Theological Journey of John Paul II to the Prayer Meeting of Religions in Assisi"). Correspondingly, the Vatican II religion falsifies Bible, Church Fathers, etc. Nor does it follow the great Founders of Catholic Orders – we have been reminded recently how Padre Pio blasted in the name of St. Francis the updated Franciscans trying to win him over to the revolutionizing of their Order. And who can without blasphemy ascribe to the Holy Ghost the fruits of Vatican II? – collapsed Mass attendance, disintegrating families, empty seminaries and convents, closed schools, decimated dioceses, etc., etc.!

Now it is true that there was a serious problem in the Catholic Church in the 1950's just prior to Vatican II, as there was in the 1520's, just prior to the Reformation: the Catholicism of too many Catholics had become hollow and external, like a husk without a kernel. But then as now, the solution was not that of Luther or Vatican II and Bishop Thomas, to throw out the husk as well. The true solution was that of the great Saints of the Counter-Reformation, to renew the inner kernel and put vigorous life back beneath the husk, which is what Archbishop Lefebvre did, as far as he could, in our own day.

Alas, Vatican II has all the power of a dream to bewitch men's minds and to make modernists like Bishop Thomas incapable of recognizing facts. Will any amount of ruins persuade him that Vatican II was a failure? One may doubt it. Nor is he any more real when it comes to Catholic doctrine, which he similarly presses into the service of his dream. Let us look at his argument on Tradition.

He recognizes that Catholic Tradition cannot change, because it is the deposit of the Faith, entrusted to the Church by Our Lord Jesus Christ to be preserved by it intact until the end of time. But he also admits — dangerous admission for a liberal — that Vatican II was a change from what went before. Therefore to avoid admitting that Vatican II broke with Tradition, he must claim that what came before Vatican II had previously broken with Tradition, so that he can then claim, as he does, that Vatican II was a change back to Tradition. This supposed previous break he makes, naturally, as recent as he can, in order to give as little weight as possible to the great anti-liberal encyclicals of the Popes prior to Vatican II. So he supposes the previous break around 1850.

Richard N. Williamson

Actually, the series of those encyclicals began at the latest in 1832, with Gregory XVI's *Mirari Vos*, or even in 1791, with Pius VI's authoritative condemnation of the principles of the French Revolution of 1789. But let that detail pass. The problem for Bishop Thomas is that these papal documents solemnly condemn, anywhere from 50 to 100 years in advance of Vatican II, the liberal principles which are at the heart of the Vatican II "change." That is why Bishop Thomas is forced to claim that these encyclicals are out of line with all previous Church teaching, so that he can claim that he is the one that is faithful to Tradition.

But Bishop Thomas is "out of the frying-pan into the fire." For indeed the briefest study of those encyclicals, notably Pius IX's *Quanta Cura* and *Syllabus*, and Pius X's *Pascendi* and *Lamentabili*, shows that those Popes not only declared that their anti-liberal doctrine was the purest continuation into 19th and 20th century circumstances of the previous 18 centuries of Church teaching, but also they put the full force of their papal authority behind that anti-liberal doctrine as being the Church's unchanged teaching (see the enclosed flyer on *Quanta Cura*). Then if Bishop Thomas claims that the anti-liberal encyclicals are outside Tradition, he has to claim that, amongst others, Pius IX and Pius X, a declared Servant of God and a canonized Saint respectively, did not know what they were talking about. But in that case why should any Catholic Pope know what he is talking about, including the Vatican II Popes? Then why be Catholic?

In other words, either Popes Pius IX and Pius X were right, in which case Vatican II is wrong, and one must follow Catholic Tradition in the true sense of Archbishop Lefebvre and not in the false sense of Bishop Thomas. Or Popes Pius IX and X were wrong in claiming that their encyclicals contained unchanged and unchangeable Catholic doctrine, in which case Popes Paul VI and

JP2 might just as easily be wrong in anything they claim, in which case there is no reason to be a Catholic. In brief, the choice is between either Archbishop Lefebvre's Catholicism (which of course is not his), or the Church's disintegration. Is this alternative not what we see taking shape all around us?

Cardinal Ratzinger's solution to the problem (problem for liberals) of those anti-liberal encyclicals was to call them "substantial anchorages" in Church doctrine and history. In other words they were good (substantial) teaching for their own time, but the Bark of Peter could no more reasonably stay at anchor with them for ever than any ship can be expected to stay at one anchorage for ever. New century, new anchorages, new doctrinal encyclicals. But that does not solve the problem either, because Pius IX and Pius X solemnly declared that they were teaching not truths substantial for their own age, but doctrine unchangeably true for all time. If they were right, Vatican II is wrong. If they were wrong, we disintegrate as Catholics. Ah, but they were half-right and half-wrong, says the artful Cardinal. That is why we see him half-Catholic and half-disintegrating!

The truth about these encyclicals is that just as the arrival of Protestantism in the early 1500's created new circumstances for the Church requiring the restatement, not change, of Catholic doctrine by new Doctors such as St. Robert Bellarmine to meet the new errors, and from then on nobody could reject his teaching (except on minor points or novelties) and still claim to be Catholic, so the mutation of Protestantism into Liberalism around the early 1800's, in the wake of the French Revolution, required new encyclicals from the Popes to restate in the new circumstances the unchanged Catholic doctrine, and all those who like Cardinal Ratzinger or Bishop Thomas reject those encyclicals denounce themselves as liberals and cannot claim to be Catholic. They are refusing the anchorage of absolute truth. Their minds are, ultimately, at sea. Ultimately, they have no idea of what it is to be a Catholic. And such men are in control of the structures of the Church!

Dear readers, pray for your part that the minds of Society priests (and bishops!) never slip anchor until God restores the Pope and Rome, not necessarily in Rome! And according to possibilities, study those encyclicals which Archbishop Lefebvre loved and taught for exactly the same reason that Bishop Thomas rejects them – they are the most brief, profound and authoritative refutation of the errors presently savaging the Catholic Church. See advertised on the next Seminary Tapes flyer audio and videotapes of Doctrinal Sessions held here from 1995 to 1997, precisely on those Encyclicals (*Pascendi* 1996, *Quanta Cura* 1997). Contrary to what Bishop Thomas thinks, we hold their doctrine to be indispensable not just to our own salvation, but to that of the entire world.

Modern Churchmen Destroy the Church

CONFUSION CONTINUES TO pour out of the churchmen now governing the Catholic Church in Rome, but, however good their intentions may sometimes seem to be, the end result every time is the destruction of the Church. By a just judgment of God, His enemies have acquired firm control over the levers of Church power – for the time being.

As someone once said of American foreign policy in the wake of World War II, if only occasionally it had failed to advance Communism one might have thought it promoted it by accident or by stupidity, but when that policy's effect was to promote Communism every single time, then one knew that that had to be its deliberate aim. If only occasionally these churchmen would effectively defend the Faith, one might think that its destruction was not their deliberate aim, but as it is . . .

The parallel is appropriate. Just as the liberals who promoted Communism were convinced they were rendering the world a service and not a disservice (which is why Alger Hiss, the famous 1940's adversary of Whittaker Chambers, emotionally repudiated his factual qualification as "liar" and "traitor" until the day he died), so the churchmen now promoting ecumenism are convinced they are rendering the Church a service, and on their deathbed they will still be convinced of it. Which is why they are so confusing as well as confused. Let us attempt to restore clarity in two cases current.

The first case is no doubt familiar to many of you: the recent moves made by Rome to strangle Tradition within the Priestly Fraternity of St. Peter. See the enclosed flyer for a very brief account of the moves, and for an extensive evaluation from "Alice through the Looking-Glass"! Yes, there is more sense in a few pages out of Alice's Wonderland than in volumes and volumes coming out of this Rome!

The truth is, as a few of the Roman liberals openly admitted from the beginning, that they only granted official status to St. Peter's in 1988 as a means of getting "Traditional" Catholics back into their Newchurch, to divide and rule the Catholic resistance. Poor St. Peter's! Could they not see that if they wanted to defend Catholicism, this Rome would never allow them to succeed? That if they succeeded they could not survive, and that if they survived they could not succeed?

No, St. Peter's did not see it. Instead of judging conciliar Rome as a whole by its consistently disastrous fruits, they wanted to judge it by this or that still Catholic part within the disastrous whole. But when a whole is no longer Catholic, then any parts still Catholic within that whole merely serve to deceive. St. Peter's is now paying the penalty for letting themselves be deceived. Maybe even now they can rouse sufficient Catholic resistance within the Newchurch to obtain a reprieve, but the death warrant of Tradition amongst them has clearly been signed. It is only a matter of time.

The second case of how apparent confusion in the Newchurch merely disguises its relentless drive towards the destruction of the Catholic Faith is the last two years' dance of Roman documents on the dogmatic question of Justification, which is the question of how a human soul is moved from the state of sin into the state of grace, or of justice before God.

To this question about 1600 years ago St. Augustine, the "Doctor of Grace," formulated, under pressure from heretics, the Catholic answer. About 470 years ago Luther set up an answer so different that it became one of the major differences dividing true Protestants from true Catholics ever since. About 30 years ago in the wake of Vatican II, "ecumenism" demanded that Catholics and Protestants get together. So discussions between them began, due to culminate at the end of this month (October 30, 31) in an official joint signing in Augsburg, Germany, of a "squarcular" document, wherein the Catholics will declare that the Catholic square is a squarcle, while the Protestants will declare that the Protestant circle is a squarcle! So everybody will be agreed, and ecumenism will have scored another squarcular triumph! (Augsburg is where the Protestants came together on June 25, 1530 to sign a joint Protestant creed! October 31 is the day on which 482 years ago Luther posted his "95 Theses" against the Papacy!)

In pursuit of clarity, let us back up. Let us see, however briefly, Catholic doctrine and the Protestant error (and its gravity) before we go dancing with the ecumenists! Such a deep question of doctrine as justification requires precision of detail to be treated properly, but what follows may have to blur some details in order to pick out the grand outlines.

Firstly, let us recall Catholic doctrine on the mode, effect and fruits of grace justifying a soul, or making it just before God. As to its *mode*, the Catholic Church has always taught that while supernatural grace can only come from God to move a man's soul to justice, never-

Richard N. Williamson

theless man being a rational creature with free will, it is not fitting that he should be merely moved by God with no participation of his own, so in fact he will not be justified by God's grace unless he freely assents to its moving him, and cooperates with it doing so. As to grace's *effect*, the Catholic Church has always taught that if a man does thus assent to grace moving his soul to justice, then his soul will be essentially cleansed of sin, both original (if not yet cleansed) and all personal sin, leaving in the soul only "concupiscence" or that inclination to sin which is the weakness Adam bequeathed to all of us, but which is not sin in the proper sense because an inclination is not an act. So for Catholics grace truly cleanses the soul and the sinner is truly justified. Finally, as to grace's *fruits*, the Catholic Church has always taught that once the soul is constituted in this state of grace, it can perform works supernatural and meritorious before God which it could not do before, indeed it must perform such works, otherwise its faith is dead (James 2: 14–26) and not working through charity (Gal. 5: 6).

Against this Catholic doctrine Martin Luther protested around 1520, and launched Protestantism. For personal reasons, it is said, of having difficulty in obeying God's Commandments, he gave up the effort to change himself and set about changing Church doctrine instead. Wresting to his own purpose St. Paul's teaching of "Justification by Faith" (Galatians, Romans), Luther taught that as to grace's *mode*, it justifies man by moving his breast to a warm feeling of trust in God, but in that process man's free will is so weak or non-existent as to be incapable of playing any part. Therefore grace alone justifies. Correspondingly, as to its *effect*, justifying grace for Luther does not clean all sin out of the essence of a justified man's soul, rather the filth of sin remains in his soul while the grace of Christ's merits is put like a lid over the top of the soul to cover the filth remaining beneath. Accordingly as to the *fruits* of grace, Luther teaches that a man "justified" in this way need not do any good works (from a still filthy soul, how could he?), all he need do is "believe," i.e., work up that warm feeling in his breast. Hence Luther's famous saying "Sin much, just believe still more" ("Pecca fortiter, sed crede fortius").

This Lutheran doctrine is (objectively) horrible. It is tailor-made to justify a man's wallowing in his sin, as it cuts off all real demands or true supernatural grace to get him out of it. It "liberates" him from the Ten Commandments, and founds all liberalism, Revolution, separation of Church and State, etc., etc. It reduces religion to mere emotions and cozy feelings, cutting it off from real life, founding all subjectivism, "Sunday Catholicism," the turning of feelings into facts, etc., etc. No wonder from the Council of Trent onwards, the Catholic Church vigorously and precisely condemned Luther's literally filthy version of justification (Session VI).

But finally came Vatican II (1962–1965) with its "ecumenism" opening up the Catholic Church to all other "religions" and to their errors, especially Protestantism. In 1997 the discussions between Catholic and Protestant squarclers finally led to a "Joint Declaration on the Doctrine of Justification" (JDDJ) which concludes (#40) that "a consensus in basic truths of the doctrine of justification exists between Lutherans and Catholics"!

The squarcling technique of the Declaration is to reduce both Catholic and Protestant doctrine on a given point to their highest common factor, and then give on that common factor a Catholic spin more or less acceptable to Lutherans, and, separately, a Lutheran spin more or less acceptable to Catholics. For ecumenical purposes, it is a clever technique, and the Lutheran World Federation swiftly approved of the Joint Declaration.

However, in June of last year the Congregation for the Doctrine of the Faith and the Pontifical Council for

Promoting Christian Unity prepared by common agreement and published a "Catholic Response to the JDDJ" (CR) which, amidst any defects it may have, nevertheless exposes serious doctrinal problems in the JDDJ. *Mode*: man is not "merely passive" when moved by grace (CR #3). *Effect*: sin does not "still live" in the soul justified (CR #1). *Fruits*: good works are the fruit of grace but also, as is not clear from the JDDJ, "of man justified and interiorly transformed" (CR #3).

Somebody in Rome still has some Catholic doctrine in him! So what does Rome do? On June 11 of this year in Geneva, the Secretary General of the Lutheran World Federation and Cardinal Cassidy, President of the Pontifical Council for the Promotion of Christian Unity, presented an official joint "Annex" to the JDDJ which blandly overrides the doctrinal objections of CR by reaffirming the squarcular ambiguities of JDDJ. And the "Annex" claims, like JDDJ, that this squarcular doctrine falls under none of the Catholic condemnations of Protestant error (notably at the Council of Trent), nor under old Protestant "condemnations" of Catholic doctrine.

Logically, media reports on the publication of this Annex with the JDDJ concluded that the Catholic Church and Protestant communities were repudiating their past. For instance, Catholics had to be giving up the dogmatic anti-Protestant definitions of the Council of Trent. Oh no, said Rome. On June 22 a press statement was issued from Cardinal Cassidy's Council which can only be called another piece of ecumenical doubletalk: the JDDJ does not fall under Trent's condemnations, but those condemnations are as serious as ever, as "salutary warnings." Yet how can a "salutary warning" be as serious as a dogmatic condemnation? Clearly, ecumenism rots Catholic minds. Freemasons within the Vatican are relentlessly destroying the Catholic Church.

For the repeat Assisi-style ecumenical meeting planned in Rome for the end of this month prior to the Augsburg signing, the SSPX's Superior General is calling for Society Chapels to hold ceremonies of reparation at the same time (Details in the USA from the SSPX HQ in Kansas City). And, to encourage you, dear readers, for the new Seminary school year the Lord God has sent us over a dozen promising young men.

Not all is lost. We count on, and are always grateful for, your continuing support.

Repeat of the Assisi Prayer Meeting

THERE IS SOME good news from the seminary, some not good news from Rome and some more good news from the Headquarters of the SSPX in Menzingen, Switzerland.

The good news from the seminary is that we have had 15 young men enter as candidates for the priesthood this autumn, and there may even be a sixteenth. True, the launching in September of an extra Preliminary Year may account for half of these candidates, but in a world where each vocation amounts to a miracle, as Archbishop Lefebvre used to say, 15 vocations amount to 15 miracles. Your prayers for vocations are bearing fruit, as are the Society's Mass Centers, Missions and churches, from which come almost all of these vocations.

More good news from the seminary is that this Preliminary Year is working well. It is designed to enable under-educated candidates to catch up on some studies within the seminary surroundings before they enter the seminary proper. The studies include mainly catechism, Latin and English, with a little History, Music and Literature. For some years now the generally falling standards of education have called for such an initiative, but only this year did Providence provide a suitable priest to handle the bulk of the extra teaching. Readers of this Letter may recognize in this Preliminary Year something like the "concentration camp" described two and a half years ago to help distracted young men to concentrate. Indeed there is a connection, but the original wide open dream has given way to a precisely seminary-oriented program. Needs must. A seminary must do a seminary's work, which is tightly directed towards the priesthood.

The bad news from Rome is the repeat in Rome itself one week ago of the 1986 Prayer meeting of World Religions in Assisi, and then the signature last weekend of the Joint Catholic-Lutheran Declaration on Justification in Augsburg, Germany. What is going on in these churchmen's heads? What are they thinking of? What do they believe in? I can remember how back in 1986 Archbishop Lefebvre was disappointed at how few even "Traditional" Catholics were scandalized by the first Assisi meeting. What is the essential difference between the mind of the Archbishop and the mind of John Paul II, for whom that meeting was a high point, if not the high point, of his pontificate up till then?

Certainly, John Paul II has in this respect the modern world on his side. The way of thinking of the mass of people all around us, caused and reflected by the truthless media, is that all men must come together, all divisions between men are bad, and all ideas that divide men must give way to the unity of mankind. And this way of thinking has got into many Catholics' heads.

On the contrary Our Divine Lord, telling the truth (Jn. 15: 6) that his Father commanded him to tell (Jn. 8: 28) and that He came into the world to tell (Jn. 18: 37), was willing to divide the people (Jn. 7: 43) and even to lose all His apostles (Jn. 6: 68) if that had to be the result of His telling the truth. Obviously Our Lord wanted to lose neither His apostles (Jn. 17: 11) nor the people (Jn. 3: 16), but there could be no question of His Father's interests (and commands) not coming first (Jn. 12: 49; 15, 31, etc., etc.).

In brief, Archbishop Lefebvre and all other faithful followers of Jesus Christ put God, and the First Commandment, first. On the contrary the modern world and all those who follow it, put men, and the unity of men, first. But how can leading Catholic churchmen, in theory followers of Our Lord Jesus Christ, come to follow the world in practice?

Through any one or all of several causes working together. Let us name a few. Firstly, lack of true prayer which keeps a soul in the truth and wanting or loving the truth. Secondly, pride which makes men want to take the place of God, and which is at the heart of, thirdly, modern philosophy which so corrupts men's minds as to confuse and dissolve altogether their grasp on any objective truth, even if they mean well, as John Paul II gives many signs of doing.

The good news from Menzingen is the letter written to the Pope by our Superior General, Bishop Bernard Fellay, on the occasion of this repeat of Assisi. As Our Lord said, if His disciples were silenced, the stones of the street would rise up to tell the truth (Lk. 19: 40).

Patience, dear readers. The Lord God will not be silenced. Pray through November for the Holy Souls who can also cry out for us.

Rome Is Now Making It Clear – The Archbishop Was Right All Along!

A FLURRY OF recent events in Rome involving the Fraternity of St. Peter suggests that the masters of Rome may be wishing to have done with the officially approved Tridentine Mass, perhaps in time for the Conciliar Church's millennial New Advent, so long spoken of by Pope John Paul II. The Fraternity is resisting as best it can, but Rome seems to be becoming impatient.

Some but not all of these events have been evoked in previous Seminary letters. Let us give here as many of them as we can in chronological order, to bring out the pattern underlying the events: there is no reconciliation possible between the Catholic Faith and the leaders of the Conciliar Church now occupying Rome. These Romans have lost the Faith and are doing their best to stamp it out wherever they can still find it.

By way of background we must go back to the Second Vatican Council (1962–1965), where, under the decisive influence of the two liberal Popes, John XXIII and Paul VI, the mass of the Church's then 2,000 bishops fell prey to the glamorous modern error of liberalism: just let man be free, and everything will be well.

In 1969 Pope Paul VI laid hands on the Mass, and "freed" it from its ancient rite, named Tridentine from the Council of Trent when Pope Pius V codified it, but actually going much further back in time, parts even to the very beginning of the Church. Paul VI was "updating" the rite of the Mass, to make it also more acceptable to non-Catholics, in particular to Protestants. And since many Catholics live their religion principally through attendance at Mass, then it was Paul VI's New Order of Mass, or "Novus Ordo," which dramatically advanced the Vatican II process of transformation of millions and millions of Roman Catholics into Roman Protestants.

Now in the same 1969, Archbishop Lefebvre, a retired missionary bishop, fully realizing the danger of the Conciliar Reform to the Catholic Faith as a whole, began his Priestly Society of St. Pius X to defend the Faith by forming true priests who would as a result celebrate only the old rite of Mass. Miraculously, as he considered, he obtained in 1970 official Church approval for his little Society. So a number of the young men drawn to his Society did not follow the Archbishop for his indepth defense of the Faith, but only for the combination he offered them, unavailable anywhere else, of priestly formation with both the Catholic Mass and Conciliar approval.

This meant through the early 1970's that as the Conciliar authorities realized what the Archbishop was up to and therefore (invalidly) dissolved his Society in 1975 and (invalidly) suspended him in 1976, so the apparent loss of official approval made many of his seminarians leave him, even if he did maintain the Tridentine Mass. However, the famous Mass at Lille in August of 1976 demonstrated that by now the Archbishop had a large popular following. The "Traditional" movement was born, and

Conciliar Rome prudently backed away from any further open persecution of the Archbishop or his Society, as such persecution risked being counterproductive.

Rome keeping relatively quiet, again a number of the Archbishop's seminarians and by now priests continued to follow him because of his unique combination of the Tridentine Mass with, sort of, Conciliar approval. Despite the Archbishop's repeated condemnations of Vatican II, they still did not understand, or want to understand, the depth of his disagreement with neo-modernist Rome. That is why, when advancing old age drove the Archbishop in 1988 to consecrate without Rome's approval four of his priests as bishops to guarantee the Society's survival, otherwise in peril, these "Tridentinists," as we shall call them, appealed to Rome to provide them with the combination of Roman approval and Tridentine liturgy which the "excommunicated" Archbishop could no longer give them.

Conciliar Rome welcomed them with open arms. Because it had converted to Tridentinism? Of course not. Rather, it saw in these refugees from the SSPX an opportunity to set up under Rome's control an alternative "Traditional" movement to keep souls away from the real Traditional movement henceforth "excommunicated" and so out of Rome's control, except by the silence and marginalization, or calumny and scorn, which have constituted Rome's treatment of the Society ever since. However, while allowing these Tridentinists to say only the old Mass, Rome required as a condition for its acceptance of them that they recognize the "orthodoxy and validity" of Pope Paul's New Mass. Which these Tridentinists did. So Rome now had a docile decoy to pull priests and people, as it hoped, away from the uncompromising SSPX.

Apparently the decoy worked well enough for Rome to give it 10 years of life, so that in October of 1998 St.

Peter's Fraternity celebrated in Rome, with kindred organizations, its 10th anniversary. However, the popular success of this meeting of some 2,500 Tridentinists from all over the world, all putting Rome under Tridentinist pressure, seems to have aggravated the Conciliar churchmen. They had only approved Tridentinism as a step down from Catholicism to Conciliarism. Now it seemed to be serving as a step back up from Conciliarism to Catholicism. This would not do.

We come at last to the recent events. We will narrate them as briefly as possible, with brief comments.

<u>Spring or early summer, 1999</u>: Grave accusations against a kindred organization of St. Peter's, the Institute of Christ the King in Gricigliano, Italy, enable Rome to threaten it with an Apostolic Visit.

The Institute was founded soon after St. Peter's by a Monsignor Wach, essentially on the same basis as St. Peter's, i.e., to practice Tridentinism under Rome's control and without attacking Rome's Conciliarism.

<u>June 11, 1999</u>: Cardinal Medina, head of the Roman Congregation for Divine Worship, to questions of the Archbishop of Sienna, replies officially that by Church law Latin Rite priests can say only the New Mass, that the Tridentine Mass can only be said by Rome's exceptional permission, or Indult (both statements are false). Nor, the Cardinal went on, can priests say the Tridentine Mass by force of Pius V's "perpetual" permission in "Quo Primum," because what one Pope (Pius V) did, another Pope (Paul VI) can undo (true, but no Pope can undo Catholic Tradition, as Paul VI tried to do with his new-fangled Mass).

The Cardinal is clearly trying to put the brakes on Tridentinism.

<u>July 3, 1999</u>: The same Cardinal drops a bomb on St. Peter's Fraternity! Allegedly in reply to questions put to his Congregation, he replies in the now notorious

Protocol 1411 that, firstly, any Tridentinist priest may always say the New Mass; secondly, no Tridentinist Superior can stop him from doing so; and thirdly, any Tridentinist priest may concelebrate the New Mass.

To the credit of the St. Peter's Superior General, Fr. Bisig, he had been trying to stop St. Peter's priests from sliding towards the New Mass. Here is Rome paralyzing his efforts, for Rome never intended St. Peter's to block the New Mass, quite the contrary.

<u>July 18, 1999</u>: A second bomb is dropped on St. Peter's, this time by Cardinal Felici of the *Ecclesia Dei* Commission, set up by Rome in 1988 to promote Rome-controlled Tridentinism. In a remarkably swift reply to complaint written only two weeks before by 16 dissident St. Peter's priests against the "Lefebvrist" direction being imposed upon St. Peter's by Fr. Bisig, the Commission writes to him that the permission previously granted for him to hold a special General Chapter in August (to stop St. Peter's from sliding) is revoked; that instead Rome will preside over a general meeting of St. Peter's in Rome in November; and that until then he can take only minor decisions for the Fraternity.

Now Fr. Bisig may accuse these 16 priests of having gone behind his back to Cardinal Felici – yet did not he himself go behind Archbishop Lefebvre's back to Cardinal Ratzinger in the mid-1980's? And he may accuse the *Ecclesia Dei* Commission of crippling his power to govern his Fraternity – yet who but he, to distance himself from the "disobedient" Archbishop, wrote "obedience to Rome" into the founding charter of St. Peter's back in 1988? In the old expression, Fr. Bisig is "hoist with his own petard" (blown up with his own bomb).

<u>July 20 (?), 1999</u>: Fr. Bisig writes to reassure members and friends of St. Peter's that beneath this double blow from Rome he is doing all he can to defend their Fra-

ternity's Tridentinism within the official Church, for the good of that Church.

But what if that Church itself determines that its good consists in ending all Tridentinism? What then can Fr. Bisig do? He himself designed St. Peter's to "obey" Rome. Truth to tell, like all Tridentinists to the left of the SSPX and sedevacantists to its right, Fr. Bisig is basically a Fiftiesist who wants to rebuild the Church of the 1950's. But that surface Catholicism is no match for the neo-modernists in Rome. They blew it out of the water at Vatican II. The 1950's are gone for ever. Clearly, when Fr. Bisig followed the Archbishop, he never understood the depth of the Archbishop's doctrinal combat. What Tridentinists fail to grasp is that the false Mass is merely the spin-off from a much deeper and more important problem, which is doctrinal.

End July, 1999: Fr. Bisig and a companion Tridentinist leader are told in a meeting in Rome with the same high Cardinals that their Tridentinist societies rest not upon Church law but only upon Rome's gracious permission, or Indult. And they are asked how they can, if they admit that the New Mass is "orthodox and valid," so obstinately go on refusing to say it.

Indeed from when Fr. Bisig made that admission in 1988 to gain Rome's approval, what did his Tridentinism rest on? On a sentimental preference for the old liturgy? He then put the noose around his own neck. Now Rome is pulling it tight.

September 8, 1999: A large number of St. Peter's priests write a letter of support for Fr. Bisig to the same Cardinals.

But who are they taking these Cardinals for? Defenders of the Faith?? It is a lack of Faith that fails to discern in these Cardinals wolves in sheeps' clothing. Archbishop Lefebvre, by his Faith, saw from the beginning who they were, but pastorally did all he could to make them return to behaving like shepherds, until 1988, when they gave the final proof that they had no care for the sheep of Our Lord. Then he took the drastic action of the Episcopal Consecrations to guarantee his Society's survival, and left the rest in God's hands, which is what the Society is continuing to do.

<u>September 26, 1999</u>: Monsignor Wach, referred to above, sees the writing on the wall and concelebrates the New Mass with Cardinal Ratzinger in a nearby Benedictine convent.

The same Cardinal Ratzinger had written a few years previously a handsome Tridentinist preface to a re-edition of the Tridentine Missal. Now he brings Tridentinists to heel. Is there a contradiction? No. For him, explicitly, as for the Tridentinists implicitly, Tridentinism is merely a matter of sentiment. New Mass or Old Mass, depending on how you feel that day!

<u>Early October, 1999</u>: Fr. Bisig speaking at a Synod of Bishops in Rome on the one hand tells them his Fraternity is doing all it can do to draw souls from the SSPX "back into the Church," but on the other hand he tells them how Tridentinism is prospering.

Did he think they wanted to hear that Tridentinism is prospering?

<u>October 11, 12, 1999</u>: Rome arranges a meeting between Fr. Bisig together with Fraternity leaders loyal to him, and leaders of the 16 dissident priests who appealed to Rome against his "Lefebvrism" at the end of June. For the first day the dissidents are accompanied (and supported) by Cardinal Mayer, for the second, morning by Cardinal Felici! Only on the second afternoon are the priests left alone, whereupon the meeting turns into something of a head-on clash. All that Fr. Bisig obtains is the postponement until the New Year of Rome's takeover of the General Meeting of St. Peter's previously scheduled for November.

Richard N. Williamson

The head-on clash was of course between the contradictory elements enshrined in St. Peter's foundation: "obedience" to neo-modernist Rome against faithfulness to the Catholic rite of Mass. How will the clash be resolved? Either Fr. Bisig comes to heel, or he will be crushed by Rome, and the same is true for St. Peter's as a whole. Rome holds all the aces, by Fr. Bisig's doing.

<u>October 18, 1999</u>: Cardinal Medina, for his Congregation for Divine Worship, issues a ten-point letter in reply to the multiple questions (or complaints) raised by his bombshell Protocol 1411 of early July. He repeats that the New Mass is the only lawful Mass for the Latin Rite, that the Tridentine Mass continues only by Indult, that diocesan bishops should be considerate of Tridentinists, but Tridentinists in return must recognize Vatican II and all its pomps and all its works. And Tridentinist priests must celebrate the New Mass for diocesan congregations where it is usual.

Thus Rome means to crush protest.

<u>November 17, 1999</u>: Una Voce International, a worldwide organization of lay Tridentinists, holds a meeting in Rome, no doubt mainly to protest against this crushing of Tridentinism by Rome. At this meeting Monsignor Perl, number two (?) official of the *Ecclesia Dei* Commission, reads a "Clarification" to the assembled Una Voce delegates.

The "Clarification" begins by attributing recent attacks on the *Ecclesia Dei* Commission to "ignorance of facts" and "questionable information" on the Internet. How can the Commission be blamed for working with the diocesan bishops when that is what was meant to do from the beginning? By what right are lay associations lobbying in this religious matter? The Commission has from the Pope full authority over St. Peter's Fraternity. For any Latin Rite priest there can be no such thing as a right to celebrate the Old Mass exclusively. If St. Peter's priests refuse to concelebrate the New Mass, are they not refusing communion with the mainstream Church?

Having read this "Clarification", Msgr. Perl immediately stepped down, giving the Una Voce delegates no opportunity for questions or comment. Apparently, this left them all more or less discontented.

Dear delegates of Una Voce, let us for charity, or for the sake of argument, assume there is no malice on the part of Msgr. Perl or his fellow Romans. Still, they are all in the grip of such a different understanding of the Catholic Faith from yourselves that it would be foolish for you to expect them ever to accommodate you. Far more is at stake than just Liturgy.

Then remember how, ever since Vatican II, lay protest in defense of the Faith has never availed against the juggernaut of neo-modernism operated by the Vatican II clergy. In real terms you have as laymen only one threat that can make these Roman prelates hesitate – the threat to go over, lock stock and barrel, to the SSPX!

The direction being taken by Rome is clear as clear can be. Can anyone still not see it? If one wishes to organize the defense of the Catholic faith, there is, alas, only the Archbishop's way. One cannot put oneself under these neo-modernist Romans.

How clear-sighted the Archbishop was! What faith he had! What a gift from God he was! Rome may crush Fr. Bisig, but it could not crush the Archbishop, nor can it crush any Catholics who like him make no compromises on Truth. The Truth is master of Rome, and not Rome master of the Truth, ultimately. The Archbishop loved Rome, in the depths of his being, but still Our Lord's Truth came first. "The Truth is mighty and will prevail," and that Truth is the strength and cohesion of the SSPX. All who seek the Truth find themselves today substantially united in holding, broadly, the Society's positions, but that is not because they are the Society's positions, it is because they happen to be the Truth.

Once again, great Archbishop, thank you, and please pray for us.

Remember also, dear friends, the Spiritual Exercises for men here at the seminary. On the night of December 31 at the seminary there will be a Benediction, with the Te Deum sung on the stroke of midnight. For Christmas, remember it is forbidden to send to the seminary Rector Christmas cards unless you first cross out the "merry" Christmas and put "scroogy" instead.

To all of you, Happy New Year, happy new decade, happy new century and happy new millennium!

Sincerely yours in Our Divine Lord, still King of Kings and Master of the Universe.

In Defense of the Family

As THIS LETTER has said before, once a year is certainly not too often to write in defense of the family. The liberal ideas possessing most people's minds today keep it under relentless attack. But the family is the nursery bed designed by God for the engendering and growth of human beings. Therefore as the family disintegrates, so everything human disintegrates.

Local horror stories continue to come to our knowledge at the seminary. In the hope of aggressing the sickly "Sound of Music" mentality, let one more story of this sort be outlined: a boy of 14 who with his three brothers of 12, 11 and 10 is forced by their father to learn how to "be a man" upon their 9 year old sister! The problem is not that such insanity has never happened before, but that it is hugely increasing, while the amount of sanity available to deal with it is diminishing all the time.

Through a married couple that this 14 year old learned to trust, and through a good "EMT" (Emergency Medical Technician!), this lad was committed to hospital (for the severe lacerations over his back from his father's belt, inflicted every time he did not want to go along with the crime being forced upon him) and to the "Social Services." Problem solved? Listen to the lad's comments:

"These adults are so dumb. We're told to listen to them, but everything they say is empty. And they try to dress and behave like teenagers!"

Indeed. How can the adults be so stupid as to send "technicians" to treat human horrors of the kind evoked above? If this EMT is a good man who succeeded in rapidly gaining the lad's confidence, it had nothing to do with his being any kind of "technician," it had everything to do with his having still some old-fashioned humanity and common sense. But these are being fast eroded.

The reason why our society drives its youngsters crazy by treating them like machines is of course that it is as strong in things material as it is weak in things spiritual, and so at every turn it wants to misconceive spiritual problems. Our society's strong suit is technology, so of course it plays off its strong suit. So it dopes its problem youngsters with violent drugs like "Prozac" or "Ritalin." But these youngsters are going to turn around and dope their elders with euthanasia! Which includes their parents! Which may start with their parents!

However, just suppose that one of these youngsters looks in the direction of the Catholic Church, and I mean the conservative Catholic Church. What will he find? "Sugar in the morning, sugar in the evening, sugar at supper time," while he is screaming out for meat and potatoes! Listen to the sales pitch for supposedly Catholic books from a Winter 2000 Trade Catalogue which just landed on my desk (before landing in the circular file. The title alone is a give-away "Beautiful Inspiring Spiritual Books, from XYZ Press")

"Transform your 'random acts of kindness' into dynamic sources of spiritual regeneration" . . . "Find your heart's rest in the peace that only God gives" . . . "Experience one of the soul's greatest and purest pleasures" . . . "The treasure of holiness" . . . "How to develop maturity, spiritual awareness and even nobility" . . . "A 'Dear Abby' for Christians" . . . "Learn by example how to be good-humored, self-disciplined, and unshakably holy" . . . "Conquer your anxiety forever" . . . "Find lasting happiness" . . . "A great benefit to all who suffer from discouragement", etc., etc., etc.

The EMT mentioned above, a good man with a distinguished track record in really helping youngsters, as above, was asked if religion helped him at all – "Oh, all those fake churches! When I can't take it any more I go off into the woods and talk alone with God." Would this "Beautiful Inspiring Spiritual" Catalogue give him any reason to think that the Catholic Church was not also a man-centered, money-making, kidology outfit?

Certainly not! Such advertising titles, which must be successful in selling books for XYZ Press, encourage the pursuit of personal gratification. And even if the gratification is "spiritual" rather than physical, it is so self-centered as to be little better. I can imagine the EMT wanting to scream at XYZ Press, "But wake up, wake up, for your God's sake – your children are perishing in your homes, and all you can do is sell books to make people feel "spiritually" good about themselves while they stuff their children with Prozac and Ritalin? Is your religion for real?"

Dear readers, is our "Traditional" Catholicism any better? What kind of Catholicism is for real?

One in which there is suffering, which does not lie, when it hurts. Let us rejoice in suffering for its ability to teach truth amidst a world of lies. However, for suffering to teach truth, it must be accepted in sacrifice of self, neither rejected in a spirit of revolt, nor wallowed in as yet another form of self-gratification. For instance, I need not ask whether the Catholicism is real of a young couple living together and staying together for the sake of their children, but striving with might and main to

Richard N. Williamson

live like brother and sister because they have discovered
their marriage is invalid before God.

Then where can such a spirit of sacrifice be learned?
Certainly not from book catalogues presenting even
good books as self-gratification. Rarely even from reading books. Then where? Especially from attending with
mind and heart the unbloody repeat of the bloody Sacrifice of the Cross, i.e., the true Sacrifice of the Mass
(which is gravely diminished by the Novus Ordo version
of Mass). And how will that put sacrifice into people's
lives? When in a world of unreality I am in the presence
of the divine reality of the man-God sacrificing Himself
for me, I cannot help feeling unworthy, so if I persevere
in attending the true Mass I will soon want to go to individual Confession (as many XYZ readers may not have
done in a long time), which means the immediate sacrifice of my pride and vanity, and the long-term struggle
(if I persevere) with the rest of my miseries and failings.
And as the state of grace reestablishes a beachhead in
our individual lives, so it must, if we persevere, spill over
into our family lives.

Sacrifice in the family. For heaven's sakes, what can
the family be without sacrifice? Answer, exactly that
which is slaughtering the children with Prozac and Ritalin.

The head of the family is the father, so the sacrifice
must start with him. "Husbands, love your wives and be
not bitter towards them" (Col. 3: 19). The husband and
father must give up his independence, selfish pursuits,
and, all due proportion observed, career and money, to
make time for his family, quantity time, because by how
much time he gives them they will accurately gauge how
much he cares for them. In particular his wife needs
from him attention, time and affection, not dispropor-
tionately much, but certainly more than many husbands
today come up with.

Love in a man's life is a thing apart,
'Tis a woman's whole existence.

A wise husband who discovered the art of husbanding has written that the wife carries the unavoidable burden of the home, which cannot easily be lightened, but her husband should let her know that despite her problems, exhaustion and dishevelment, he loves her, that he is sorry she is suffering and that he would change things for her if he could. That is all she wants, and yet it is everything. A Fr. Hesburgh said that the greatest thing a man can do for his children, is to love their mother.

As for the wife, sacrifice is inscribed by God in the depths of her feminine nature, only sin and the modern world's crazy falsification of woman get in the way. Let her with the help of her Catholic Faith rediscover her deep-down instinct to give herself to husband, children, family, and she will be as happy as she can be in this "valley of tears," while preparing for eternity.

"Wives, be subject to your husbands," says St. Paul, "as it behoveth in the Lord" (Col. 3: 18). For "The head of every man is Christ; and the head of the woman is the man" (I Cor. 11: 3). (From which it follows that if a man wishes to be obeyed by his family, the first thing he should do is himself obey Christ.) Let the wife then sacrifice her own will, her emancipation, her trousers, her money and pseudo-career in order to attain the glorious freedom of motherhood to bring into the world and raise whatever children God sends – "The woman," says St. Paul again, "shall be saved through childbearing; if she continue in faith, and love, and sanctification, with sobriety" (I Tim. 2: 15).

However, for this purpose it is, again, essential that the husband know how to honor and love his wife in her role as mother, because almost nobody else will. And as for accepting the children God sends, both of them must trust in God. As a mother recently wrote to me, "We have a few more child-bearing years in which to exercise trust in God. As our family increases, this has been the most difficult of crosses and the richest of blessings."

I must say that as I visit the various churches, chapels and missions of the SSPX in the United States in particular, I am impressed by the number of lovely young mothers with many children, looking feminine and fulfilled. I imagine they are the delight of their husbands, and I imagine that few of them wear trousers or slacks, even during the week. Am I under an illusion? God bless them, almost none of our women wear men's wear to Mass.

As for bringing children into the world, everything going on around us would seem to discourage it. But how could God through His Church so strictly forbid sinful means of avoiding children, and not be willing to bless and protect the homes where His law is obeyed? For parents to obey God is the key to their being obeyed by their own children. Contraception and teenage revolt rise and fall together. Let the home be filled with the Faith in the form of sacrifice, not in the form of self-gratification disguised as "spirituality," and the children will have a strength of God inside that need fear little that the Devil can throw at them from the outside. Only if we adopt the principles of the Devil for marriage and family need we fear him or the world. Our Faith is our victory over the world (I Jn. 5: 4).

Dear friends, whatever looks dark or threatening around us in the New Year or Millennium is only allowed by God to drive His friends closer to Him. Let us use it that way.

The Jubilee Year

FOR THE CALENDAR year 2000, Rome is organizing both a Holy Year Jubilee, which is Catholic, and a series of ecumenical celebrations, which are not Catholic. For early August the SSPX is organizing a Pilgrimage of Tradition to Rome for the Jubilee, not for the ecumenical celebrations! Let us turn to the Old Testament to think about what the Society is doing.

The word "Jubilee" comes from the Hebrew "yobel," meaning trumpet. Amongst laws laid down by the Lord God for the Israelites in the Old Testament and transmitted by Moses (Leviticus 25), there was the command that every seventh year was to be for the Israelites a sabbatical year in which all debts were forgiven, and all work on the land was forbidden, the land's natural produce then belonging to and sufficing for all. After seven such sabbatical years, every 50th year was to be proclaimed – by trumpets – as a year of special forgiveness: besides all debts being cancelled, all property that had been sold since the last Jubilee came back to the original owner (so that all property sales must have been like leases, decreasing in value as the next Jubilee Year approached), and all Israelites that had been sold into slavery since the last Jubilee recovered their liberty.

At first sight these Jubilee laws of the Old Testament can seem shocking to our modern way of thinking. However, like all Moses' laws they were inspired by God to prepare His people for the coming of the Messiah, and so not only were they materially wise for the Israelites, but also that material wisdom pointed to the spiritual significance of Jubilees under the New Testament. Let us consider that wisdom of Moses as to slavery, debts and real property.

As to slavery, modern minds will have no difficulty in grasping the wisdom of its grip being broken every 50 years. Perhaps some of the slaves liberated in this way will have immediately sold themselves back into slavery, just as some convicts released today from prison immediately act to get themselves back into prison, but if one wished to get out of slavery at least there was no hopelessness of the prospect of being endlessly trapped in it. The Lord God placed limits on human bondage so that men would not forget that "the children of Israel are my servants, whom I brought forth out of the land of Egypt" (Lev. 25: 55). Children of God are not meant to be in chains.

However, debts and usury are another way of reducing men to slavery. How many marriages and homes today can be broken up by either spouse blaming the other for letting the family fall into a debt trap by, for instance, those tempting credit cards with their usurious rates of interest? Not all debt is unjust, but that it is often used as a means of enslaving one's fellow men (or whole nations!). By regularly dissolving all debts, Moses' sabbatical law breaks such chains, and if one thinks such a law is unjust, notice how today's bankruptcy courts are nevertheless tending to fulfill the same function.

Finally the Mosaic Jubilee law cancelled the enslavement of land to money such as we have everywhere today. In modern cities nobody has a stable environment wherever there is more money to be made by tearing the city buildings down. In the country money uproots every farmer who can be replaced by more or less poisonous chemicals and machines. Moses' law cut this stranglehold of money and put people back on their land where God meant them to be, for "the land is mine" (Lev. 25: 23).

In brief, the Mosaic Jubilee broke various kinds of chains by which men will always tend to enslave one another materially. As then the Old Testament points to the New Testament far surpassing it, so the essence of the Catholic Jubilee is that it breaks various chains of sin by which men enslave themselves spiritually. For if the remission of material debts, perhaps foolishly or unintentionally incurred, can be a weight off a man's mind, like a new start in life, an immense natural relief, how much greater will be the supernatural relief, if it is properly understood, of there being lifted off a man's spiritual life the crushing expectation of all the temporal punishment still due in Purgatory to his sins, punishment which he can see little normal chance of paying off in this life!

That is why down all the Christian centuries Catholics made penitential pilgrimages to the tombs of Saints Peter and Paul in Rome. In 1300 Pope Boniface VIII regularized this practice by pronouncing that year a Jubilee Year. In other words he pronounced that by his power as Pope he was opening up the Church's treasure chest of merits and graces to make available to all pilgrims fulfilling certain conditions in their pilgrimage the full remission, or plenary indulgence, of all punishment in Purgatory still due to their sins once a valid sacramental confession had obtained remission of the eternal punishment due to them in Hell.

Popes following Boniface VIII proclaimed Jubilees at various intervals until 1475, since when they have been given to Catholics by the Pope every quarter century. Thus Pope Paul VI and Pope John Paul II were in line with Catholic Tradition when they proclaimed Jubilees for 1975 and 2000 respectively. In 1975 Archbishop Lefebvre led all his seminarians from Ecône down to Rome to take part in the Jubilee, although Rome turning neo-modernist gave us a cold welcome. In August 2000 Bishop Fellay will lead all Society members available and willing to Rome, although Rome with 35 years of the Council now behind us it risks giving us an even colder welcome.

This is because the Newchurchmen organizing this millennial Jubilee are doing what they can to dilute and distort its Catholic character. The dilution is achieved in a way typical of the "reforms" following on Vatican II: to the classical disciplinary requirements of a Jubilee are added conditions so loose and imprecise that they can mean almost nothing.

Thus in the November 29, 1998 decree of the Apostolic Penitentiary, laying out what works one must do to obtain the Jubilee indulgence, the first two sections prescribe the visits, normal for a Jubilee, to one of the four patriarchal basilicas in Rome, to which are added two more basilicas and a shrine and the catacombs near Rome, and three basilicas in the Holy Land. These two sections clearly specify the places to be visited and the prayers or acts of piety to be performed there. So far so good.

The third section is looser and less demanding. In any Catholic diocese of the world, the diocesan cathedral will serve the same purpose as the basilicas mentioned above, and so will any other diocesan church or shrine designated for that purpose by the diocesan bishop. Also it will suffice now, in addition to a Pater Noster, Ave Maria and Creed, to do "for a certain time a pious meditation." However, such extended conditions for a Jubilee are still traditional.

What is not traditional is the fourth section. Anywhere in the world it will be enough to visit a brother in need or difficulty, such as "prisoners, the sick, old people, the handicapped, etc"! The usual conditions of Confession, Communion and prayer are still mentioned, but the penitential character of a pilgrimage is gone. As if to make up for that, the last paragraph is penitential, but then it is even looser! The Jubilee Indulgence can be obtained by merely going without anything superfluous for a day like tobacco or alcohol, or by fasting or abstaining for a day, or by some "proportional" alms given to the poor, etc., etc. But what does "proportional" here mean? It can mean all or nothing. Such vagueness destroys law. Is not the Sacred Penitentiary dissolving the Indulgence?

As for the Newchurch's distortion of the Jubilee, that is of course by ecumenism. Here are three examples.

At the end of this month they are organizing a "Study Convention on the implementation of the Second Vatican Ecumenical Council," in other words how to push into effect even more the revolutionary principles that have been devastating the Church for the last 35 years.

On Ash Wednesday, March 8, they mean to hold a "Request for Pardon" ceremony in the Coliseum in which the Pope himself will apologize to all the world for Catholic features of the Church's past, like the Inquisition, or the condemnation of Galileo, or the condemnations of the Synagogue. But the Inquisition rendered extraordinary service to "Western civilization" (then called Christendom) by picking out those heretics who were its worst enemies. The condemnation of Galileo was designed to block not scientific truth but his personal arrogance in the name of science which has been giving "science" a bad name ever since. And the condemnations of the Synagogue, which is the religion not of Abraham and Moses, but of Annas and Caiphas, have been elementary self-defense on the part of the Catholic

Richard N. Williamson

Church, because the spiritual descendants of those two judicial murderers of Jesus Christ have for 2,000 years been continuing their work of hatred against the Mystical Body of Christ, the Catholic Church.

This Pope may mean well, God knows. It looks like it. But he lost his Catholic head, when, in his own words, he "discovered" it at Vatican II!

Finally they promise us for the Holy Year in Rome on Sunday May 7 an "Ecumenical service for the 'new martyrs'." The media tell us that these are to include numerous non-Catholics. But it is of the essence of martyrdom in the true sense that the martyr is being killed because of his Catholic Faith. "Martyr" in Greek means witness. He is witnessing to the Faith by the testimony of his death. If he does not have the faith, how can his death witness to it? Madness! These Newchurchmen are, as such, dissolving the Catholic Faith!

However, Catholics need not content themselves with the loose conditions diluting the Jubilee, nor need they attend the ecumenical happenings that distort it. The SSPX is making the Pilgrimage of Tradition to the tombs of Saints Peter and Paul in Rome in order to pray for the Church (and for the Pope!), to gain the Jubilee Indulgences in the normal way, to attach themselves more firmly to eternal Rome and to give witness to the true Faith. Despite our failings, we and all who share our Faith are the Roman Catholics. Despite their virtues, the Newchurchmen are Roman Protestants. Rome, its Basilicas and its Jubilees belong to us, not to them.

Dear readers, please pray for my stricken mother approaching death without the Catholic Faith. She has led a good life in the eyes of the world, but she will need much grace to die a good death in the eyes of God. I thank you in advance.

Our Lord's Agony & Vatican II

"**J**ESUS CHRIST, YESTERDAY, and today; and the same for ever" (Heb. 13: 8). At the Second Vatican Council (1962–1965), a host of leading Catholic churchmen sought to bend Our Lord out of shape because they thought that His Church had become out-of-date. Let us for the beginning of this Lent meditate briefly upon the beginning of our Lord's Passion in the Garden of Gethsemane to see how closely the Gospel fits our own times.

Let us start with the background to Our Lord's Agony in the Garden, which was His isolation from the mass of men. True, a few days before there were, on Palm Sunday, crowds of Israelites crying out "Hosanna, Hosanna to the son of David" in jubilation at the entry into the Holy City of the Rabbi of Nazareth who had been so good to many of them, but events one day after, when many of the same Israelites would be crying out "Crucify him, crucify him," were going to show that this jubilation, like the weeping of the daughters of Jerusalem on the Way of the Cross, was mainly sentimental.

Among Western peoples at this turn from the 20th to the 21st centuries there are still the vestiges of a gen-

eralized good will towards the teacher Jesus and His
Christianity in general, but that good will is largely
sentimental and it is being fast eroded by the media,
politicians and universities which are, by those peoples'
fault, controlled by the successors of the "chief priests
and ancients persuading the people to make Jesus
away" (Mt. 27: 20). In reality, it is Our Lord who is solely responsible for the benefits of what is called "Western civilization," but the peoples are letting the media
persuade them to the contrary, such that if things continue without interruption on their present course, it
is merely a matter of time before the peoples will, following their democratic media, be baying for the blood
of Christians: "It is all the Christians' fault! Away with
them to detention camps! Death if necessary! We want
Barabbas' New World Order!"

Our Lord was nevertheless accompanied by a handful of faithful friends into the Garden of Gethsemane,
the twelve Apostles minus Judas. These Apostles had
no idea what Judas was then doing to plot and contrive,
with the chief priests, Our Lord's destruction, but of
course every detail had been known to Our Lord by His
divine omniscience from eternity. In fact without at all
partaking in Judas' sin, Our Lord had sent Him on his
way to betray (Jn. 13: 27), because through that sin freely
chosen by Judas, our Lord would work the Redemption
of mankind.

A few years ago, Archbishop Lefebvre used to say that
we have little idea of all that the Freemasons and their
collaborators inside the Vatican are plotting and con-
triving in order to deliver the Catholic Church bound
hand and foot into the power of Christ's enemies, but
God has obviously known every detail from all eternity.
If then He chooses to allow His enemies such a seeming triumph over Him as today's chaos in the Catholic
Church, we can and must be sure that without in any

— 80 —

way causing their sin, God is making use of it to bring about tomorrow some great good.

The Apostles in Gethsemane might have understood this if by prayer they had enlightened their minds to enter into the ways of God, which are not men's ways (Is. 55: 8, 9). As it was, Peter and his fellow Apostles were full of a confidence all too human (Mt. 26: 35), so that even when Our Lord urged them to watch and pray that they might not enter into temptation, the spirit indeed being willing but the flesh weak (Mt. 26: 41), still they did not keep awake, but nodded asleep, while Judas Iscariot was hard at work.

At Vatican II, the mass of the world's Catholic bishops cannot have been watching and praying in the sense here required by Our Lord, because they were caught asleep at the switch by the very active enemies of Our Lord, blueprinting the destruction of the Church by the votes of those bishops (see Fr. Ralph Wiltgen's *The Rhine flows into the Tiber*). Since that time Catholic Tradition has reawoken, but it had better now watch and pray with its suffering Master if it is not to fall asleep again and get taken by surprise again like the Apostles in Gethsemane.

Interesting question – supposing the Apostles had stayed awake to pray as Our Lord asked, what would or could they have done? Firstly, they would have given human consolation and support to the human heart of Our Lord in His hour of terrible agony. Then they would not have prevented Our Lord's capture, nor, enlightened by prayer, might they even have tried to do so, because how then should the Scriptures be fulfilled? (Mt. 26: 54) But they would not have shamefully fled, and even so they would not have been harmed themselves, because Our Lord guaranteed their safety. (Jn. 18: 8, 9)

Through the triple prayer of His Agony, Our Lord in His humanity, without human support, found in God the strength to go through with His Passion. When His enemies at last arrived in the Garden of Gethsemane, led by Judas betraying Him with a kiss, Our Lord far from reproaching Him, appealed to Him – "Friend, what have you come for?" This "Friend" is astonishing in the circumstances, but such is Our Lord, thinking only of souls and their salvation – Judas, think what you are doing, and repent, before you cast yourself into a terrible and eternal damnation!

In today's crisis of Church and world, our strength is in God alone, because humanly speaking we are powerless in the face of the trials confronting us. Our enemies are all-powerful, those inside the Church being much more dangerous than those outside. Just as the chief priests and ancients hated Jesus unto death, but they needed an Apostle to betray Him, so we may blame Jews and Freemasons and others like them for engineering the destruction of the Church, but it has taken churchmen from within to do the actual betraying and destroying. Does Our Lord hate these traitors, as we can be sorely tempted to do? No, He seeks only their salvation, although their punishment will be horrible if they do not repent.

After being betrayed with a kiss in Gethsemane, Jesus calmly asked the Temple rabble whom they sought. "Jesus of Nazareth!" they cry out. "That is me," says Our Lord, but in such a way that they all crash to the ground (Jn. 18: 6)! Obviously it is Our Lord who is in control. But He wishes to suffer, so He smothers the power of His majesty and lets them arrest Him – "This is your hour and the power of darkness" (Lk. 22: 53). Obviously at any moment today the Lord God could stop the Church wreckers dead in their tracks, but in March of 2000 it looks as though He is still choosing not to do so. Because God is holding back, the Devil has virtually a free rein and we are undergoing the bitter experience of the power of darkness. But God's hour will come.

However Simon Peter could not wait. Single-handed with one sword he was ready to take on the whole Temple rabble that had come out to arrest Jesus. Virile and courageous, adoring Our Lord, he could not stand by inactive. He had to act! He slashes off an enemy ear, only to be told to sheathe his sword by our Lord, who proceeds to look after the enemy! How many good men there are today who similarly cannot bear to stand by inactive, as it seems, and watch the rabble of mankind (as they can seem to us) tearing to pieces every last shred of truth and decency. Surely we can DO something! Surely we MUST do something! Let us slash the ears off a few Jews and Freemasons, etc.! But then we would find Our Lord only stooping over them to look after them! "You know not of what spirit you are." (Lk. 9: 55)

To Peter he gave three reasons why he wanted him to put away his sword (Mt. 26: 52–54). Firstly, those who take the sword will perish by the sword. Secondly, if Our Lord wanted to defend Himself by force, He could have 12 legions of angels at His side in a flash. Thirdly, if He was delivered from the hands of His enemies, how then would Scripture (e.g., Isaiah 53: 10) be fulfilled? All three reasons bear closely on our situation today.

Firstly, if the friends of Our Lord make the cause of Our Lord into a trial of force, then as sheep amongst wolves (Mt. 10: 16) they can easily be overwhelmed by force. We think of those well-intentioned souls in Waco, TX, who seven years ago took guns and perished by flame-throwers. Not that resorting to force is always wrong, but it will rarely win over men's hearts. If Our Lord's friends make Him into the Knave of Clubs and sticks (Mt. 26: 55), they will never make Him what He wants to be, the King of Hearts. All hearts He will draw after Him by being raised on the Cross (Jn. 3: 14, 15). Even today when sin has gone so far that God may use the force of a Chastisement to set things straight, still we will see the Church revived by the free and not forced love of men for God. Noah was not forced to love God as he did, either before or after the Flood.

Secondly, in any trial of force between good and evil, the Creator could crush His creatures whenever He wished. A few mere legions of angels could do that. But, again, the Creator seeks conversions, not concussions! Supposing all today's corrupt churchmen were liquidated, would the Church's problems be solved? Of course not. So long as souls were not converted, other churchmen would merely take their place and become equally corrupt.

Thirdly, God decreed from eternity that His Son would die on the Cross to redeem mankind. This decree was progressively revealed to the Old Testament prophets, notably Isaiah, who consigned it to Scripture. There is no way in which such a prophecy can be not fulfilled. Similarly Scripture reveals that at the end of the world to which we are now winding down, the Catholic Church will be very small (Lk. 18: 8) and fiercely persecuted by the Antichrist (Apoc. 13: 7). It may be mysterious that God should have decreed to allow this virtual disappearance of His Church, but there is no questioning the decree or its fulfillment. "Thus it behooved Christ to suffer, and rise again from the dead" (Lk. 24: 46). The Mystical Body of Christ, the Church, must suffer in like fashion today, and while each of us must do his duty of state, none of us is going to change that decree.

But since Peter and his companions did not pray in the Garden when Our Lord told them to, they could not grasp what He was saying. Did He not want to defend Himself? Did He not want them to defend Him? Was He out of his mind? What kind of a Master was this? He had betrayed them! In the hour of Satan the Apostles' minds were overwhelmed by such thoughts of darkness, and as we say today, "they lost it." They fled, and abandoned

Our Lord. If Catholics today attempt to grasp by any merely human measure this crisis of the Church, unique by its scale and depth in 2000 years of Church history, they risk being overwhelmed by darkness. As Archbishop Lefebvre repeatedly said, "What is happening is unimaginable, inconceivable." But it is here. And whereas the Apostles had only verbal warnings from Our Lord of His coming Passion, Catholics ever since have had the extraordinary events of that Passion to throw light upon the sufferings of Christ's Mystical Body, the Church.

Then let us this Lent meditate on Gethsemane (Mt. 26: 36–56; Mk. 14: 32–52; Lk. 22: 39–54; Jn. 18: 1–12) in order neither to rage uselessly at the enemies of Our Lord, nor join them, nor run away from His Church in its hour of need, but to stand by in prayer and if necessary in suffering, to await the hour appointed by God for the triumph of His cause.

I thank and bless all of you praying for my mother (Helen by name), but I have to warn you that she will not be easy to convert. Into God's hands...

The Pope's Millennial Apology: Deeply Confused, Deeply Confusing

THE MARCH 12 ceremony in Rome, known to many of you from the media, when the Pope apologized for all kinds of past sins of the Catholic Church, is so confusing that it will take a long letter to try to sort out the confusion.

This letter divides into three main sections. Firstly, general <u>principles</u> governing how Catholics should or should not apologize. These principles were hardly respected in the ceremony of March 12. Secondly, the confusing <u>way</u> in which JP2 and those who think like him express themselves, and why they express themselves in this way. Thirdly, the confusing <u>content</u> of their thoughts, because they are trying to make the Church think like the world, instead of making the world think like the Church.

For easier reading, we will use again the question and answer format.

Q: Firstly, may we get straight exactly what happened in Rome on March 12?

A: Some time ago the Vatican announced that amongst its plans for the Catholic Church's celebration of this Jubilee Year, there would be a new ceremony in which the Pope with high Church officials would pray to God for pardon for various sins of the Church. This ceremony took place on the first Sunday of this Lent within a High Mass concelebrated by Pope and Cardinals in St. Peter's Basilica, Rome.

In his sermon at this Mass, the Pope said, "As Successor of St. Peter I have asked, in this (Jubilee) year of mercy, for the Church . . . to kneel down before God and beg pardon for the past and present sins of her children."

Next five Cardinals and two archbishops successively introduced seven categories of sins of Catholics for which the Pope then recited a prayer to God asking for pardon. Each time a cantor and the assembly sang a triple Kyrie eleison and a lamp was lit before a Crucifix. The ceremony concluded with a general prayer by the Pope and with his kissing the crucifix. What interests us here is of course the text of those seven prayers for pardon which specified the supposed seven categories of sins.

SECTION ONE: PRINCIPLES OF CATHOLIC APOLOGY

Q: What is wrong with apologizing? Catholics are decent people. Is it not a decent and honorable thing to recognize one's past mistakes, and to admit them in public?

A: To apologize is an honorable thing to do, but on three conditions. Firstly, for anybody at all, it must be for a genuine and not imaginary error or sin. Now a number of sins apologized for by the churchmen on March 12 are

Richard N. Williamson

highly fashionable but very unclear, e,g., "anti-semitism," "racism," "sexism." To apologize for them promotes the unclarity, i.e., confusion.

Secondly, for anybody in authority, he must not apologize in such a way as to undermine his own authority, because that authority exists not for his own benefit but – when properly exercised – for the benefit of all beneath that authority. When on March 12 Pope John Paul II implicitly condemned many of his predecessors (for instance for approving of the Inquisition), he implicitly undermined the Papacy and himself. If we need not listen to previous Popes, why should we listen to him?

Thirdly, for any Catholic, he may apologize for human sinfulness in the Church (on the two conditions above), but he absolutely may not apologize for anything divine in the Church, because that is implicitly to criticize or condemn God, which is blasphemy. So a Catholic apologizing for sins of Catholics must be extra careful that nobody can take him to be apologizing for any of the many divine things in the Catholic Church, for instance its being guided down the ages by the Holy Ghost. But anybody listening to the apologies of March 12 could easily think that Church principles and practice have been wrong for centuries.

Q: But the Catholic Church is a human institution full of human beings capable of making human errors, surely all of them matter for apology.

A: True, the Catholic Church is human, it exists only in humans and these humans God chooses to leave capable of sinning. But the Catholic Church, alone amongst human institutions, is also divine.

Q: Why?

A: Because the Catholic Church is the institution established amongst men by Our Divine Lord to continue

His Incarnation amongst men in its work of saving souls down to the end of the world. As Our Lord was prophet, king and priest, so His Church saves souls by teaching (prophet), governing (king) and sanctifying (priest). And as Our Lord was and is true God, so His Church is truly divine by its infallibility in teaching, by its authority in governing, and by its supernatural power in sanctifying, especially by the seven sacraments.

Q: But all human beings err, and churchmen remain human beings. How can any church be infallible?

A: It stands to reason that God's own Church, the Catholic Church, must be infallible. For if God creates souls with free will and commands them on pain of eternal damnation (Mk. 16: 16) to make the right use of that free will, how can He not provide them with a source of certain or infallible truth as to how to use that free will rightly? Either there is no God commanding any such thing, or, if there is, then somewhere, and clearly recognizable, there must be an accessible and totally reliable source where I can be sure of finding those truths upon which the eternal salvation or damnation of my soul depends.

Q: But everyone knows how churchmen are always into church politics. How can such men have divine authority in governing?

A: It stands to reason, again, that God's own Church – nobody else's – must be endowed with full authority to command those actions upon which salvation or damnation depends. The crowds in our Lord's time noticed how he taught them "as one having power, and not as the scribes and Pharisees" (Mt. 7: 29). How often (especially in St. John's Gospel) Our Lord told the Jews not just to listen to Him as a man, but to believe His miracles and to accept that He was speaking on behalf of His Father in heaven. Similarly the Catholic Church must speak the truth of God and with the authority of God. If it pretends to souls that it is speaking with merely human authority, it is betraying those souls.

Q: *Then a divine authority perhaps, but how can the merely human beings who make up the Church possess a divine power to sanctify?*

A: They do not possess it by themselves, because sanctity is of God, so sanctification must come from God. But God gives to His Catholic Church the seven sacraments which the churchmen (mostly) must administer. In these sacraments is His own sanctifying grace, and in the Holy Eucharist in particular is, mysteriously, God Himself, Body, Blood, Soul and Divinity, truly and really and substantially present. Men administer. God sanctifies, but usually through men.

Q: *If the Catholic Church is as divine as you say it is, then how can it also be human?*

A: Just as Our Lord was true God and true man, and to deny either truth leads into great errors, so the Catholic Church is not only divine in its origin, design, institution, mission and endowments as said above, but also it is truly human, and to deny either aspect of the Church is to expose oneself to serious danger of error. The Church is truly human because it consists in a society of men (it is nowhere to be found where there are no men), and these men, even those singled out by God and called to be leaders in His Church, remain sinners with free will and sinful tendencies until the day they die. We think of Peter, the first Pope, whom Our Lord once had to call "Satan" (Mt. 16: 23), who denied his Master three times (Mt. 26: 74), and who had to be, even when Pope, corrected by his brother Paul on a point of major importance for the future of the Church. (Gal. 2: 11–14)

Q: But if the Catholic Church is so laden with divine things as you say, how can God have left these in such sinful hands?

A: It is a mystery, but that is what God chose to do. However, ask yourself: if Our Lord had not been truly human, could He have drawn men to follow Him as He did? If the Church was administered by angels and not by men, would men feel that such a Church was for them? God works through and with the good churchmen whom He rewards, He works through and around the bad churchmen who do not escape His punishment.

Q: Divine and human, human and divine, it is all rather confusing!

A: In the Catholic Church as in our Lord, the human and the divine are never separate but they are always distinct. And in considering Our Lord or His Church, to separate the divine and the human, or not correctly to distinguish between them, leads likewise into error. If I do not distinguish clearly, either I am liable to credit human error with divine infallibility, like all the liberals at present following blindly the errors of this Rome, or I risk dismissing the divine institution together with its human sinfulness, as one may think sedevacantists do who say these liberal popes are too sinful to be popes. Or I can commit both errors at once! (Sedevacantists are closer than they think to liberals!)

Q: How does all of this apply to the March 12 apologizing in Rome?

A: First and foremost, it is clear as clear can be to anybody who has the Catholic Faith that if I undertake to apologize for past errors of the Church, I cannot possibly apologize for anything which is divine in the Church, I can only be apologizing for what is human and sinful, like St. Peter's mistake, mentioned above, of showing too

Richard N. Williamson

much respect for the religion of the Synagogue after it had perished with Our Lord's death upon the Cross.

Q: But on March 12 the Pope seemed to be apologizing for Catholics having too little respect for the Jews and their Covenant, i.e., the religion of the Synagogue!

A: Exactly. Instead of drawing the line between human sinfulness and the divine Catholic Church which condemns all other religions, JP2 gives the impression of drawing the line between the old "judgmental" Church needing to be apologized for, and the post-conciliar Newchurch which tolerates and greets all other religions. Put simply, Catholics always used to say, "Catholic is good, new is bad." JP2's apology seems to say "That old Catholic thing is bad, the new is good." He is turning the Church upside down.

SECTION TWO: THE MODE OF
EXPRESSION OF THE APOLOGY

Q: But why do you say JP2 "gives the impression of drawing the line"? Did not the media quite clearly understand what he meant?

A: We hit a major problem which is best tackled before we look at the Pope's own words. They are nearly always ambiguous, i.e., capable of meaning two things at once.

Q: Why?

A: Because JP2 believes not only in the Newchurch, he ALSO believes in the "old" Church.

Q: But that is impossible! The Newchurch, as you just said, turns everything in the "old" Church upside down! The two contradict one another at every point!

A: When men want to have their cake and eat it, they have a remarkable way of being able to live in contradiction. When they want to dance with the Devil and be on good terms with God, there are remarkable things they can do with their own minds. Like Paul VI, JP2 wants to be both modern AND Catholic. He lives in between Catholicism and modernity, so he breathes ambiguity and contradiction, so he by instinct finds ambiguous words to express what he lives and breathes.

Q: That is ridiculous! How can anything ambiguous be Catholic? Does not the Lord God say He hates a double tongue?

A: Indeed He does (Prov. 8: 13). But try arguing from the texts we are going to argue from that the Pope is turning the Church upside down, and you will find that "conservative" Catholics, for instance, to defend their Pope, will nearly always be able to find a Catholic escape hatch in his words, so that these can be given a Catholic meaning.

Q: Well, a Catholic meaning is certainly not what the media found in his words. These may contain escape hatches, but the whole drift of their meaning is modern.

A: JP2 instinctively and deliberately chooses words both defendable by Conservatives and pleasing to modern liberals. Instinctively, because he himself lives a double life and breathes it. Deliberately, because he wants the whole Church to get modern without breaking with its roots, as he sees it.

Q: What you say is hair-raising! Can you give some examples?

A: Let us start with John Paul's own words in his sermon of March 12, just preceding the ceremony of apology. He said, for instance, "We beg pardon (1) for the divisions that have arisen amongst Christians, (2) for the resort to violence by some Christians in the service of truth, and (3) for the attitudes of distrust and hostility sometimes shown towards followers of other religions."

(1) When he begs pardon "for divisions," does he mean, with the mind of the Church, any sins of Catholics contributing to those divisions, or does he mean, with the Newchurch, that all those movements breaking away from the Catholic Church, like Orthodoxy and Protestantism, should never have been condemned? We fear he means the second, but he avoids clearly saying so.

(2) When he mentions "the resort to violence in the service of truth," does he mean, with the mind of the Church, any sins of Christians wrongfully resorting to violence to serve truth, or is he expressing the mind of the Newchurch, namely the liberal principle whereby any and all resort to force in the service of truth is wrong? Everything points to him meaning the second, but putting in the word "some" enables him still to be taken as saying the first.

(3) When he refers to "the attitudes of distrust and hostility sometimes shown towards followers of other religions," does he mean, with the mind of the Church, blameworthy acts of distrust and hostility, or does he mean, with the Newchurch and against all common sense, that centuries-old enemies of the Church are really nice people and are never to be distrusted? We fear he means the second, but the "sometimes" serves as an escape hatch to allow him still just to be interpreted as meaning the first.

Q: In context, don't these words of JP2 have to be stretched to be pulled back to a Catholic meaning?

A: Yes, indeed, the whole drift and push of his words is towards the Newchurch which was likewise implicit in the documents of Vatican II. But try telling these liberals that they are not Catholic, and they can nearly always find that escape hatch in the words to get back to a Catholic meaning, because they put the escape hatches there deliberately.

Q: In plain English that is called duplicity! Do these liberals realize how two-faced they are being?

A: God knows whether they realize it, but in many cases one may think they do not, because, bathed in the modern world, many of them are sincerely persuaded that Catholicism needs modernizing, only the modernizing must go easy on the old religion which was good in its day and still has something to offer.

Q: But what you call the "old religion" directly contradicts the Newchurch!

A: That is what liberal Catholics like Paul VI or JP2 do not see, or, do not want to see. Either way, they are blind.

Q: But could there be anything more destructive of the true Church than Church leaders who mean well by "the old religion," but, because they do not understand it, do all they can to remould it?

A: You are right. Archbishop Lefebvre used to say there can be nothing worse for the Church than a liberal on the Seat of Peter. Had Pilate hated Christ, he would have made Him suffer less by condemning him straightaway to be crucified. It was because Pilate was half for Christ and tried half-heartedly to spare Him, that in the event he subjected Christ to the extra sufferings of Herod's court, Barabbas, the scourging at the pillar and the crowning with thorns. "Well-meaning" liberals wreak havoc! Yet they do "mean well," and you will get nowhere with many Conciliar Catholics if you deny that JP2 means well by the old religion.

Q: Then, I would rather nobody ever "meant well" by me in that way!

A: Correct. But it was necessary before looking at the text itself of the apologizing to see how it reaches forward to the destruction of the Church even while it can be stretched backward by those denying the destruction.

SECTION THREE: THE CONTENT
OF THE APOLOGY

Q: *What did the text consist in?*

A: On March 12 in Rome the Pope's sermon was followed by the "Universal Prayer" of "Confession of Sins and Asking for Forgiveness," in which between a brief introduction and conclusion by the Pope, five Cardinals and two archbishops introduced seven categories of sins for which they and the Pope then prayed for pardon.

Q: *What was the first category?*

A: "Sins in general." It was a general prayer for "purification of memory," meaning presumably that Catholics should clean out of their minds errors of the past, or "disobedience" to God which "contradicts the faith we profess and the Holy Gospel." What disobedience? What Gospel? Not yet specified.

Q: *What was the second category?*

A: "Sins committed in the service of truth." The Pope prayed here for the "firm knowledge that truth can prevail only in virtue of truth itself." These words clearly suggest the false liberal principle that force used in the defense of truth is always wrong. On the contrary St. Louis of France, speaking as king, said that in dealing with a heretic, you argue, argue, argue with him, but if he remains obstinate, you run him through with a sword. This is because there is only one Heaven and only one Truth by which to get to that Heaven, so heretics who insist on corrupting that Truth are criminals murdering the eternal life of souls, whereas by comparison even serial murderers in this life are merely shortening the brief life of bodies here below. There is no comparison.

If I believe in one Heaven and one Truth, the need for the civil authority sometimes to use force, for instance on heretics, is easy to understand. But if I have any doubt in one Heaven or one truth, then this life becomes all, and force serving truth becomes incomprehensible (as does capital punishment. It appears that JP2 is now lighting up the Coliseum to celebrate each nation renouncing capital punishment!).

Q: Then does he believe in one Heaven and one Truth?

A: By his actions, no. This is indicated also by his prayer for pardon for the third category of sins "which have harmed the unity of the Body of Christ." Here he said amongst other things, "Believers have opposed one another, becoming divided, and have mutually condemned one another and fought against one another."

Q: What is wrong with that?

A: If we consider the Catholic-Orthodox split finalized in 1054, and the Catholic-Protestant split of the 16th century and since, it is obvious that the Catholic churchmen on these occasions have shown various human weaknesses in their dealings with those breaking away from the Catholic Church, but there is no comparison – unless one does not believe in Truth – between the Catholics condemning error and the non-Catholics condemning Truth! When the Orthodox deny papal primacy, they are wrong. When Protestants deny the Real Presence, they are wrong. The mutual condemnations are in no way equivalent, as JP2's silence on their difference implies. By slurring the Catholics in the way that he does, he also slurs the divine doctrine. Any Catholic apologizing for Catholics' human sins must in no way allow the slur to pass over to the divine doctrine, to Catholic faith and morals.

Q: Does this Pope have an inkling of the absoluteness of Catholic truth?

A: That is the question. In the fourth category, "Sins committed against the People of Israel," he says we are saddened by all those who have caused Jews to suffer, and "we wish to commit ourselves to genuine brotherhood with the people of the Covenant." But firstly, Catholics are the people of the New and Eternal Covenant, which did away with the Old Testament or Covenant made on Mount Sinai between God and the Israelites, as substance replaces shadow (Heb. 10: 1). The Jews are no longer the people of a valid Covenant, in fact any religious practice of their dead covenant, because it looks forward to the Messiah coming, has been, ever since the Messiah came, mortal sin, at least objectively.

And secondly, down 2,000 years Jews have repeatedly sought to undermine the Catholic Church and to take Christ out of Christendom (leaving only -endom or end-doom!). In praying to commit the Church to "genuine brotherhood" with these people, does the Pope take into account this lesson of two millennia? He makes no mention of it in his prayer for pardon.

Q: Isn't it against all common sense to want to make friends with your enemies?

A: Yes, unless you are passing over to the enemy . . .

Q: Does this Pope know what he is doing?

A: One wonders. One may think not. One may think he is, in Sister Lucy of Fatima's description of modern churchmen, "diabolically disoriented." One may think he means to serve the Church but is hopelessly – or willfully – confused as to how to do so. God knows.

Q: After the famous sin of "anti-semitism," what next?

A: Racism! "Sins committed in actions against love, peace, the rights of peoples, and respect for cultures and religions." Here the Pope said, "Christians have often violated the rights of ethnic groups and peoples, and shown contempt for their cultures and religious traditions." But how did mankind treat, for instance, black Africa before the Catholic missionaries went inland? As a slave-pool! Any "racist" sins of Catholics pale in comparison with what Mother Church, i.e., Catholics, have done for Africans and for all races. As for despising ethnic cultures, are we to suppose that before the Spaniards arrived the weaker peoples enjoyed being human-sacrificed by the culture of the ethnic Aztecs? Where would JP2 himself be if Catholic missionaries had never gone into pagan Poland those many years ago and destroyed its idolatry?

Q: And I suppose after "anti-semitism" and "racism" he apologizes for "sexism"?

A: How did you guess? The sixth category is "Sins against the Dignity of Women and the Unity of the Human Race." The Pope said here that "At times the equality of your (i.e., God's) sons and daughters has not been acknowledged," because women are "all too often humiliated and pushed to one side." But again, what institution on earth can remotely compare with the Catholic Church for the true (not false) honor and glory it gives to womanhood through, especially, the Blessed Virgin Mary but also through all the women Saints? The Catholic Church alone raised up woman to the level of Mary from the level of Eve to which she otherwise necessarily falls and is today again, according as the Church is despised, falling.

Richard N. Williamson

Q: But the Pope no doubt thinks he is promoting women by thus highlighting the "sexism" of "some" Catholics.

A: But is he accusing human sins or Church doctrine? He is certainly trying to make Church doctrine fit the crazy modern notions of "gender equality." Of course man and woman are equal before God and eternity, which is all that really matters, but they are not equal in this life where even before Adam and Eve fell, Adam was to be the head and Eve as close as a rib to his heart. Modern man desperately needs to be retaught, not untaught, the difference between the sexes.

Q: What was the Pope's last category of sins to beg pardon for?

A: "Sins in relation to the fundamental rights of the person." The Pope accuses Christians of having often not recognized Christ in "the hungry, thirsty, naked, persecuted and imprisoned" and in the unborn. But who has taught mankind to look after all these "little ones so dear to God," if not the Catholic Church, i.e., Catholics? The track record of Catholics in creating the very notion of human rights (except insofar as these defy God) is, thanks to the Church, second to none. Instead of thinking like a child of the Church, proud of her incomparable glory, the Pope is seeking to adapt to the mentality of the world which perversely blames the Church for all sorts of fabricated but fashionable sins, like anti-semitism, racism, sexism, etc.

Q: What is Catholic doctrine on these questions?

A: Ever since Eve, God has meant men to lead women (Gen. 3: 16). Ever since Noah, the sons of Japhet, as a broad rule leaving ample room for exceptions, are to lead the sons of Cham and to occupy the tents of Sem (Gen. 9: 27). Sons of Sem, Semites, set up the Catholic Church, God bless them eternally, but it is nearly all

Gentiles (sons of Japhet) who came in after that beginning and for two thousand years built up the Church all over the world. The problem of today's world is not that white gentile males are leading it, but that they are not leading it in the Catholic Faith as they are meant to be doing, because they have lost their Faith, and as a just punishment for their apostasy they are being scourged by the uprising of the non-whites, non-Gentiles and non-males whom they have betrayed.

Q: Do you realize you are not being very "politically correct"?

A: Political correctness is for imbeciles. For the Catholic churchmen to be trying to make the Church "politically correct" is a disaster of the first magnitude. The world will love them briefly for doing so, but that love will soon turn to contempt. Possibly the Pope is already disappointed with the apparently low turnout for his unprecedented apologizing. The Catholic salt that loses its savor is soon trampled upon.

Q: Does this Pope have the Catholic Faith?

A: He seems sure that he does. God knows. But Jesus Christ is certainly not for him the Truth that condemns all errors. For him, Jesus Christ's Church is merely the most valid amongst all other more or less valid religions. If the Pope does believe in the Catholic Faith, he does not understand what he believes.

Q: Is he then really Pope?

A: The scandal of something like his March 12 apologizing is so great that one can be tempted to ask such a question. However, this "apology" is merely unfolding the evil folded up inside Vatican II 35 years ago. Archbishop Lefebvre knew all about it back then (see his book *I Accuse the Council*), but he never said these recent Popes were not real popes, he always said they were liberals. By his fruits in this crisis, his judgment is the most reliable.

Q: How can I grasp liberalism in depth?

A: Through the Popes' Encyclicals from the early 1800's through to the 1950's. For an introduction to these Encyclicals, get audio or videotapes of this Seminary's Doctrinal Sessions on the Encyclicals, especially the 1996 Session.

Q: How will Mother Church get out of this incredible problem?

A: By the intercession of the Blessed Virgin Mary. What the Church needs is a Pope who will stand up to the modern world and say, as nicely as you like, "You are all of you liars and you are on the way to Hell." "We will kill you for saying so!" "Kill me, but until you change your ways, I can say nothing else." And if only there were enough such Popes, one after another, to let themselves be killed for the Truth, at last the Truth would prevail.

That was how the Catholic Church was built in the first place, by a long series of martyr Popes. That is how it must be rebuilt today, and if anyone reasonably argues that the state of mankind presently makes such a thing impossible, then there remains only a Chastisement to straighten out mankind.

So let us be prepared for hours darker yet before the dawn, and meanwhile, as Our Lord tells us to do, let us "possess our souls in patience." (Lk. 21: 19) And let us, as Our Lady told the children at Fatima to do, pray for the Pope, and for all the misguided churchmen, in Rome especially.

Dear Readers, spring is coming again, and the prospect of summer. God does not change, and He continues to be good to us.

Our Lady of Fatima

A FASCINATING ARTICLE in a recent issue of an American Catholic periodical, *All These Things*, told me a little fact about Our Lady of Fatima that I had not known, and which is most revealing, and reassuring. For Our Lady's month of May, let us present this proof of her presence and power amidst all the wickedness of the world around us. But we must begin with quite a bit of background.

Most readers will be familiar with the main outlines of the story of Our Lady of Fatima, referred to also in this month's accompanying issue of *Verbum*. From May to October of 1917, on the 13th of each month, Our Lady appeared to three little shepherd children in the village of Fatima, Portugal, to teach to the modern world Heaven's answer to the Communist revolution with all the horrors it would bring in its train from October 1917, when it took over the great land of Russia.

Most readers also know that on July 13 Our Lady gave a message to one of the children which is known as the Second Secret. In it she said amongst other things that the war then raging, World War I, would end. "But if men do not cease offending God, another worse one will begin in the reign of Pius XI. When you see a night lit up by an unknown light, know that it is the great sign given you by God that he is about to punish the world for its crimes, by means of war, famine and persecutions against the Church and the Holy Father."

She concluded, "To prevent this, I will come to ask for the consecration of Russia to My Immaculate Heart, and the Communion of Reparation on the first Saturdays of the month. If my requests are granted, Russia will be converted and there will be peace. If not, she will spread her errors throughout the world, raising up wars and persecutions against the Church. The good will be martyred, the Holy Father will have much to suffer. Various nations will be annihilated."

Now most of you know that this Consecration of Russia to Mary's Immaculate Heart which Our Lady called for, has never been properly performed with all the conditions fulfilled as Our Lady requested. The result is that Russia's key error of atheistic materialism has spread all over the world, so that even the United States which once appeared to be a valiant enemy of Communism, is now a Communist country in all but name. Then when was the night "lit up by an unknown light," signifying that the still offended God was going to punish the world "by means of war," etc.?

That light appeared all over the sky of Western Europe and then in Northern America on the evening of January 25, 1938. Over a large part of the northern hemisphere "the sky was ablaze like an immense moving furnace, provoking a very strong blood-red glow. The edge of the furnace was white, as if the sun was about to come up," said a newspaper report. It lasted from about 6:30 to 9:30 p.m. in Europe. The "experts" said that it must have been the northern lights, or an "aurora borealis," but those northern lights are caused by sunspots, of which only a minimum were recorded at that time. Also the nature of the light was quite different from that of an "aurora borealis" – on January 25, 1938 in many cities the fire engines rolled out to look for the fire, something they never do for an "aurora borealis."

Lucy, by then Sister, immediately recognized in the unusual night light the warning that Our Lady had told her of 20 years before. And of course in September of 1939, the terrible Second World War began with England and France declaring war on Germany because of Hitler's invasion of Poland. Ironically, this war would result by 1945 in Poland's being betrayed soon after to the Communists, along with the large part of Eastern Europe, a huge triumph for Russia's errors, just as Our Lady had warned at Fatima if Russia were not consecrated to her Immaculate Heart.

Yet when the Second Secret became known, its accuracy in this respect was questioned on two grounds. Firstly, as everybody is told, it was the wicked Hitler and not "Uncle Joe" Stalin who was responsible for the start of WW II. So what sense did it make to call for the consecration of Russia and not of Germany? And secondly, the Second Secret said that "another worse war will begin in the reign of Pius XI." But Pius XI died on February 10, 1939, while the Second World War was only declared on September 3, 1939, under the reign then of Pope Pius XII, not Pius XI. Opponents of Fatima seized on these "mistakes" to discredit the Second Secret.

However, in Brother Michael of the Holy Trinity's wonderful three-volume series "The Whole Truth about Fatima," published in English as part of Fr. Nicholas Gruner's heroic efforts to get the Fatima message out to the world, Brother Michael answers these objections (Vol.II, pp. 688–702). He shows that in reality it was Stalin who cleverly maneuvered Hitler into declaring war on the Western democracies, which means that Communist Russia was really the one to blame. Stalin calculated that once another huge fight between Germany,

France and Britain had exhausted them all, then Russia would step in and take over Europe. Indeed World War II resulted in Communism taking over the Eastern half of Europe. So the real criminal who started the war could be identified as the one who finally profited from it, not Hitler but Stalin.

The second objection concerning Pope Pius XI or XII then solves itself: the Second World War began not really with Hitler's invasion of Poland, but with the prior dealings between Hitler and Stalin culminating in the famous German-Russian Ribbentrop non-aggression Pact of August 23, 1939, which by covering Hitler to the East enabled him within ten days to defy his enemies to the West. (So it turned out. War between Germany and Russia broke out only in June of 1941). Thus WW II started in secret well before it started in public, under Pius XI's reign as Our Lady said, and not under Pius XII's. It is remarkable confirmation of this explanation which appeared in the recent *All These Things*.

Many of you know of the great struggle in the 1930's between nationalist and internationalist Communists. Inside Russia, the nationalist Stalin had succeeded in ousting his former ally, the internationalist Trotsky, but the internationalists, then and now real rulers of the modern world, were plotting inside Russia to oust Stalin in turn. He discovered their plot, imprisoned the ringleaders, put them on trial in the famous show trials of the Great Purge of 1937 and 1938, and had them shot.

However one victim who escaped death was a certain Christian Rakovsky (Christian only in name), one of the internationalists who considered Stalin had betrayed Communism by putting the interests of Russia and himself first. Rakovsky, to save his life, promised to tell Stalin secrets of great value to Stalin. Stalin who knew that Rakovsky was one of those few men who are the real rulers of the world, agreed to listen. The resulting interrogation of Rakovsky by one of Stalin's agents inside the prison was recorded by the interpreter present for the interrogation, and by him it was smuggled out of the prison. By remarkable circumstances it reached the West, where it should be far better known that it is, but of course the modern world has a thousand ways of smothering its own dirty secrets. God puts in men's hands the *Protocols of the Sages of Sion* and the "Rakovsky Interview," if men want to know the truth, but few do.

What Rakovsky told Stalin's agent was that as far as "they" were concerned (meaning the internationalist plotters for world control by money) he, Stalin, had betrayed their Communist Revolution in Russia. So to bring Stalin down, "they" had brought Hitler to power by giving to his Nazi party crucial financial support in the late 1920's. However, Hitler, by issuing his own money to replace their debt-money, was now liberating Germany from their control, a liberation so threatening to their world power that they were now willing to forget their feud with Stalin and join with him in crushing Hitler. So here was the deal, said Rakovsky: if Stalin would put out feelers to Hitler for a Hitler-Stalin pact, to include a joint invasion and partitioning of Poland, then Stalin would get all kinds of decisive help from the USA and from other unexpected quarters, and when the Hitler-Stalin deal had produced the desirable war to crush Hitler, then Stalin could be given Europe (in the event he got half of it). But if Stalin would not put out those feelers towards Hitler, then he could expect from those same quarters to be crushed himself!

Rakovsky's interrogator required confirmation of such secret realities. Rakovsky told him to check out his truthfulness with – the USA ambassador in Moscow! This Mr. Davis duly confirmed everything Rakovsky had said. Rakovsky's life was spared. Stalin put out the feelers to Hitler, and the Ribbentrop Pact and World War II were well on their way.

Now when exactly did the Rakosvky interview take place? From midnight to 6 am, Moscow time, in the night of Jan. 25–26, 1938, or, from 9 pm to 3 am West European time! In other words, the beginning of that interview overlapped exactly with the end of Our Lady's warning light in the night sky!

Dear readers, God is in command. He and His Mother know exactly what they are doing. They do not expect all of us to know such details as above of the plotting of wicked men, but especially when we do know them, Heaven expects us to take the simple remedial action which it puts in the hands of all of us – the prayer of the Rosary and the five first Saturdays. We cannot see, but we must believe in, the world-saving power of these simple remedies. "In that same hour, Jesus rejoiced in the Holy Ghost, and said: I confess to Thee, O Father, because thou hast hidden these things from the wise and prudent, and hast revealed them to little ones. Yea, Father, for so it hath seemed good in thy sight." (Lk. 10: 21)

Towards the Mother of God we need to have the boundless trust and obedience of little ones.

Promises to Reveal the Third Secret

INTERESTING PIECES OF information come out of Rome. No doubt many of them are known to you from other sources where they are more fully and accurately reported than in this Letter. Let us give here a composite picture of events with the factors at work today which must govern the details also for tomorrow.

Firstly, when I was in Italy for several days after Easter, I came across a book called *Bugie di sangue in Vaticano* or, *Bloody Lies in the Vatican*. Cast your minds back two years to early May of 1998. You may remember the media at that time reporting the bloody triple killing, in the Pontifical Swiss Guard's quarters inside the Vatican buildings in Rome, of the Commanding Officer of the Swiss Guard, and his wife, and a young vice-corporal of the same Swiss Guard.

The Pope's spokesman or main officer for the Press, Joaquín Navarro-Valls, immediately gave out, and the world's media followed him in declaring, that the young vice-corporal had in a fit of clinical madness or out of personal jealousy (of a kind in accordance with or against nature – we could take our pick) gunned down his commander and wife, and then turned his gun on himself. With this version of the events coming from the Vatican and the media, the world seemed to be content, and so in the great flow of world news the sensational shedding of blood inside the headquarters of the Catholic Church soon dropped out of view as a nine- or perhaps three-day wonder.

The story told in *Bugie di sangue* is somewhat different. Inside the Vatican the liberal-liberal organization of Freemasonry is all-powerful, and it has since the 1970's established its own police force inside the Vatican, called the *Corpo della Vigilanza* (Vigilance Brigade), to control happenings around the Pope. Now rises in the 1980's "Opus Dei," a conservative-liberal organization favored by Pope John Paul II, because he can like liberal principles to be applied in a relatively conservative way. To exploit and consolidate its own influence around the Pope, "Opus Dei" set up in the late 90's one of its members to become Commander of the Swiss Guard, so that the Swiss Guard would become the effective police of the Vatican. For months the Freemasons succeeded in delaying this man's nomination as Commander, but at last on May 4, 1998, his appointment was announced. Within nine hours of that official announcement he lay in a pool of blood with his wife and a "culprit" conveniently dead on the floor of his apartment.

The Vatican Secretariat of State wanted the Commander and his wife to be buried with all honors, the young vice-corporal to be treated like a suicide. The previous Swiss Guard Commander, called back in haste to fill provisionally the gap left by his successor's untimely death, would have none of it. He had all three victims buried with equal honours. He knew. He does not talk. Nor do a host of people inside the Vatican talk, although they also know, just like in Dallas after the 1963 murder of J. F. Kennedy. People have a funny way of wishing to live. Freemasonry is powerful. And it is ruthless. And it is in command (humanly speaking) inside the Vatican. That is why out of the Vatican in its present state there is nothing to be expected except worldwide lies and bloody murder. As Archbishop Lefebvre used to say, we do not know the small part of the evil reigning inside this Vatican. And of course the media fall in line, being controlled by the same people as control the Vatican.

This Vatican plays with organizations under its control that seek to defend the Catholic Faith, like a cat plays with mice. Apparently Msgr. Wach, head of the Institute of Christ the King, sent the Institute's seminarians home from its seminary in Gricigliano after Easter, with no date fixed for their return – "for financial reasons." Like putting their money on the Traditional Liturgy?

As for St. Peter's Fraternity, it appears that the Superior General, so "generously reinstated" by the Vatican, as we were told, at their crisis meeting in February, wanted to demote a disloyal District Superior (no names), but was prevented from doing so by the Vatican – because the latter was loyal to Rome? Some "reinstatement"! Nor is Rome accepting any longer the "secret" agreement it accepted in February whereby priests of St. Peter's will not celebrate the New Mass at any other time so long as they may concelebrate it with their diocesan bishop on Maundy Thursday – because so few actually did so this last April 20?

But if you let the fox into the henhouse, how do you expect it not to eat the hens? Just how long will all these conservative Catholics go on blaming Archbishop Lefebvre for not letting the Roman fox into his chicken coops? How much more evidence do they need? One person in the case of the Swiss Guard murders who at least for a while – and maybe still – would not keep her mouth shut, was the mother of the murdered vice-corporal. But then she is a Protestant. What Americans might call the

"knee-jerk" obedience of "Catholics" was hugely responsible for Vatican II, and still is for these on-going crimes
of the Vatican.

It seems that Monsignor Perl, secretary of the Vatican's *Ecclesia Dei* Pontifical Commission which was designed and created in 1988 to bring "Lefebvrists" back
into the "Church," was not pleased by any of the four
copies he received of a flyer comparing him to Lewis
Carroll's Carpenter who with the Walrus ate up all the
petrified oysters. Yet he continues to invite those not yet
petrified to take that fatal walk with him! Thus, numbers of you saw in last month's issue of *Inside the Vatican*
the article entitled "Rome's new 'Game Plan': Heal the
Lefebvre schism." One has to ask: is the journalist who
wrote it (no names) an idiot, or is he (like so many of
his profession) a prostitute? The article relates how Monsignor Perl appealed with "openness" and a "warm pa-
ternal welcome" for Lefebvrists to "unite" their "living
forces" with those of the mainstream Church in order
to resist the common enemy, triumphant atheism! Some
"change of game plan"! The same mouth that is dripping
from its meal of petrified oysters appeals for a meal of
pious oysters, and it is supposed to have changed? This
Perl is a jewel in the crown of world atheism! At least
objectively he is another worldwide liar and bloodless
murderer of the Catholic Church.

We come to the most important news items of all
coming recently from Rome – the promises to reveal the
so-called Third Secret of Fatima. Readers will recall that
the Mother of God, after giving to the three little shepherd children of Fatima, Portugal, in July 1917, a terrifying vision of Hell (first Secret), and after giving her
famous prophecy of Russia spreading its errors all over
the world if her requests were not heeded (second Secret),
finally gave to Sister Lucy a message which she was to
give to her bishop, and which was to be made known as

soon as she died, or in 1960 at the latest, if Sister Lucy was then still alive. This message, known as the Third Secret, was taken out of that bishop's possession by the Vatican in 1957, and it was guarded in Rome. When 1960 came, since Sister Lucy was still alive, the Catholic world awaited with bated breath the revelation of the Third Secret by the Vatican. But the Vatican refused to reveal it. It declared that instead of the Third Secret's having to be made known by 1960, it might be made known from 1960 (lie), a decision depending on the Pope (lie), who, then John XXIII, read the Third Secret and declared that it did not concern his pontificate (lie).

This refusal of Rome to publish the Third Secret is merely one amongst several indications that, in the words of Cardinal Oddi to an Italian newspaper in March of 1990, "The Blessed Virgin was alerting us against apostasy in the Church." It stands to reason that neither John XXIII nor his entourage, planning in 1960 their revolution of Vatican II, wanted to make known that the Blessed Virgin condemned it. That is why the Third Secret has remained smothered in a Vatican drawer and Vatican lies ever since.

That is, until May 13, one month ago. Then Pope John Paul II visited Fatima to celebrate there the beatification of Francisco and Jacinta, Sister Lucy's two little companions of 1917, who both died within a few years of the original apparitions. At the end of the Mass of Beatification, the Vatican Secretary of State, Cardinal Angelo Sodano, gave an address in which he announced that "the Pope has charged the Congregation for the Doctrine of the Faith with making public the third part of the Secret, after the preparation of an appropriate commentary." What had happened?

It looks as though the Mother of God reached through to Pope John Paul II. It looks as though, moved by grace at beatifying two of the three Fatima children and/or at recalling his own rescue from assassination on May 13, 1981, a rescue which he attributed to Our Lady of Fatima, he made two personal decisions, both opposed by his Secretariat of State. The first was himself to go to Fatima one month ago for the occasion. The second was to reveal on that occasion the Third Secret.

The Secretariat of State tried but failed to prevent his going. It arrived at a compromise with the Pope over the Third Secret's being published, firstly by the Secretary of State and not the Pope being the one to announce the publication, secondly by that publication being delayed for "the preparation of an appropriate commentary." The announcement's being made by Cardinal Sodano enabled him immediately to start the Vatican's "spin doctoring" and "damage control," in case the Third Secret does finally have to appear. As for the delay in publication, it may enable the Vatican's criminals to stifle the Third Secret once more.

For indeed, to begin with, the world was told by Vatican spokesman... Joaquín Navarro-Valls . . . that the Secret would be published "within days" of Cardinal Sodano's announcement on May 13. Then the Vatican promised publication for the end of May. Most recently Cardinal Ratzinger wrote in a May 19 Italian newspaper article, which continued the "spin-doctoring," that the Third Secret will be published "at the latest" by mid-June. I do not know about you, dear readers, but I for one will not be holding my breath in a few days' time.

Yet all of these human shenanigans will not stop the Mother of God from achieving her purpose in God's good time. She wishes and she works to save the souls even of her bitterest enemies. If the Third Secret is, by a miracle of hers, finally published in its true text, it will make its own way despite the worst that this Vatican can do. It might even mark the beginning of the end of our 40 years in the desert of the neo-modernist revolution in the Church. That is why the Devil is doing all he can to smother it. Let us have patience. God will of course have the last word.

In the late evening of Ascension Day my mother died in England. She did not die in the Catholic Church. She had free will, and her mind was strong to the end. But I know that many of you prayed for her, and I wish to thank every single one of you. Now she knows. May God have been able to have mercy upon her soul. How wisely He keeps such secrets from us.

I continually recommend the Doctrinal Sessions on the papal Encyclicals, because here is the ever old, ever new, teaching of the Popes against the errors of the apostasy engulfing us. "The truth is mighty, and will prevail."

Third Secret of Fatima

So the Third Secret of Fatima was made public after all, by the Vatican, one week ago. Or was it? Amidst all the confusion generated by the Vatican's distraction maneuver of June 26, we will need experts on Fatima (of which I am not one) to disentangle the Truth. And the SSPX will before long give its best judgment on the matter, which I do not mean here to preempt. However, it seems to me that a few essential guidelines can be laid down already, especially if one knows the third volume of Brother Michael of the Holy Trinity's excellent work *The Whole Truth about Fatima*.

First and foremost, it seems to me that there is one very clear and simple proof that what the Vatican released on June 26 as being the text of "the Third Secret" is not at all that text of the Third Secret which was sealed in an envelope by Sister Lucy in 1944, was opened by Pope John XXIII in 1959, was eagerly awaited by Catholics all over the world in 1960, but was kept disappointingly hidden by the Vatican at that time and ever since. Here is that proof:

The Third Secret as sealed in an envelope by Sister Lucy and handed over by her to the Church authorities on June 17, 1944, was written on a single sheet of paper.

Sister Lucy, who wrote it, said so. Msgr. Venancio, who carried it, said so. Cardinal Ottaviani, who read it, said so (*W.T.F.*, III pp. 481 and 651). On the contrary the June 26 text, as reprinted by the Vatican in Lucy's own handwriting, spreads over four pages.

Therefore the text which on June 26 the Vatican did all it could to make us think is the text of the Third Secret, is at any rate not the text of the crucial Third Secret which Lucy sealed in an envelope and which all true Catholics are waiting for. The real Third Secret is still hidden. What else was to be expected from this Vatican?

Then what is the June 26 text? Let the Fatima experts decide. If it was written down by Sister Lucy on four pages of a notebook handed over with the sealed envelope on June 17, 1944 (*W.T.F.*, III, p. 49), then maybe it can be called part of the Third Secret in a broad sense, but that is certainly not what people usually mean by the expression "the Third Secret," which here also we will use exclusively for the one-page text sealed in the envelope.

Having then clarified our terms, let us give further reasons why the June 26 text is not only different from, but also, at least apparently and for now, rather less interesting than the Third Secret.

Firstly, we know that when Sister Lucy made known in 1942 the first two parts of the Secret, she held back what she called the third part because she said she had not received permission to reveal it (*W.T.F.*, III, p. 35). Even after her diocesan bishop ordered her to write it down, she could not put pen to paper for two months because of something like a diabolical interference. It took an apparition of Our Lady to overcome all the obstacles (pp. 45–48). But what comparable difficulty could Lucy have had in penning the June 26 text of multiple martyrdoms?

Secondly, we know that the Third Secret was framed between two sentences revealed by Lucy in her fourth version of the Second Secret: first comes "In Portugal will be kept always the dogma of the Faith . . . ", then comes the Third Secret, then comes "in the end my Immaculate Heart will triumph." This means that the Third Secret consists in a prophecy uttered by the Mother of God. But the June 26 text consists, like the first part of the Secret, in a vision revealed by Lucy.

Thirdly, the Third Secret sealed in an envelope by Lucy in 1944 and opened only by Pope John XXIII in 1959, was, as everybody knew, to be made public at the latest in 1960. This was at the request of the Mother of God (*W.T.F.*, III, pp. 469–479) because, said Lucy, by 1960 the prophecy would be clearer. Yet the Vatican authorities, from Pope John XXIII onwards, have kept the text a close secret. But what ever in the June 26 text needed to be so closely hidden for the last 40 years?

Fourthly, over the same 40 years a certain number of high-up churchmen like Cardinals Ottaviani and Ratzinger have notwithstanding been allowed to read the Third Secret. When questioned about it afterwards, their guarded words all nevertheless pointed in the same direction, namely, the Third Secret concerns the Faith. Which makes sense. For how could Lucy have had no problem penning the second part of the Secret with its threat as grave as that of Russia spreading its errors throughout the world, and yet almost have been broken by the penning of the third part of Secret, unless the Third Secret were much graver still? And how could it be that much graver unless, instead of concerning Russia and the world, it concerned the Faith and the Church? But the June 26 text does not concern the Faith. It concerns only an Angel, penance, climbing a hill, martyrdoms, etc.

On the other hand if the Third Secret contains a prophecy of Our Lady that the Catholic churchmen around 1960 will gravely endanger the Faith, does that not perfectly explain, firstly why the pious Sister Lucy could hardly bring herself to write it down, secondly why it fits in between, on the contrary, Portugal keeping the dogma of the Faith and the Immaculate Heart in the end triumphing, thirdly why the Vatican churchmen especially in 1960 sought to silence the Third Secret directly condemning the revolutionary Council they were on the brink of launching, and fourthly why the Third Secret directly concerns the Faith?

Thus what we know for certain about the hidden Third Secret does correspond to a dramatic warning from Our Lady to the Conciliar churchmen and their followers, it does not correspond to the June 26 text. It certainly looks as though on June 26, once again, the Vatican authorities kept hidden, as they have done for the last 40 years, the message of Our Lady directly condemning the One World religion of their man-centered Newchurch. Is it wishful thinking to hope that this June 26 evasive action or distraction maneuver will serve merely to rouse Catholics to demand even more the release of the Third Secret? The Mother of God is far mightier than the Devil, but she does need our prayers with which to go before her Son to obtain such a grace.

Meanwhile here are two other versions of the hidden Third Secret, neither of them authoritative but both of them interesting. The first is the reconstruction of the Third Secret's contents by Brother Michael of the Holy Trinity, at the end of his third volume's patient detective work on all the available clues and evidence (*W.T.F.*, III, p. 841):

> While in Portugal the dogma of the Faith will still be kept, in many nations, perhaps throughout the world, the Faith will be lost. The Church's shepherds will fail gravely in their duties of state. Through their fault, consecrated souls will in large numbers let themselves

Richard N. Williamson

be seduced by pernicious errors spread everywhere. The time will have come for the decisive battle between the Virgin and the Devil. A wave of diabolical disorientation will sweep over the world. Satan will reach up to the topmost height of the Church. He will blind the shepherds' minds and harden their hearts, because God will have left them to their own devices as a punishment for their refusal to obey the requests of the Immaculate Heart of Mary. It will be the great apostasy announced for "the last times", the "False Lamb", the "False Prophet" handing the Church over to "the Beast", according to the prophecy of the Apocalypse.

And here is another version of the Third Secret, as supposedly heard by a French priest in Germany in 1994, in the middle of listening to a CD of religious music. At one point the music faded into the background, and he heard a normal (not inner) voice say quite clearly, "The Church will bleed from all her wounds." Then he heard the following:

A wicked Council will be planned and prepared which will change the face of the Church. Many souls will lose the Faith, confusion will reign everywhere. The sheep will seek in vain for their shepherds. A schism will rend my Son's tunic. It will be the end of the times, announced in Scripture and recalled by me in many places. The abomination of abominations will reach its peak and call down the chastisement announced at La Salette. The arm of my Son that I can no longer hold back, will come down on this world which will have to expiate its crimes. All that one will hear of is wars and revolutions. The elements of nature will be shaken and will strike anguish into the best (most courageous) of men. The Church will bleed from all her wounds. Blessed those who persevere and seek refuge in my Heart, for in the end my Immaculate Heart will triumph . . .

After which, all that the priest heard was, "That is the Third Secret of Fatima." The identity of this priest is known, but he prefers to remain unnamed. He is apparently Traditional, without belonging to the SSPX or the Fraternity of St. Peter. He is always in a cassock. He is not sedevacantist. He passes for being worthy of belief.

Of course what he says that he heard carries with it no proof that it is the authentic text of the Third Secret. Note however that it corresponds in full to Lucy's anguish, to the Second Secret frame, to the Vatican churchmen's silence and to the centrality of the Faith, as listed above. Note also that it is a text perfectly clear, like the first and second parts of the Fatima Secret, but unlike the text of June 26. Finally, this priest's version of the Third Secret corresponds fully with the real situation of Church and world around us for the last 40 years.

Dear friends, let us pray and do penance. As Our Lady prophetically told the three children of Fatima, our duty of state is, today, penance enough. Just to live like a Catholic maintaining the state of grace in a world decomposing around us becomes daily more heroic. In patience we shall possess our souls, and if we persevere to the end, we shall be saved. Make if at all possible the five first Saturdays – in reparation to the Immaculate Heart of Mary.

Realities from the Modern World

THINGS ARE GETTING bad, but it is good to think about them, not in order to get depressed, but in order – as Americans say – to get real. In the days of sailing ships, when a storm approached at sea, the captain and sailors watched the weather like hawks, in order to pull down the sails, batten down hatches and take all measures for survival.

Let me quote the testimony of two men and a woman leading ordinary lives in today's world, but reading it with Catholic eyes. Firstly, a family father with growing children, who having had to take a job in a large department store, sees afresh what others may no longer see, because they have grown used to it. Here is the working world of many men:

> In this nation-wide department store, for the employees, it is survival of the fittest. The company is going through a major re-structuring, and therefore many people are being laid off. Only money matters. The severance packages are made as small as possible. The large organization allows for no human relations.

In the work environment everything centers on self. There is no room for the supernatural. Christ is driven out everywhere. The frantic pace allows no time to look upwards.

Inside the company it is a strange world, a strange reality to explain. It is an abstract world, based on profit, working a great deal from computers. It is an artificial system with no reference to nature, let alone to grace. For the sake of some fantastical profit, it rests on unreal speculations and debt, not on real production. It recalls the nightmare world of Big Brother in George Orwell's "1984."

Because of the divorce from reality, even natural reality, there is a process at work of decay, decomposition and death, but death does not come so quickly. One senses inside people their loss and frustration. They are giving up any hope of truth or happiness, they are learning just to survive. Their only hope is the weekend, the vacation and their electronic toys. It is amazing that this world continues. It is a tinder-box waiting to explode, but it goes on and on.

If I think about our Society of Saint Pius X parish and watch our parishioners, it seems to me that a number of them passively accept this Dilbertian world. I am even afraid that some of them are more comfortable in it! Attendance at Mass is a duty and an obligation, but some parishioners are putting in an appearance rather than the reality of Catholic life. Parish activity is to that extent somewhat of a façade. Of course I am not speaking of all parishioners, but a number of them have grown numb from learning to survive out in the world, and also from being accepted by it. The material comforts and the glittering technology act like opiates to dull the inner sense, and to counter-act any uneasy feeling that something is really wrong . . .

End of the first testimony. The second is from a mother of growing children who is watching and describing women of her own generation between 35 and 55 years old. Of course she too is not describing everybody, but she does discern a common trend of women under pressure throwing away some key principle of womanly sanity:

We children of the sixties or seventies are now approaching our change of life. I thought years ago that we would go over the edge, and now I see it happening. My generation knows the problem, but is ceasing to deal with it. I would say three-quarters of these women are going on some Prozac-style drug because life becomes so stressful that they just can't handle it, whereas if you go on drugs it doesn't matter. They reject common sense and good advice, they have thrown up their hands and are refusing the pain. But these drugs have terrible side-effects. I see women beginning to treat pet animals like children . . .

One friend could not sleep or think. She went on Prozac, she dumped her husband, she is filing for divorce. Another friend – or ex-friend – was a Novus Ordo Catholic who did not want children, she had only one, later in life. Recently, she was coming closer to the Truth but then threw it all away, went back to war with her husband and divorced him, so her daughter is now on Prozac, and nature is coming back to haunt her unabsolved past sins against womanly nature.

A third friend has four children aged between 6 and 10 who are growing up like animals. She ignores their needs and now has taken a new job. Her home is in uproar. Her 10-year old attempted (or pretended) suicide. "I don't care, the job is what I want", she says, and she won't listen to anybody. She and this daughter are now on Prozac! And a fourth friend is a good-hearted but impulsive mother, intelligent and highly cultivated, but rejecting what she knows is good advice and setting her lovely children at risk for the sake of a crazy affair.

These poor women are turning ugly. Two cut me off just before they went over the edge. It is frightening. I am a product of the same world. I have pulled up the drawbridge at home for this summer, and I am only letting in the influences that I can deal with. The force out there is getting stronger. It used to be some ways away, but now it's closing in, all around. The children of these women I know are going to be WILD!!

End of the second testimony, concerning women and children. The third concerns old age and death, which a Catholic friend has been running into in his home environment. He says:

This summer I have had three encounters with today's world of the dying. Firstly, the aging of a beloved old aunt obliged me to make a tour of the local hospices and old folks' homes. Tragic! The old people are simply shunted aside. Nobody seems to even consider keeping grandma' at home. Partly because there is nobody at home! So to daycare for infants at the beginning of life correspond hospices for the aged at the end. But where are the true family homes?

Secondly a good friend, only in his fifties, has been told he has cancer and has only six months to live. He was born Presbyterian so he quit religion as soon as he grew up. He became a worshipper of science and materialism, and he married a like-minded woman. They aborted their only child. Now she is bitter, as well as being confined to a wheelchair. He does love music, but that initial Protestantism has left him with an insidious pride. I have given him a Rosary, but if I tried to talk religion in front of her, no doubt she would roll at me, tooth and claw!

Thirdly, I have long known a Protestant man who was patient and kind all his life, but who as he approaches death is now angry every day, lashing out in terror. The Protestantism was an easy religion to live with. You go to church when you want, and when you go, you are told how wonderful you are. Lies, lies! But the lies take a grip, and when it comes to dying, you cannot go back on them. The great questions of life should have been tackled when one was young and strong, but because of the comfort, they were left alone. Then the body gets worn out, the spirit gets lazy, and it is too late. Television always served to cut out nature, and with old age television is turned on more and more, to keep out the questions.

Yet so many of these older Protestants are decent people, sweet people! But they are terrified of death. In truth, it is their generation that let the United States go down the drain. They took no care of the country they received, nor of their own souls that God gave them. Yet they are decent. With my Faith, I know I can give them all they need, but they do not want it. As the tree has stood, so it will fall, and as it falls, so for eternity it will lie. Protestantism damns souls. Now with the Second Vatican Council even the Catholics have turned Protestant!

Dear readers, all we need do is keep our undefiled Catholic Faith, and share it around us in St. Paul's "patience, benignity, goodness, longanimity, mildness, faith, modesty" (Gal. 5: 22, 23). And do our Catholic duty, keeping God's ten Commandments, especially perhaps the worship and love of the one true God, the honor of parents and care for children, and the telling of the truth (1, 4, 8). The Lord God may today be asking of us a great deal, but He is not asking of us the impossible, and He offers us all the means we have need of to do what He wants. May His Name be blessed for ever!

Enclosed is a flyer advertising a set of three tapes that Bernard Janzen and I made towards the end of last year. In it we discuss the principles and forces at work in the war between today's Rome and Catholic Tradition. Since then several more battles have taken place in that war, especially on the battle-field of the Fraternity of St. Peter, but the principles and forces have not changed. The analysis remains timely, and even kindly towards the petrified oysters! Order the tapes from Canada.

Dear readers, may God bless each of you with supernatural light and courage to stay on the road to Heaven, when so many people and things would pull us down to Hell!

Jubilee Year Pilgrimage

MANY OF YOU have heard by now of the triumphant Jubilee Year pilgrimage by the SSPX to Rome last month, but let none of you think that such a triumph means that Rome is reconciling itself to Tradition. Alas, events before and after the pilgrimage showed how little this is the case . . .

SSPX JUBILEE YEAR PILGRIMAGE

The pilgrimage itself took place from Tuesday to Thursday, August 8, 9 and 10, Some 3,500 SSPX pilgrims from literally all over the world gathered together in blazing sunshine outside the great Basilica of St. Paul Outside the Walls on the Tuesday morning. There the pattern was established of some 250 priests, seminarians and nuns leading the pilgrims, grouped by the main languages present, solemnly through the Jubilee Door into each Basilica. This procession would last a prolonged five mysteries of the Rosary and would fill the Basilicas, filling Santa Maria Maggiore twice. Once inside, there would be a meditation on the Basilica, prayers, chants, a brief sermon, the whole lasting from 20 to 30 minutes. Then the pilgrims would leave, in an equally solemn and impressive procession.

A high point of the pilgrimage was, of course, the Tuesday afternoon visit to St. Peter's, the central and most famous Basilica of all. In sunshine still more blazing, some 4,500 pilgrims lined up in the street leading to St. Peter's, the Via della Conciliazione, and for a good hour the SSPX occupied, in peace, the Basilica! Bishop Fellay preached a five-minute sermon, wisely evoking from Scripture the need to pray for Peter.

As a no doubt villainous but not stupid Italian journalist remarked, it was the first time in 2,000 years of Church history that thousands of "excommunicated" Catholics had come to St. Peter's to pray for the Pope! For, of course, the SSPX pilgrims did again and again pray for the Pope.

On the Wednesday, the pilgrimage was to the two other leading Basilicas of Rome, St. John Lateran and St. Mary Major. The high point here was no doubt the procession up the Via Merulana joining these Basilicas, which are not far apart. Until the day itself, the Italian police had said they could do nothing to assist the movement of the now 5,100 pilgrims through the streets concerned, but at the last moment, within 10 minutes, they had the route perfectly sealed off (ah, these Italians!). Imagine a whole street of Rome filled from top to bottom with our people marching 10 or 12 abreast, and chanting "Lauda Sion, Salvatorem"! It was a sight for sore eyes, and a joy for sore hearts! For a few moments, Rome was back in Rome, or, Catholic Rome was back in geographical Rome.

The official pilgrimage concluded on the Wednesday afternoon with a Pontifical Mass celebrated by Bishop Fellay on an improvised altar in the open air, on the site of what was once Emperor Nero's palace on the Oppian Hill. The Coliseum, clearly visible not far off, was a poignant reminder to the SSPX pilgrims, forbidden to celebrate Mass in any of the Basilicas, that the persecution of Catholics did not begin with Vatican II! Rome might have eased the Society's passage through the Basilicas, but emphasize the word "through"! It was easy to imagine, going up from the Coliseum as from a modern sports stadium, the howl of the crowds baying not for a home team goal but for the Christians' blood . . . The equivalent happened as recently as 1848 . . .

However, as pilgrims left the Oppian Hill Mass in procession, a few from each SSPX group in nine different countries of Asia carried a succession of national banners. Now Asia is the least Catholic of continents. Rarer still are the Catholics there keeping to Tradition. Yet a few representatives of the tiny remnant of this slim minority had wanted to be there, and to show they were there! They were applauded (ah, these French!), as another inspiration to all!

The SSPX's Jubilee visit to Rome continued unofficially on the Thursday with the classic pilgrimage to the seven Basilicas. Over 1,000 of our pilgrims in groups of 50 made the 14-mile walk, still in the blazing sunshine of Rome in August! A light sunstroke from Tuesday kept me out of it personally, but all the Winona seminarians present at this climax of their six-week visit to Europe made the round. They were totally uplifted by the pilgrimage and they thank you all who helped to make their European trip possible. As an English priest quoted a pilgrim saying, "Our pilgrimage must have been a Jubilee Year present of Our Lord to Himself"!

All of which is much sunshine, but every event around the pilgrimage was there to remind us that we are still under the reign of the enemies of Our Lord. The first such event took place at the end of the week preceding the pilgrimage.

"SI SI, NO NO" CONGRESS IN ROME

From August 3 to 5 some 100 priests and laity, mainly of the SSPX, participated in the bi-annual Congress of the twice-monthly anti-liberal Italian periodical *Si Si, No No*, known to many of you from its extracts and articles published in *The Angelus*. The Congress consisted of some dozen speakers analyzing in depth problems raised by the Second Vatican Council. Such analysis is valuable, as preparing for the day when the Catholic Church will have to clean up the whole present mess.

In effect, one speaker after another made clear that the problem of Vatican II is not only in the aftermath of the Council, but it is in the Council itself. The Council's documents themselves are loaded with a mind-rotting doublethink of a kind to enable (or cause) Catholics to dance with the Devil while still pretending to serve God. Two contradictory religions, one centered on God and the other on man, are blended there with a diabolical skill. Eventually the Catholic Church will be obliged to trash the entire documents and start all over again, because they intertwine truth and lies inextricably.

For instance the Council document on the priesthood ("Presbyterorum ordinis") passes for being one of the more acceptable Council documents, yet Bishop Fellay in the closing lecture of the Congress had no difficulty in showing that in that document the seeds of the destruction of the Eternal Priesthood of Christ are well and truly planted.

MEETING OF SSPX SUPERIORS IN ALBANO

Immediately after the pilgrimage took place the next event to bring pilgrims down to earth. Some 30 SSPX superiors of Seminaries, Districts and independent Priories met in the SSPX house in Albano, 40 minutes out of Rome, to deliberate on current problems. Two questions stood out in the deliberations: vocations and the Internet.

The lack of vocations – which is making itself felt all over the world – seems a real puzzle. For 30 years now the SSPX has been up and running with a number of boys' high schools, and for several years now SSPX priests and laity have been called on to pray for vocations, yet still they are scarce. I said that the whole of modern life takes its toll, because godlessness is built into the very fabric of industrialized suburbia, and I quoted Archbishop Lefebvre telling the 20,000 faithful attending his 60th Priestly Jubilee Mass in Paris in 1989, to "go back to the country."

Of course nobody pretends that such a return to the country is always possible or easy, but unless the virtues of the old-fashioned country way of life are recreated, be it in city, suburbs or country, there will simply not be, except by miracle, the human material out of which to fashion priests. Already in the 1970's, Archbishop Lefebvre used to say that any vocation was a miracle. (Take heart, dear Americans. We have what looks like a dozen miracles entering Winona this month!)

To the Superiors' debate whether priests should have Email or the Internet in their houses, I made a similar contribution to the effect that technology and the machine way of life take their toll. Pope Gregory XVI was opposed to the railways being laid in his pontificate. Absurdly behind the times? But who can deny that these marvels of transportation destabilize a way of life? Who can deny that the motorcar is a major facilitator of individualism and rootlessness? Similarly Email and the Internet may facilitate communications and access to information, but who can say that either promotes real thought? Both change the very notion of "thinking." Who can claim that they change it for the better?

However, the consensus of my colleagues seemed to be that priests should make use of these tools while establishing safeguards to protect against their dangers. Which I can understand. But I am not sure that either Email or Internet has any place in a seminary where future priests must fill their minds and souls with old truths, not their in-trays with novelties. Dinosaurs too have rights!

At this meeting Society Superiors were reminded of the distress of the Newchurch clergy by the Society's First Assistant, Fr. Franz Schmidberger, describing his recent outreach to all the Catholic priests in Austria. He told how in the space of one year he had visited personally 170 priests likely to be at least sympathetic to Tradition. Amongst these he found eight saying the old Mass, 20 saying both Masses, perhaps 60 ready to work with the Society, but in general the priests he visited would not discuss the real issues and they lacked direction and authority. A few were leading truly heroic priestly lives, but the overall picture was of a clergy in dissolution, neither lead nor leading, sheep dogs astray between the struck shepherd and scattered sheep. Kyrie, eleison!

Altogether, the mood amongst the SSPX Superiors present in Albano seemed tranquil and united. Given present circumstances, that is surely a remarkable grace of God, even a miracle. If we are thankful for the Society's existence, let us be mindful how much we have to be thankful for.

WOODSTOCK IN ROME

If, leaving Albano, Society Superiors came back through Rome, another event reminded them of the official Church's distress: the World Youth Day organized by the Vatican for the Feast of the Assumption, when 300,000 youngsters gathered in St. Peter's Square where the Pope-mobile was to make its tour, while another 200,000 gathered outside St. John Lateran. Any disagreeable taste left in the Vatican's mouth by the Society's pilgrimage must have been more than washed away by this huge demonstration for the media: masses of youngsters walking for days around Rome, often hand-in-hand, singing or clapping together, sweet, innocent, nice boys and girls, dressed often immodestly, but what does that matter? Here was the new religion.

Here was what Rome has worked for: a sweet, innocent – innocent? – dream of everyone living happily ever after – ever after? How many of these youngsters believe in eternity? How many of them believe in the Creed? How many even have any notion of the Creed? How many of them are being taught that Catholic Faith without which they cannot save their souls?

SSPX BISHOPS LUNCH WITH CARDINAL

Alas, the problem comes from high up. The Vatican had done its best to keep the SSPX pilgrimage as quiet as possible. So the recently appointed President of the *Ecclesia Dei* Commission, set up by the Pope in 1988 to stop Catholics from following Archbishop Lefebvre into "schism," 71 year old Columbian Cardinal Castrillón Hoyos, knew nothing (he says) of our passage until he saw news of it on television. Now two months previously, desiring to meet the four SSPX bishops, he had written a letter to us (beginning "My dear Brother"), in which he invited us to come and see him at any time. Seizing the opportunity of our presence in Rome, he invited us to lunch with him there and then!

Three of us accepted the invitation. He was most hospitable and kind, welcoming us in and, after an ample two-hour luncheon, embracing us on our way out. "Come and see me at any time," he said. Yet this was the same Cardinal who only a few weeks previously had taken firm action to cripple Tradition inside the Fraternity of St. Peter by replacing four of their own choice of leaders by four of their number chosen by Rome! He smashes what he invites, he invites what he smashes. "Go figure," say Americans!

Was he insincere? Humanly judging, I did not think so. I think he simply belongs to the new religion. "We have the same Holy Trinity, the same Incarnation, the same Holy Eucharist," he said, and he surely does believe in the Real Presence because he said that when the experts begin disputing about it, he tunes out. "I'm nice, you're nice," he seemed to say, "so where's the problem? Why not join in the happy-ever-after religion?" Concerning St. Peter's Fraternity, he did admit that he had acted unpleasantly now, but it was only in order to avoid having to act more unpleasantly later. In other words, St. Peter's had had to be stopped, from getting away from happily-ever-afterness, while we were to be drawn towards it by the attraction of all niceness possible. Were we not back to the sweet, innocent religion of the zillions of nice youngsters holding hands and singing in the streets? And since this is the religion of the Holy Father (whom the Cardinal venerates and often sees) and of the Holy Eucharist, then what else can there be in "Tradition" for "Traditionalists" to be making such a fuss about? I think the Cardinal really cannot see.

For this reason I would be (humanly) sure that Cardinal Castrillón Hoyos is not one of the real villains in Rome who for their part can see, and who know exactly what they are doing – getting rid of the Catholic Church to replace it with the Satanic One-World-Religion. There need not be many such real villains, but dear old men who still believe in the Real Presence are mere instruments in their hands. If the Cardinal really is nice, one day he will have to be nasty, either to his handlers or to us. War is war.

Richard N. Williamson

SUMMING UP BY BISHOP FELLAY

An accurate view of this war is how the SSPX Superior General concluded the Superiors' Meeting in Albano:

Firmness pays off. It is Rome which is wrong. We have no reason to back down. We must continue as we have done. Has Rome changed? See what they told St. Peter's: 'Traditionalists must recognize that there is only one rite of Mass in the Church, and that rite is the new rite.' So Rome is hardening its position. Under pressure it may make a few exceptions for the old Mass, but its principles are unchanged.

However, little by little Rome is growing weaker, by its loss of authority over its own bishops." Cardinal Ratzinger said recently in France that authority within the Church is becoming by consent only. So we must stand firmer, not less firm. We must say to Rome, 'If Tradition no longer works, why was our pilgrimage such a success? And if Tradition works, why destroy it?' Yet Rome knows where it is going, and it means to go there. It set up St. Peter's Fraternity against us, and now it is destroying that Fraternity with a cynicism that is stunning. We are at war!

The same can be said for the mainstream bishops and episcopal conferences. Paris is as solidly anti-Tradition as Rome. A bishop here or there may sympathize with us, but that does not mean much. Their conversion is in Providence's hands, not ours. Until then, let us pray for them, and give them a hard time!

It is with mainstream priests that we have better hopes of fruitful action, long-term. The Vatican II generation of priests is passing. The younger priests are more open. They have had a bad formation, but a number of them still have the Faith. In France, Austria and the Argentine we know of possibilities ... it is slow work for ourselves, but not to be neglected. The SSPX has been blackened in their eyes. That is why it is so important to make ourselves known. It is our actions which speak, and make people think.

As for the Church, it is still there, even if only just. It is relatively easy to sift in it Catholic words from non-Catholic words. It is not so easy to sift the persons. Have they all left the Church? It is dangerous to say so. For the moment, we are lucky to be cut off from Rome which only wants us to compromise, either on the Mass or on the Council or both. However, we should not therefore refuse all personal contact with them, but let us be under no illusion! The Cardinals are hanging lock-tight together!

What is the degree of guilt of any one of them, taken singly? Much more difficult to say. But word for word they stick together, to the party-line coming from the Secretariat of State. The machinery is well-oiled! The dicasteries form a network. For example, for the last two years we were asking Rome for permission to make this Jubilee pilgrimage in the Basilicas, and we know that our request went the rounds, from one Cardinal to another, from the Congregation for the Clergy to the Secretariat of State, to *Ecclesia Dei* to the Secretariat of State, etc., etc. It was a trial of strength. They were caught in a double dilemma. Firstly, their open-to-all ecumenism – how could it be closed to us? Secondly, the scandal we risked causing if with 5,000 pilgrims we had run into closed doors. So they let us in and out as smoothly as possible, and their charm was all part of their technique!

ROME OF THE MARTYRS

Such wise words remind us how far the Church crisis is from being over. Just a few days later Rome went ahead with the supremely confusing joint beatification of a Saint, Pius IX, and no saint at all but the Founder of the Newchurch, Newsaint John XXIII. How can poor Catholics think straight when they are thus told that 2 and 2 make 4, and at the same time they make 5? Repeat, at the

Richard N. Williamson

same time! Heads can no longer think! Words no longer have meaning!

What will it take to give back to words their meaning, to enable heads once more to think, to reestablish the Truth? We pilgrims in Rome were reminded of the answer, by the multiple churches and shrines there of glorious Martyrs. It took a sea of blood to float the Catholic Church. She has run aground. It will take another sea of blood to float the Church off again . . . the signs of the next bloody persecution are showing.

Meanwhile, dear Friends, do pray for the seminary as we pray for you, and please continue to support us. We do have vocations for the runup to martyrdom!

Bishops' Meeting With Cardinal Castrillón Hoyos

I HAVE BEEN thinking about the August 14 meeting between Cardinal Castrillón Hoyos and three of us bishops of the SSPX. How could he be so ruthless with the Fraternity of St. Peter and then so charming with ourselves? And I came to a broad conclusion: the minds of these hard Church leaders of the world's soft apostasy are so messed up with contradiction that they can no longer see a contradiction when it stares them in the face. The prince of their faculties, their mind, is gone, and the rest follows.

This is approximately what I said when I described briefly in September's letter the lunch date in the Cardinal's apartment in Rome, where he so warmly welcomed and embraced three of us SSPX bishops, who are after all, from his point of view, much worse enemies of his Rome than the Fraternity of St. Peter leaders that he had so firmly called to heel a few weeks before. However, the subject merits a longer analysis because here once more is the whole vast problem of these "nice" men wrecking the Catholic Church. Several Seminary Letters have considered this problem, but the niceness of these

Richard N. Williamson

Church-wreckers can be so misleading to Catholics that
it is well worth another letter to go over it again in the
light of this "eyeball to eyeball" meeting with one of the
leading wreckers. Too many Catholics follow our sentimental world in thinking that wherever there is niceness,
there there is truth. So at the risk of going over ground
gone over many times before (but there are always new
readers), let us start with the clear proof that the Cardinal is a wrecker.

In April of this year the 71 year old prelate from Co-
lombia, South America, was appointed by Pope John
Paul II to be President of the *Ecclesia Dei* Commission,
set up by the Pope in 1988 at the time of the SSPX Episcopal Consecrations to prevent Traditionally-minded
Catholics from following Archbishop Lefebvre and his
four ugly ducklings into "schism." The Commission
would offer to such Catholics all they could desire from
Tradition but under, and with the approval of, Rome.
This the Commission mainly but not exclusively pretended to do by the founding of the FSSP with a dozen
or so priests who were leaving the SSPX because of those
consecrations.

Now – and here is the key to all that follows – Vatican II Rome contradicts Catholic Tradition, and Catholic Tradition contradicts Vatican II Rome. That is why,
from the beginning, the SSPX warned that sooner or later neo-modernist Rome would clamp down on the FSSP.
However for ten years Rome cunningly allowed them a
certain expansion and prosperity. After all, Rome wanted to catch as many mice as possible with one trap! In
this appearance of prosperity the FSSP exulted at their
10th anniversary celebration held in Rome in the autumn
of 1998.

But Rome was only waiting, and in the summer of
1999, Rome struck. By supporting a band inside the FSSP
of pro-Rome priests rebelling against the "Lefebvrist"

tendency of the FSSP leadership, Rome let loose through the remainder of last year a series of disputes, divisions, actions, reactions within the FSSP, until in February of this year the FSSP leader-ship managed to restore a measure of calm and unity. But then Rome struck again.

At the FSSP General Chapter held in Rome this July, a devastating letter was read out coming from the authorities in Rome in which they imposed on the FSSP three decisions: firstly, by a ruling upon the FSSP Constitutions, they stopped the Chapter from reelecting Fr. Josef Bisig, the FSSP Superior General who had more or less held the FSSP together on its more or less Traditional course up till then. Secondly, in the name of preventing dissension, Rome in this letter imposed on the FSSP its own choice of successor to Fr. Bisig as Superior General, a priest who will certainly be more amenable to Rome's anti-Traditional directives. Thirdly, it imposed new rectors upon the two FSSP seminaries, in South Germany and the USA. The letter did not name these rectors, but it traced their portrait: they will "eradicate a spirit of rebellion against the current Church," and they will have "a caring and love of the Church and its supreme Pastor."

In conclusion the letter warned against giving too much importance to the Tridentine rite of Mass. The FSSP must "forget no more that the reformed rite of Paul VI is the common rite of the Church," and the FSSP must stop saying that the new rite is not as good as the old. The letter recalls that Rome founded the FSSP (merely) "to help Catholics who have an attachment to the old rite, to better find themselves in the Church." Clearly, Tradition is to be integrated into the Newchurch on the Newchurch's terms, in other words Rome decrees that Tradition is to be crippled inside the FSSP. And who signed this June 29 letter? Why, the new President of "*Ecclesia Dei*," Cardinal Darío Castrillón Hoyos.

Now actions speak louder than words, and this letter is action – crippling action! By this letter the Cardinal is a clear enemy of Catholic Tradition. How then could he on June 1 have written a letter to the four SSPX bishops beginning "My dear Brother," and warmly inviting them to visit him at his home or office in Rome at any time? And how could he on August 14 welcome three of them to lunch in his home, embrace them on their departure, and repeat the invitation? There is a problem here!

Immediately, one might think that Cardinal Castrillón Hoyos was being insincere with us on August 14, that he was putting on a sweet front to lure the SSPX into a trap. But as one judges men, "eyeball to eyeball" as Americans say, I do not think that was the case. I think he really wishes us well. He really wishes we were "inside" the Church instead of "outside." The next explanation is, that if the Cardinal wants us "inside the Church," then he is not intelligent enough to understand the clash between Rome and Tradition. He certainly did seem to be ignorant of the issues at stake on August 14. But see above. His June 29 letter to the FSSP General Chapter showed a clear grasp both of how Tradition is working inside the FSSP against his Rome, and how his Rome must act in order to cripple that Tradition. It is not the letter of a man ignorant of the clash!

Well then, third explanation, that letter may be the letter of a puppet. Sinister forces inside the Vatican composed that letter, and the "dear old man" (quotation from last month's letter) merely signed it, not worrying too much about what he signed. Meanwhile his "dearness" might serve to draw the disarmed SSPX bishops within the range of the sinister forces' guns... I still give a little credit to this explanation, because I do believe that behind the Cardinal, as I said last month, there are villains at work, either Judeo-masons or prelates working for Judeo-masonry, who are far more sinister than this Cardinal is. These villains, I do believe, are using frontmen like the Cardinal for as long as he is useful to their Revolution. He is, in Lenin's phrase, "a useful idiot," who will be cast aside the moment he no longer serves their forward march to the One-World-Religion. The Revolution is famous for eating its own children.

However, "useful idiots" are the more useful for being less idiotic. On reflection, I doubt that the Cardinal merely signed like a puppet his June 29 letter. For instance, as he began his June 1 letter sweet-talking the SSPX bishops by "My dear Brother," so he began his June 29 savaging of the FSSP by "My very dear Friends"! And, surely, just as he savaged Tradition inside the FSSP to stop the FSSP sliding out of what he considers to be Church unity, so he sweet-talked the SSPX bishops to begin restoring them to that unity.

It is surely this notion he has of Church unity that explains not only the oneness of the Cardinal's contradictory behavior, but also the contradictions flowing out of the one man. This is because his Vatican II notion of the Church mixes love of God with love of that modern world which is opposed to God. So his notion of Church unity, like that of Vatican II prelates from the Pope downwards, contains contradiction in itself, and continually spills contradictions.

In a recent *Remnant* article (August 31, page 13) there was a long list of Pope John Paul's permanent contradictions. On September 3 there was the joint beatification of Popes Pius IX and John XXIII, whose pontificates mix like oil and water. Most recently there was Cardinal Ratzinger's *Dominus Jesus* which said that the Catholic Church is the one true Church, but that other churches also subsist in the true Church! Contradictions spill out of Rome like muddy waters out of a muddy fountain. For how can minds force-fed on contradiction think straight? These minds are no longer the royal servants of Truth, but the dethroned followers of their owners' wills, which wilfully choose contradiction in the hope of enjoying both God and this world. Such wills are correspondingly degraded, which is why, thirdly, sentiments become so important, and why sentimentality so easily takes over. Instead of the Way, the Truth and the Life, we have "luv, luv, luv." Hence the Cardinal's August 14 luv, luv, luv, for the SSPX bishops!

The problem then with this Pope, with the dear (?) Cardinal and all followers of Vatican II like them, is not a lack of nice sentiments, nor even of good will, except insofar as they will to love the modern world in its modernity. The problem is that their minds are self-disabled. They could not recognize the Antichrist if he hit them in the face!

What to do, dear readers. Firstly, pray with mind and will for the grace of love of the Truth. Secondly, apply the mind to discovering the Truth, the whole Truth, and nothing but the Truth. Thirdly, apply the will to living by that Truth, because if God sees us not profiting by His grace, He will take it away again. On the other hand, if He sees us doing all we can, however poorly, to put the Truth into action, He will give us grace upon grace, unto life everlasting.

Death, Through the Eyes of St. Paul and John Keats

I N A SPARE day after the Society's official pilgrimage to Rome in August, I made a personal pilgrimage to two sites in Rome, the first of which probably and the second of which almost certainly no other of our pilgrims visited: the grave of the English poet John Keats in the Protestant Cemetery, and the church of San Paolo alla Regola in the Arenula. Keats they will hardly have visited because he is not a Catholic poet, San Paolo alla Regola because it is closed to the public for repairs, yet the two sites fit together like lock and key!

John Keats (1795–1821) is a famous figure in English Literature. A handful of his best known poems are to be found in almost any collection of poetry in the English language: "On first looking into Chapman's Homer," "When I have fears that I may cease to be," "La Belle Dame Sans Merci," "Ode to the Nightingale," "Ode to Autumn," etc. He belongs to the Romantic period of English literature, so much so that more than anyone else he incarnates what the word "poet" has come to mean to most of us: an imaginative young man, not altogether masculine, finding beautiful language with which to put on paper his sensitive dreams.

In our times such poetry is on the one hand so despised that if newspapers quote it, they will print it out as though it is prose for fear of alienating readers by anything so effete as "poetry." On the other hand such "poets" reign supreme in the world of greeting cards which get sent on all sentimental occasions. As Oscar Wilde said, "Sentimentality is the bank-holiday of cynicism."

Keats contributed towards this disintegration of modern man. He came to Rome with a friend in November of 1820 in the hope that the warm climate would alleviate the tuberculosis ravaging his lungs. It was too late. After four months of distant exile and severe pain, he died in March of 1821 at the early age of 25, in rooms overlooking the Piazza di Spagna which have become a pilgrimage center for lovers of English literature.

He was buried in the Protestant Cemetery just inside Rome's old city walls, in the shadow of the pyramid of Caius Cestius. He lies in the far corner of a well-kept lawn scattered with the gravestones of other distinguished or famous non-Catholics who died in Rome. Amidst shady trees in the warmth of a sunlit August morning one would have thought anybody there could lie in peace, but then one comes to the gravestone of the famous poet. The inscription concludes with the one sentence Keats himself had wanted to be engraved there: "Here lies one whose name was writ in water"!

What had happened? In fact, the great Romantic had lived in virtual despair for many months before he died. At some point after he left school and had become a medical student in London and, showing promise as a poet, had begun to mix in a group of the capital city's artistic intellectuals, he picked up liberal ideas and turned his back resolutely on Christianity. During his last illness he admired and envied the Christian faith enabling his artistic friend Severn to watch over him faithfully, but Keats could not or would not believe in like manner.

In his short life, he had come to stake everything on human feelings of beauty. In a letter to a friend in 1819 he wrote the charter of Romantics: "I am certain of nothing but the holiness of the heart's affections and the truth of imagination – what the imagination seizes as beauty must be truth." To his brothers: "O for a life of sensations rather than of thoughts." His "Ode to a Grecian Urn" concludes with the famous lines:

> Beauty is truth, truth beauty. That is all
> Ye know on earth, and all ye need to know.

So when the full ugliness of slow death by tuberculosis struck, Keats had none of what worldly people called "the consolations of religion," he had only feelings, the darkest of feelings, left to him.

In fact Keats had envisaged literature as a kind of substitute religion, with poets like himself serving as substitute priests to bring happiness to mankind. And it is surely because his best poetry expresses the quasi-religious longings of the human heart without religion that he is like the incarnate poet for our apostate age. Here is a famous sonnet of Keats, meditating on death (it goes well on retreats!):

> When I have fears that I may cease to be
> Before my pen has gleaned my teeming brain,
> Before high-piled books in charact'ry
> Hold like rich gamers the full-ripened grain;
> When I behold, upon the night's starred face,
> Huge cloudy symbols of a high romance,
> And think that I may never live to trace
> Their shadows, with the magic hand of chance;
> And when I feel, fair creature of an hour
> That I shall never look upon thee more,

Richard N. Williamson

> Never have relish in the faery power
> Of unreflecting love! – then on the shore
> Of the wide world I stand alone, and think,
> Till Love and Fame to nothingness do sink.

The first eight lines present the tension between human Fame and Death: will the young poet live to unlock all the treasures in his heart? And given the beauty of his words, we need not doubt the treasures were there. In the next four lines is the tension between human Love and Death: the brief glimpse of a "fair creature" makes his heart resonate with the love that might be. But then – last two lines – what do all of Fame and Love mean when they can be cut down by Death? The heart says there must be a meaning – but there is none in sight. The heart lifts – and falls back. The heart longs with a longing as deep as the sea – but it is left with its longing.

The truth in Romanticism is the lift and the longing. The falsehood is the lack of corresponding object. Like Keats, not finding the answer or else refusing it, his many followers lifted and longed less and less, until the post-Romantics had nothing better to do than wallow in the mud and finally blow their brains out. Severn had had to persuade Keats several months before his death not to take his own life by a drug overdose, in those days, of laudanum.

From Rome's Protestant Cemetery to the unknown Church of San Paolo alla Regola is a brief taxi ride into what used to be the Jewish Quarter of Rome by the bend in the river Tiber where it turns southeast. Rome's Synagogue is still nearby. The church, going back to the earliest times, was built on the very spot where St. Paul spent his first imprisonment in Rome, from perhaps 61 to 63 AD (Acts 28: 30, 31). From here it was that for at least two years under house arrest, by example and by instruction of Rome's Catholics, he helped Peter to build the vital new church at the heart of the great empire. Here it was that he wrote what are known as the four Epistles of the Captivity, in each of which he refers to his imprisonment: Ephesians (3: 1), Philippians (1: 13, 14), Colossians (4: 3), Philemon (1). Are there any other books of the Bible of which we know the exact location where they were written?

In any other city than Rome such a place would be an outstanding shrine, but in Rome and in Roman guidebooks it is overshadowed by dozens of shrines and sanctuaries more outstanding still. The result is that the church of San Paolo alla Regola fell into disuse and material decay, which the State is now slowly paying to restore (materially). I could only gain entrance by ringing at a side door through which a Peruvian Brother of a small congregation kindly let me in. The main church is chock-full of builders' rubbish and materials. The side chapel on the exact site of St. Paul's house captivity is choked with scaffolding and planks and builders' dust!

To think that from this place of ruination flashed forth a Prince of the Apostles, and Epistles of his which have built the Roman Catholic Church ever since! Here was penned the answer to poor John Keats:

St. Paul has all the lift of Keats: "Mind the things that are above, not the things that are upon the earth," but the lift is not adrift with feelings, it is anchored in Christ, "for you are dead, and your life is hid with Christ in God" (Col. 3: 2, 3). There is all the longing of Keats: "To live is Christ, to die is gain . . . and what I shall choose I know not," but St. Paul's yearning to live is anchored in serving Christians, his yearning to die is anchored in Christ, "having a desire to be dissolved and to be with Christ, a thing by far the better" (Phil. 1: 21–23).

In St. Paul there is any amount of the "heart's affections" and their "holiness": "For the rest, brethren, whatsoever things are true...just...holy...lovely...think on these things," yet all these things that are not Christ St. Paul would let go "for the excellent knowledge of Jesus Christ my Lord, for whom I have suffered the loss of all things, and count them but dung, that I may gain Christ." (Phil. 4: 8; 3: 8)

So Fame and Love are nothing to St. Paul, except in Christ, but Christ he can reach once and for all only through Death, therefore Death is no longer the problem that cuts down all Fame and Love, as for Keats. On the contrary, it is the only gateway to true life and infinite love, Christ Himself: "Death is swallowed up in victory. O death, where is thy victory? O death, where is thy sting?" (I Cor. 15: 54, 55).

Keats staked all on the human heart's affections, but all they told him at the end was that his name was writ in water. St. Paul staked all on Christ, and at the end of his life he knew on the contrary that the just Lord would render him a crown of justice, however, "not only to me, but to them also that love his coming." (II Tim. 4: 8)

Should then Catholics renounce literature and the arts, and all their pomps and all their works? Not at all. Firstly, if pagan or non-Catholic artists or poets are famous, it is because of gifts of imagination, or affection, or expression, all of which come from God and all of which by being rightfully imitated can be made to serve Him – St. Jerome, translator of the Latin Bible, was soaked in Cicero. For, secondly, a stairway built downwards can always be climbed upwards. If the audiotapes on not necessarily Catholic literature of, for instance, a Dr. David White, are so popular with traditional Catholics, is it not because they use even non-Catholic materials to build a firm bridge from our non-Catholic world back to the Faith?

And let us pray in what remains of November for all the souls in Purgatory, poor by their suffering yet rich in salvation and in power to pray for ourselves.

The Suburban Way of Life

THE SEASON OF Advent which started today means the season of preparation of our hearts and minds for the coming of Our Lord. But in what real environment will he find these on December 25, 2000? At least surrounded, if not more or less tainted, by the sentimentalization and commercialization of everything "Christmassy"?

This primacy of feelings and money is basically to be blamed on Protestantism, but through the environment which it has created, Protestantism gets to all of us in ways we think not of. A year and a half ago, this letter accused the suburban environment of being the immediate cause of the notorious school shooting in Colorado. Yet most "Traditional Catholics" come from suburbs. For the penitential season of Advent, let us reflect further on the modern suburban way of life.

Preliminarily, we must recall that environment is only environment. No soul is determined to salvation or damnation by its environment. Some souls have become great saints by rising above the worst of environments, and the best of environments have not prevented other souls from becoming the worst of sinners. The inner governs the outer. It is, ultimately, souls that determine

Richard N. Williamson

environments rather than environments that determine souls. Salvation and damnation are by grace and free will, neither of which are determined by surroundings.

Nevertheless, for human beings supernatural grace has to come in to land within their natural surroundings, within which their free will also has to be exercised. Man is by nature a social animal, always reaching out to the human beings who surround him. Therefore a man's surroundings play a large part in his life on earth and in his eternal destiny. St. Paul quoted from a Greek poet that "Evil communications corrupt good manners." (I Cor. 15: 33) And in 1989 Archbishop Lefebvre told a congregation of 20,000 Catholics celebrating his 60th priestly anniversary to "go back to the country." Suburban surroundings are something relatively new in history. Catholics need to think about them.

"Suburbs" are defined (by Webster) as "city environs." A suburb is "an outlying district of a city or town." Now did not cities always have their outlying districts, or suburbs? So what is new? What is new is that as long as men traveled on foot or on horseback or in horse-drawn carriages, they would, if they left the city, find themselves soon in the country. See maps of Philadelphia or Boston in George Washington's time. On the contrary, modern suburbs are apt to sprawl for dozens of miles around city-centers.

Modern suburbs were created over the last 200 years firstly by the rise of industrialization, and secondly by industrialized means of transportation. Beginning in England in the 18th century, the Industrial Revolution, by its invention of new machines to create heavy and light industry, also created a new kind of city. Multitudes of workers had to be herded together off the land around the new factories where the crowding, smoke, grime and noise often created an environment which by all previous standards was disagreeable and inhuman.

The middle classes with some money began to look for somewhere else to live, but still close to the factories or populated centers where the money was to be made. Thus began the suburbs, and with them the custom of separating all day long the father from his family, with unhappy consequences for both.

However, the underpowered means of transportation available at that time strictly limited how far those suburbs could reach out from any city or center, which is why the late 19th century saw a tremendous push to invent new machines of transportation, of which some failed like the steam bus, some succeeded for a while like the trolley bus, some succeeded well like the motor bus, and one succeeded sensationally – the motor car.

Winston Churchill once wondered if the invention of the internal combustion engine had really been a blessing for mankind. In any case, from being the tail wagged by the dog, the motor car rapidly became the dog wagging the tail. From being created by modern man's need for transportation, the motor car became the virtual creator of modern man's way of life: his horizons, his work, his leisure, his holidays, the relations between his muscles and his nerves, his morals, his countryside and his cities are all revolutionized by his motor car. And when, thanks to what most men call "progress," nearly every man owns a motor car, then, necessarily, it becomes next to impossible to live in his new suburban surroundings without a motor car. At which point, although few people (outside the despairing rock musicians) seem to stop to think about what has happened, we are into a new world.

We are into a new world! Given how important a part man's surroundings play in his life, and given the decisive part a man's earthly life plays in his eternal destiny, how can so apparently few Catholics be thinking about our revolutionized environment?

We are into a new world. The old-fashioned city and the old-fashioned country are both virtually gone. In the place of agriculture is agri-business. In the place of country farms are ever larger corporations exploiting by machines and chemicals enormous tracts of land to generate the quantities of cheap food demanded by the democratic multitudes now cut off from the land. In the place of towns or small cities focused around – as it often used to be – a church or cathedral, there are now dozens upon dozens of square miles of drive-in banks, drive-in cinemas, drive-in eateries, etc., etc., focused around – mega-shopping malls! What community life do the youngsters – or oldsters – here have? Doing the "wave" at a sports stadium, and drifting around the shopping mall! Look and see! How on earth does anyone expect vocations out of these new heavens and new earth?

The contrast between the pre-suburban and post-suburban worlds is most striking in a historic country like France, where the network of motorways with their attendant liens has been slapped down upon the ancient landscape of farms and villages like a machine stamp on a medieval manuscript. How can anyone make it boring to drive through France? By constructing a motorway. But democracy and the motor car are in command. Too many people want the motorized way of life for the construction of motorways to be about to slow down.

For what does the motorized and suburban way of life give people? Independence and comfort. In other words, pride and sensuality. No wonder the new world has such an apparently irreversible grip on the fallen sons of Adam! But nature (let alone the Lord God) has not spoken her last word. Nature is speaking through the young who are not "grown up" enough to "fit in" – through the children who have to be dosed with Prozac and Ritalin to stop them breaking down their so-called homes and schools, through the adolescents screaming in rock music at the meaningless adult life that lies ahead of them. As for the adults, the independence of their motor car and the sensuality of their suburbs have, as it were, reconciled most of them to any lingering sufferings of their higher nature. They are in a comfortable stupor and do not want to be woken up.

But by their nature men need to belong to a family and to a community of families. The tightness of modern city street-gangs under their leader shows how boys (and girls) need brothers and a father. The mindless fanaticism for this or that sports team shows how adults need to feel part of a larger association or community. Alas, the suburban way of life undoes the family by undoing father and mother, and it undoes community by making all associations unreal.

The suburbs undo the father by taking the virility out of bread winning. No longer is his manhood at a premium by his muscles handling the horses to plough the fields, which mother's muscles could never do. Instead it is at a discount by his working week being spent in an overheated office pushing papers at underdressed secretaries. As for mother, the suburbs take the integrity out of her homemaking. Washing for the family yesteryear at the village well, she could talk with other real wives about real husbands and children, but now the isolation of her luxurious home and the leisure provided by her washing machine drive her, if she stays in her man-less home, to fulfill her need for family interest by watching the notoriously popular and improper soap operas on television. As for suburban associations, reality has been emptied out of them by industry and electronics. The chemical food and synthetic clothing arrive by the ton at the local shopping mall in massive motorized trucks, while the entertainment is disgorged trouble free in the home on a series of magic lanterns, each more unclean than the last. If no real need associates men together,

Richard N. Williamson

how can their associations still be real? Needs cannot be artificially fabricated to be real.

Therefore the suburban way of life may suit original sin, but it goes against nature, and it will not last. And since the suburbs are now interlocked on a global scale, the ending risks being dramatic.

"Fear not, little flock", says Our Lord, "for it hath pleased your Father to give you a kingdom." (Lk. 12: 32) The Catholic Church, however reduced, will survive all upheavals. The Second Vatican Council, wrought, precisely, by suburban popes and bishops, was a tremendous upheaval, but the Church is still here. Like a cork on a storm-tormented ocean, it may seem to have disappeared, but when the storm dies away, it will reappear, serenely floating on the water.

Probably most readers of this letter live in suburbs and many cannot "go back to the country" even if they wanted to. Nor would a merely physical move into the country make much difference if they took their suburban way of thinking with them. But, wherever a Catholic finds himself, he must "watch and pray." I must stop and think. Can I deny that in my way of life, men are unmanned and women are unwomanned? Can I deny that this is, with the rest of the suburbs' undoing of reality, a major cause of the lack of vocations? Is this also stopping people from being saved? Is it going to stop my own salvation?

Dear readers, no human obstacle can stop Our Lord coming to the soul that seeks Him. The Vespers Antiphons of Advent are beautiful, drawn mostly from the Old Testament prophets. Here are three: "Behold the Lord will come, and all His Saints with him: and on that day there will be a great light, allelujah" (Zach. 14: 15). "Behold our Lord will come with power, and illuminate the eyes of His servants, allelujah" (Is. 40: 10). "Sound the trumpet in Sion, because the day of the Lord is close:

behold, he will come to save us, allelujah, allelujah." (Joel 2: 1)

May Our Lord find a real landing place in our hearts and minds this Advent and Christmas.

Back to the Land, Back to God?

L AST MONTH's LETTER on the undesirability, from a Catholic point of view, of the suburban way of life brought in a few thoughtful replies. I was glad. I love independent minds – as long as they agree with me.

Actually, I do believe that the December letter contained in advance, however briefly, the answer to many of the objections against it. Notably, it did not say that modern suburbs are the real disease, but that they are a major symptom of the real disease. To attack the suburban symptom is to challenge Catholics to stop taking it for granted as a natural and normal way of life, and to start thinking whether it may not even be one serious threat to their eternal salvation. "Watch and pray," said Our Lord. Let us "watch" by answering readers' objections:

CONTEXT OF SIN

Q: *Surely you are not attacking cities, which have always been centers of Catholic civilization and culture? St. Paul's Letters are all addressed to early churches in cities*

(Rome, Corinth, etc.). Medieval Cathedrals were all built in cities.

A. Correct. But industrialization, in particular the motor car, changed radically the structure of cities, and the mentality of city dwellers. For instance the people who had socialized, and the children who had played, in the city streets were chased off them by the motor car. Similarly, as long as the country outweighed the cities, city dwellers shared more or less of the country men's common sense (e.g., you cannot fool with day or night, winter or summer), but as soon as industrialism enabled the cities to outweigh the country then that common sense began to be worn away (e.g., with electricity and central heating we can change night and winter). The modern city and suburbs easily erode this natural sense of there being a nature of things. Now without nature, where is grace?

Q: But the suburbs, like television, are merely neutral, and can be used for good or bad. The problem is sin. Attack sin, not suburbs!

A. It is precisely to attack sin that one attacks modern suburbs, because their way of life favors sin. Their softness and comfort favor sensuality (Second Sorrowful Mystery). The anti-socialness and independence of their way of life favor pride (Third Sorrowful Mystery). True, television is in theory neutral, but not in practice. As installed in the (suburban or modern city) home, it strongly tends to be misused, discombobulating mind, will, the sense of reality, activeness, humanness, and family. Similarly the suburbs in practice strongly tend to discombobulate human beings. Listen to the Rock musicians, voice of now two alienated generations (1960's to 1990's). This alienation cannot go on.

Richard N. Williamson

Q: But priests (and dinosaur bishops) should be attacking sin, which is the heart of the problem, and not suburbs, which are obviously not the heart of the problem.

A. Granted, of course, sin is the real problem. But if a child complains of its shoes hurting, is it foolish to point out that it has put the right shoe on the left foot, and vice versa? If Catholics complain of finding it very difficult to lead Catholic lives, is it foolish for priests to point out where they are not realizing that the whole context of their lives is carrying them towards pride and sensuality?

Q: What do you mean by "a context carrying towards sin"? Sins are committed by free choice, not by context!

A. Yes, but contexts can exert more or less pressure on free choice, which is why many of them are branded as "occasions of sin," which a Catholic must avoid.

Q: Then you are saying that modern suburbs are an occasion of sin? Ridiculous!

A. Let us take a different example. A car radio is, as such, not the best context for listening to classical music, because I am distracted by driving, I am purely passive to the music being played, I am by my "Seek" or "Scan" buttons master of the Great Masters, to replace them at will with umpteen Rock stations. Now I <u>can</u> listen to classical music on a car radio. But the context of attending a live concert is much better, where I am neither distracted, nor purely passive, nor master of the Masters by the push of a button. Similarly I <u>can</u> lead a Catholic life in the motor-car-suburbs, but the whole context is man-made, man-centered, man-controlled. It is a <u>context</u> that shuts out God, making Him not impossible, but rather more difficult, to reach. Contexts count!

Q: For Catholics on a small tropical island, this whole question of suburbs or city against country is unreal!

A. How many Catholics are living today on small tropical islands? Get real!

NOSTALGIA RULES?

Q: You are like so many Society of St. Pius X priests, you just want to go back to the Middle Ages, which were not as great as all that.

A. SSPX priests at least appreciate that the Middle Ages were the height of Catholic Christendom, by which to measure its present depths. However, few SSPX priests (none that I know of) want to go back to those Middle Ages, which is obviously impossible. They do however, wish to go forwards <u>upwards</u> instead of forwards <u>downwards</u> into the future, and going forwards <u>upwards</u> means aiming at those Catholic heights achieved in the Middle Ages despite all their faults. Hence our regard for the Middle Ages.

Q: You just want to go back to the peace and quiet of mid-19th century hypocrisy!

A. Peace and quiet, where suitable, yes. Hypocrisy, God forbid!

Q: You just do not like anything new.

A. Much wiser (Prov. 22: 28) to like nothing new than to like nothing old, which is the condition and conditioning of modern man! But anything new that will help me to save my soul, like a new set of officials in Rome, truly Catholic, I will grab with both hands! A truly renewed Catholic Church, a new truly Christian World Order, yes please!

Q: But time passes, and things change. It is no use lamenting the "good old days."

Richard N. Williamson

A. There is no question of lamenting the good old yesterdays, only of judging correctly our present todays, in order to save as many souls as possible tomorrow. Of course time passes and things change. That is exactly why we must think about what time has brought us to now so that we can make things now change for the better. Otherwise they will go on changing for the worse. Change is inevitable, but God requires of us to direct that change in the direction of His will.

Q: But people have always praised times past as though they were better. Which strongly suggests that they were not really better at all.

A. The arguments for the Reign of Christ the King having – broadly – deteriorated for the last 700 years are clear and convincing. A car without brakes can free-wheel down a hill without crashing for a certain length of time, but finally it must crash. To the remains of Christendom in the 20th century, God sent three major warnings – World Wars I and II, and Vatican II. But still mankind is freewheeling downhill, and faster than ever.

COUNTRY DRAWBACKS

Q: But country people are now as full of drugs and vices as city or suburban people.

A. Probably not quite, but that is much more true today than yesterday, precisely because the motor car with all its pomps and all its works has overtaken the country. When Our Lady (allegedly) appeared in the mountain village of Garabandal in Northern Spain in the early 1960s, it was still an isolated mountain village. Now it is just an outrider of the nearest town.

Q: But even before industrialism, the supposedly lovely English countryside was full of Protestants.

A. Protestant England was supernaturally mad. Protestant industrialized England is supernaturally <u>and</u> naturally mad.

Q: As for the American countryside, or heartland, it is full of Protestants, the farms are laid out in an anti-social way, and life is led there in a manner downright selfish.

A. As December's letter said, Protestantism is the heart of the problem of "suburbanism," so that to attack the symptom of suburbanism amounts to a way of alerting Catholics to how the disease of Protestantism <u>is most likely infecting them without their realizing it</u>. To be Catholic is, in itself, far more important than to live in the country, but, circumstantially, not living in the country can incline many Catholics to cease being Catholic at all. Accordingly, let any Catholic think twice before he moves away from the Mass to be in the country, and let him think thrice before moving into the country to recreate suburbs there, or to rejoin an industrialized, mechanized, anti-socialized way of life if that is truly what the country has now become.

Q: Yet we Catholics are not Amish!

A. By the Truth of our supernatural religion, no. But does that mean that there is nothing in their natural way of life that we could profit by imitating? Not necessarily. There is "method in their madness." To live on the land is not the same as to live off the land.

Q: But check in your seminary to see if most of your vocations do not come from the suburban way of life.

A. It is true that Catholic Tradition is, broadly, a middle-class movement. The "upper" classes are, broadly, enjoying their corruption too much to seek the Truth, the "working" classes are, broadly, too unthinking to defy Church Authorities. And middle-class often means suburban in today's world. If then Tradition arises from suburbs, it must be that "where sin did abound, grace did the more abound." (Rom. 5: 20) If suburbanites reached Tradition "the firstest with the mostest," it may be because they were the mostest exposed to the falsity of modern life. In any case, Tradition is "a remnant saved according to the election of grace" (Rom. 11: 5), so there is a mystery of God involved.

Q: Traditionalist country elitism is odious!

A. Is it widespread? Is it anything like as widespread, or as dangerous to the Faith, as the blindness of suburban-technological complacency? We poor men will always be sinners, but country Traditionalists sound as though they have got at least some of their principles in place.

Q: But why should white collar work be less valid than blue collar work? Are only men who do physical work masculine?

A. Read the cartoons of Dilbert!! Every society by nature needs a certain number of "white collar" workers to be able to run, so by no means all "white collar" work is unreal. The fact remains that Dilbert is for real, in other words masses of suburbanites are doing work that is modally and/or substantially unreal! Similarly any society requires some unphysical work to be performed by real men, but woe to that society if widespread unphysicality unmans a mass of its men.

Q: Didn't the Conciliar Popes come from small towns and villages? So the country was to blame for Vatican II?

A. Paul VI came from middle-class Milan, a big city, and he was hugely responsible for the Vatican II disaster. John XXIII and JP2 were from the country, but both followed the essentially (sub)urban movement of modernism.

Q: This despairing of modern society is for Rock musicians, not for Catholics.

A. Like, in fact, many intellectuals (so called), Rock musicians have a point, at least when they state the problem, but they have no solution. On the contrary Catholics have the solution, only many of them lose their grip on the problem, <u>and so they lose their grip on the solution</u> ("Going My Way," "Bells of St. Mary's," etc., etc.). No Catholic can despair, but he had better be able to see why he could despair.

Q: Oh, do let us stop being negative! Let us Catholics be positive and full of luv – I'm sorry – full of l-o-v-e! Let us be an example in the world, and not just hurl abuse from the safety of our bunkers!

A. One cannot love Truth without hating error. He who so hates being "negative" that he agrees with everything that everybody says, must agree with many errors, and so he does not love truth. He who is so "positive" that he luvs everybody and everything they do is going to luv a good deal of sin, and so he is not positive in any true sense at all. All Catholic Saints hated error and sin as much as they loved God. Great Saints of the past would have had much compassion on our world had they lived today, but from the bunkers of God-given truth they would not have ceased—prudently—to "hurl abuse" at today's tidal wave of heresy and sin.

PRACTICALITIES

Q: OK, OK! Supposing I do move into the country, close enough to get to Mass each day, with time enough to recite the Rosary each day, and on too few acres to get sucked into industrial farming. What then?

A. First, let no suburbanite pretend that the move back into the country is easy. Farming is a hard way of life, which is precisely why many people in the 20th century left the land for the cities. Cows take no holidays, they must be milked every day, which includes at dawn in the dead of winter! But "no sweat, no sweet." In the hardness of the life lies its salutary discipline, for youngsters and oldsters. If people had stayed on the land, Communism could never have arisen. Who would dream of going on strike against land, animals or weather? Conclusion: in order to achieve what you would have moved to the country to achieve, do not expect, and do not reconstruct, the easy life for yourselves. "In suffering is learning."

Secondly, proximity to the Mass would be a crucial part of your move into the country, not only because of our Sunday duty and absolute need of the sacraments to save our souls, but also because of the Catholic's need of community. If Catholics fled the modern city or suburbs because of that whole context damaging to the Faith, it would not be worth fleeing into a Protestant context of isolated and individualistic country life, where there would be no Catholic families for miles around. In the early Middle Ages (500–1000 AD), the villages, towns, cities of Christendom formed around a monastery or church.

Q: *But in the Middle Ages the altars of the Catholic Church were rather more stable than they are in today's crisis of the Church!*

A. As we look back in time, it may seem so, but at that time amidst the ruins of the Roman Empire and the threat of barbarian invasions, the altars may in fact have seemed hardly more stable than they do today. At some point God requires of us to take reasonable risks, and to trust in Him for the rest.

NEED OF ADAPTATION

Q: So I flee the suburbs and I relocate in the country within striking distance of a group of Catholics where there is the Mass. What will I have achieved positively?

A. In the country, much more of the environment is God-made, or natural, instead of man-made, or artificial. Every creature of God speaks directly of God, if one has ears to listen. So if one moved into the country, one should not make the move too humanly abrupt, with too many sudden changes, because the temptation might then be to come racing back to the good old suburbs one is used to. On the other hand one should envisage leaving behind, little by little, more and more of those artificialities which are the pride and consolation of suburbanites, and which fill the glossy color catalogues stuffing our mail-boxes. Life in the country should simplify, and as it did so, so the <u>important things in life would come back into view</u>, presently blocked out by multiple artificial distractions.

Q: But no museums, no concerts, no culture – just the beauties of Nature? How boring!

A. Moving into the country would require a period of adaptation, to survive which I would need to have well thought out why I had moved into the country in the first place. But if I had thought it through, I would stand a good chance of adapting successfully.

For instance, in the cities, museums have to constantly make up new exhibitions from the same old artists, or else patronize the modern anti-artists. In the country, no two sunsets or sunrises are exactly the same, and each one is a fresh masterpiece painted in moving technicolor, but of course one must have eyes to see. Similarly concert halls have to go round and around the same favorite pieces of the classical composers, or else descend into the bear-pit of "modern music," whereas in the country each dawn-chorus of bird-song is a new symphony conducted by our Maker, but concert hall ears have to be adjusted to hear it. (In one sense, the museums and concerts died some time ago.)

Q: *But life in the country would be boring!*

A. The adults would have to adjust, for sure, and the older children, but the younger children should take to country life like ducks to water. Most parents can see how much more healthy it would be for their children to grow up in the country, only circumstances of all kinds prevent them from thinking that they could make the move.

RESCUING NATURE

Q: *What is the advantage for children?*

A. Fresh air. Freedom to play outside. Manual labor, apt to teach discipline and responsibility. The handling of live animals for which children have a God-given affinity, and which by their God-given nature can teach many lessons of life that no machines can teach. For instance, what child born and bred in between stallions and mares, bulls and cows, cocks and hens, is ever going to buy into the absurdity that there is no difference between males and females? Dare I say that the animals without reason will have taught the child a significant part of the difference between the males and females that have reason?

Q: *But all of these advantages of country life are situated on the merely natural level. It is grace, or supernature, that counts for salvation!*

A. Of course, but grace builds on nature. Grace does heal nature, but it does not violate it. Grace works against sin, but it works with our God-given nature. That is why a wise education works with grace and nature in tandem. The problem with the ever increasing artificiality of suburban life is that nature is being so shattered that grace has nothing left to work with. The total suburban context makes stony ground on which the seed of grace has little chance. That is a major reason why so many pious suburban parents see their teenagers become disinterested in the Catholic religion. Grace and nature, as presented to the teenagers, just do not integrate or fit one another. That is also a major reason why we have few vocations at present, and it is a deep reason why at the seminary we have needed to introduce a preliminary year of Humanities.

Q: Tell me some good news of the Seminary!

A. Gladly! It looks as though we may have seven new priests ordained at Winona on Saturday, June 23. That is a larger number in any one year than we have had for a few years.

Dear readers, do not lose heart. The Lord God pays each of us the compliment of demanding a great deal of us, but He does not demand the impossible. Thank you always for your spiritual and material support of the seminary. We begin a new calendar year quietly and steadily, with the help of God and of His Blessed Mother, and with 42 seminarians.

Contacts With Rome

A S MANY OF you know, official contacts have been renewed between Rome and the SSPX in the last few months. In theory we should all be reassured by this proof that the Society is not after all a non-entity in Rome's eyes, as Rome has since 1988 been pretending. In practice, all kinds of rumors are flying around, and many Catholics who love their Faith are anxious. What is going on?

Now on the one hand, nobody reasonable will expect somebody in my position to tell everything I know. On the other hand, the interests of the Society are the interests of every Catholic, so in this sense every Catholic has a stake in the Society, and in this sense it is reasonable to tell every interested Catholic as much as may help him both to understand the issues involved and to take his part in the defence of Mother Church, wherever Our Lord has placed him on the battlefield. Here then is less a blow-by-blow account of recent contacts than an overview of all such encounters, their framework, their parameters. For it is less important to know exactly what is happening than to know why whatever happens does happen. Similarly, none of us at this point in time knows exactly what will come of the recent contacts but all of us need to know how to react if this or that does come from them.

Firstly, let us be <u>very clear</u> that the initiative for these latest contacts came from Rome. It was Rome that opened up these latest contacts last summer with the Society, and not the Society that opened them up with Rome. Cardinal Castrillón Hoyos opened the fire with a letter to each of the Society's four bishops, beginning "My dear Brother," and declaring that the Pope's arms were wide open to embrace us (I almost wept with emotion on reading this – but not quite!).

Secondly, it was inevitable that Rome <u>would reopen</u> the contacts with the Society, not because the Society is the Society or has nice blue eyes or whatever, but because by the grace of God and by a measure of human cooperation with His grace, the Society happens to have guarded the Deposit of the Faith around which Our Lord's Church officials, if they themselves lose it, must hover like moths around a flame. Therefore if the Society loses the Deposit – humanly, more than possible – and if Rome continues to reject that Deposit, then tomorrow Rome will be hovering around whatever other flame God will have subsequently lit to take the entrapped Society's place.

Thirdly, so long as any organization like the Society has the Truth while Rome has not, then the Society is in the driving seat <u>for all Catholic purposes</u>, and any behavior, shape, size or form of negotiations which would allow this Rome to get back into the driving seat would be tantamount to a betrayal of the Truth. Of course from the moment when Rome returned to the truth, Rome would be back in the driving seat, because that is how Our Lord built His Church: "Thou art Peter, and upon this rock I will build my Church." (Mt. 16: 16) However, when Peter has for a prolonged period of time, as now, demonstrated in word but above all in action that

Richard N. Williamson

he has to a significant extent – albeit not entirely – lost
the Truth, then however much the organization which
is in the Society's position may even supernaturally long
to scuttle back under the skirts of Rome, the burden of
proof lies with those who say the moment for negotiations has come, and not with those who say it has not
come. To enter into negotiations at the end of such a period without that proof would, again, amount to virtual
betrayal of the Truth.

This is because, fourthly, Roman Church officials are
<u>masters</u> of negotiating, of dealing, of maneuvering, of
out-maneuvering their opponents. They have top-class
brains, state-of-the-art networks of informants and information, and 2,000 years of experience in out-witting
whoever happens to be facing them. When all these as-
sets are used truly in the service of Our Lord, the results
are magnificent. But when they are used, as today, in the
service of Vatican II, then automatically the Society is in
peril if it tries to cut a deal with these Romans. Our Lord
said to His disciples, "I send you out as sheep amongst
wolves," but that is no excuse for putting oneself between
the wolf's teeth, outside of extreme necessity. True, the
Romans may always convert, but, again, given a track-re-
cord such as the Vatican's over the last 40 years, then the
burden of proof lies with those who claim they have converted, and not with those who assume, by the Romans'
fruits, that they are still wolves and foxes and sharks!

However, fifthly, Rome still being, by Our Lord's design, the command-center of the Catholic Church, it follows that if an organisation like the Society can, by negotiating, wring important concessions from the "sharks,"
then those concessions may benefit the Universal Church,
and this is the best-case scenario which must tempt an
organisation in the Society's position. But if the "sharks"
remain sharks, in the service, for instance, of Vatican
II, how can they possibly put into honest practice the

concessions? And if in exchange they have succeeded in putting a leash and/or muzzle upon the Society which was until then free to serve God as best it understood, what will such a Society have gained in exchange for the freedom to serve God which it will have lost?

Moreover, sixthly, even if negotiations, for all kinds of reasons such as above, come to nothing, then the simple fact of having entered into negotiations will have played for Rome and against the organisation in the Society's position. This is because any Catholic organisation re-sisting Rome in crisis suffers from the unavoidable inter-nal tension between staying close to Mother Rome and keeping away from her neo-modernist leprosy. So mem-bers of the Society will stretch all the way from those for, to those against, any negotiation. Let Rome but make an offer calculated to please the ones as much as it dis-pleases the others, and the Society will be stretched to breaking point. Rome will at least have divided, if not conquered.

In 1921 the Irish rebels had fought the British Em-pire to a standstill. Cleverly, the British stopped fighting and offered a Peace Treaty which split the Irish down the middle. The immediate result was that in 1922, in-stead of fighting the British, the Irish began fighting one another! Now the British were cunning rulers of a great Empire at the time, but compared with these Church of-ficials of Rome, the Brits were mere beginners!

All of which means, seventhly, that any organisation in the Society's position stands a good chance of falling into a Roman trap. At best, it obtains unsure concessions in exchange for a sure loss of freedom; at worst it obtains nothing at all and is divided into the bargain. Wise after the event, we might say that the Society's best course in the circumstances would be not to talk with Rome at all, but that is for Catholics easier said than done.

Richard N. Williamson

However, eighthly and finally, "The Truth is mighty and will prevail." What is unique about the Catholic Church amongst all organisations of men on earth is that it rises with the Truth and falls with untruth. Neo-modernist Rome has fallen with the untruths of Vatican II. The SSPX has, at least until 2001, risen by being faithful to the Truth of Catholic Tradition. As soon as Rome comes back to the Truth – as it will – Rome will rise again, to the joy of us all. Equally, if the Society turns unfaithful to Tradition, it will inevitably and deservedly fall. But "fear not, little flock," as Our Lord told us, "your Father knoweth that you have need of all these things." (Lk. 12: 32; Mt. 6: 32) Souls seeking God will never be left without the means of finding Him. That is because God created the whole world only for souls to come to Him. And that is why, as Our Lord on Palm Sunday told the Pharisees who were angry at His disciples crying out Hosanna to the Son of David, if all human beings were to stop crying out the Truth, the very stones of the street would rise up to proclaim it. (Lk. 19: 40)

This Rome may then – worst-case scenario – succeed in reducing the Society of St. Pius X to paralysis and silence, but if it did, that would only be a just judgment of God, and the Truth would be upheld elsewhere. What does the Society presently deserve? Time will tell.

Personally I think that in the United States, in France, in fact all over the world, most Society priests are quietly working at ground level to sanctify and to save souls, that such real and humble work is blessed by God, and so I think most Society priests – and the laity who are with them – will be protected by God from falling in with Roman corruption. However, even if I am right this time round, there will certainly be a next attack on the Society from the Devil or from his Rome, and since these days are such that if they were not shortened, even the elect would not be saved, then I do not know if the

Society will survive in its present form all the way until that shortening of these evil days.

<u>But it does not matter whether it will or not, whether I know it or not</u>. I do not have to worry today about the problems of tomorrow – "Sufficient for the day is the evil thereof" (Mt. 6: 34). Let me be the best Catholic that I can, day by day, and the rest I can leave in God's hands. The rest is <u>His</u> problem!

Dear readers, spring is not far off when one can look around and say with the poet:

> The world is so full of such wonderful things,
> Why can't we all be just as happy as kings?

Nobody will be able to do away with God, however hard they try. So let us by all means pray for the SSPX, because things will be that much easier if it does hold up. But at the same time let us be prepared, if it goes the way of all flesh, not to be stricken with panic. "God alone suffices" – St. Teresa of Avila.

May He love you and bless you.

From Rome, Good News

FOR THE MONTH of the tenth anniversary of the great Archbishop Lefebvre's death, we have the pleasure of offering you not only the enclosed portrait of him (from Virginia), but also good news of the SSPX which he founded; it is standing firm in the face of Rome's recent efforts to buy it back into the Conciliar Church. One may never put one's trust in man, as last month's letter sternly recalled, following Jeremiah (17: 5–8). But one may, and must, put one's trust in God, with whom the Archbishop will certainly have been interceding for us.

Here is the sequence of events. In early December of last year, Cardinal Castrillón Hoyos, with a mandate from the Pope to bring to an end the 13 year old "schism" (as Rome sees it) of the SSPX, invited Bishop Bernard Fellay, the Society's Superior General, to Rome to see the Pope. On December 29 and 30 the Cardinal had two long talks with Bishop Fellay, including a brief encounter with the Pope where New Year greetings were exchanged, and little else. On January 13, SSPX leaders meeting in Switzerland to consider the Cardinal's generous-looking proposals, decided that Rome must first liberate the Tridentine Mass and declare null the 1988 "excommunication" of the four SSPX bishops, before the SSPX will even sit down to negotiate with Rome an end to the "schism."

A few days later Bishop Fellay conveyed this decision to the Cardinal. A few weeks later the Cardinal replied verbally (not in writing!) to an SSPX priest in Rome, firstly that the Tridentine Mass is not banned but that Rome cannot be expected to say so in public (!); secondly that the "lifting" of the "excommunication" would form part of a package deal reintegrating the SSPX into the mainstream Church.

On February 19 two SSPX priests, mandated by Bishop Fellay, gently but firmly brought the Cardinal to understand that the SSPX had meant what it said when it said one month previously that either Rome must liberate the Tridentine Mass for all priests, or the SSPX will not even sit down to begin negotiating. The Cardinal has the reputation of a powerful negotiator who gets what he wants, and in a variety of ways since last summer he has made it clear that he and the Pope want to get the SSPX "back into the Church" (as Rome sees it). That is why he did not want to accept that the Society was taking such a principled stand on the Mass of the old religion, hated by all Conciliarists, but after three and a half hours of talking, he had to accept that that was the Society's pre-condition for any further negotiations.

One need wish the Cardinal no ill. Bishop Fellay's spokesman at this February 19 meeting commented that in any normal circumstances the Cardinal's loyalty to the Pope and his desire to serve him would be touching. Cardinal Castrillón surely desires to bring the SSPX "back into the Church" and he may even sincerely wish the Society well. But so little does he (or, then, the Pope) grasp the issue at stake that our spokesman was at a loss "in what language to speak to him." And it was horrifying, he said ("effroyable" in French), to realize how the

highest of churchmen in Rome today could be so ignorant of the essentials of the true Faith!

We are reminded of the carefully weighed words of
Archbishop Lefebvre shortly before the "excommunica-
tions" of June 1988: "I do not think we can say that Rome
has not lost the Faith." Also of what he said more than
once after that "excommunication," namely that Rome
having thereby given final proof of its unwillingness or
inability to look after the Faith, then from that time onwards any discussions with Rome could no longer be ju-
ridical or canonical, they would have to be dogmatic. In
other words the problem between the SSPX and Rome
was no longer a question of legal nuts and bolts, it was
a question of basic doctrine, and could only be handled
as such. The February 19 meeting in which the Cardinal
insisted on nuts and bolts, shows how right the Archbishop was. Coming out of the three and a half hours
with the Cardinal our spokesman said he was more convinced than ever that the Society's firm stand was the
right one. But how few Catholics can yet see that! The
basic theology of Conciliarism, that infernally subtle
falsification of Catholicism emerging from the Second
Vatican Council, is the real problem between this Rome
and the Society.

However, Cardinal Castrillón is not a man easily
stopped. On February 19 he told our priests that four
new members would be added to the *Ecclesia Dei* Commission (set up to handle the 1988 refugees from "Lefeb-
vrism") in order to prepare for the new Commission due
to replace *Ecclesia Dei* as soon as (!) there is an agreement with the SSPX. On February 24 these four names
were publicly announced by Rome, and they are heads of
the four departments that will be most concerned by a
Rome-SSPX deal: Cardinal Ratzinger (Doctrine), Cardinal Medina (Liturgy), Archbishop Herranz (Canon Law)
and Cardinal Billé (primate of the French bishops).

Now these are four heavyweight churchmen being added to a lightweight Commission, given the fact that important Congregations or dicasteries of the Roman Curia rarely include more than one Cardinal. But when we add Cardinal Castrillón, here there will be four! There are two opposite interpretations of this unusual move.

Either, as I was told by an English journalist who claims to have contacts high up in the Roman Curia, these four celebrities are being added to *Ecclesia Dei* in order to put brakes on Cardinal Castrillón, who is moving towards a Rome-SSPX deal altogether too fast for the liking of Conciliar Romans who fear the SSPX acting like a Trojan horse if it is given re-entry within the walls of their official Church. Or, on the contrary, as Cardinal Castrillón told our two priests on February 19, these powerful men are being brought on board in order to make the supposedly imminent Rome-SSPX deal work. In this case the unusual move corresponds to the Cardinal's expressed desire to have the agreement concluded by Easter!

Such a hurry may also correspond to Rome's public announcement on February 26 of an extraordinary Consistory of Cardinals to be held from May 21 to 24 of this year in order "to analyze, among other things, the Petrine ministry and episcopal collegiality." A Roman newspaper interprets this announcement as meaning that the Cardinals will study "the role and functions of the primacy of the Bishop of Rome as well as . . . the ministry of bishops united among themselves and in communion with the Pontiff."

In plain English, the Conciliarists in Rome are planning, in accordance with Vatican II, to do away with the Pope, and replace him by some committee of cardinals and/or bishops. But the Conciliarists are well aware that for many Catholics still within their Novus Ordo, this might prove the last straw. If in addition to everything else Catholic which "the spirit of Vatican II" has taken away from them, Catholics lost also their Holy Father, then they might really look for some Catholic refuge in which to ride out the storm. At which point, if there simply was no longer any such refuge, many could lose heart and feel obliged to go along even with the destruction of the Papacy. But if there was still in existence a refuge like the SSPX, proclaiming itself the staunch defender of the old-fashioned Catholic Papacy, then such distressed Catholics would have somewhere to go, and the numbers and strength of the SSPX might grow alarmingly.

So, is the unprecedented extension of the temporary *Ecclesia Dei* Commission proof that Rome wants to bring in the SSPX, or proof that Rome wants to push it away? Either way, the story is by no means over.

If the Cardinal has his foot on the accelerator, then he must come up with new enticements to draw the SSPX out of its Traditional fortress, and we must continue to trust God and to pray to the Archbishop that the Society neither flinch nor waver. On the other hand, if the Cardinal's colleagues have their foot on his brakes, then Rome must fall back on its 13 year old policy of smothering the SSPX in silence, a silence so remarkably broken by the recent initiatives of Cardinal Castrillón. And in that case we clergy and laity of the Society must possess our souls in patience, and continue to practice humbly and steadily the Catholic Faith of all time. But if quiet does return, for sure and certain it is simply a matter of time before another Cardinal Castrillón will be coming back to busy himself with the Society! Roman error cannot leave the Truth alone.

Inevitably our thoughts come back to the great Archbishop Lefebvre. Ten years since he died! But as we always knew, he is the master of Rome. What a man of God! What a man! He is by no means yet generally vindicated, but by his magnificent fidelity to the Truth when everyone else was, in a collective madness infecting even Cardinals and Popes, abandoning it, he sits astride the Catholic Truth for all future generations, so that tomorrow or the day after, all Catholics without exception will be profoundly grateful to him.

And we have known him sooner than most. Dear readers, you and I are lucky creatures! Let us only be faithful! Let us do Lenten penances for fidelity!

New Mass Depth-Charged

A T THE RISK of, as they say in French, drowning the fish, let me come back once more to the recent contacts between the churchmen in Rome and the SSPX, to give one major news item but, more importantly, to present the Society's depth-charging of the New Mass.

Amidst a flurry of misinformation and disinformation coming out of Rome, we know for sure what Cardinal Castrillón told the Society's District Superior in Italy a few days ago: at a March 22 meeting in the Vatican of important heads of Church government departments (called Congregations or Dicasteries), with Pope John Paul II present, the liberation of the Tridentine Mass was again blocked, so Rome–SSPX "negotiations" are, for now, off.

At an interdicastery meeting of this kind, it appears that one of the Cardinals or churchmen present lays out a problem of his dicastery. Then each of the churchmen gives his judgment. Finally the Pope decides what he will or will not do. On March 22 Cardinal Castrillón presented the problem of the "reintegration" of the SSPX into the "mainstream Church" (inverted commas, because of course the SSPX has never ceased to belong to the true Catholic Church, as recognized by its four distinguishing marks of being one, holy, catholic and apostolic).

The "problem," as we all know by now, is that in February the SSPX made clear to Rome that before the SSPX will even sit down at a negotiating table to begin negotiating its "reintegration," Rome must both undeclare the "excommunication" of the SSPX bishops declared upon their consecration in July of 1988, and it must liberate the Tridentine Mass from all restrictions at present making Catholic priests think they may not say it.

Apparently the "excommunication" seemed to the heads of Dicasteries on March 22 to present no great problem – by means of discussions it could at any time be talked out of the way. But the release of the Tridentine rite of Mass so that any priest would be free to celebrate it whenever he liked, seemed altogether more difficult. Cardinal Castrillón told our Superior in Italy that a strong majority of the Cardinals present was opposed, including Cardinal Ratzinger. To prove his point, the latter brandished in his hand on this or a similar occasion a copy of the new book that the SSPX has just brought out, which depth-charges Pope Paul's new Mass of 1969.

This book, called *The Problem of the Liturgical Reform, the Mass of Vatican II and Paul VI*, was written by SSPX priests, and 17,000 copies have been sent out to priests all over France, where it is being heavily discussed. Clearly and briefly it lays out a mass of quotations from the fabricators of the New Mass themselves to show how coherent and un-catholic are the principles behind the New Mass' fabrication. No wonder Cardinal Ratzinger referred to the book to persuade his fellow Cardinals that the SSPX's insistence on the Tridentine Mass is no slight affair, and it seems that they agreed.

However, by the time the March 22 meeting came to an end, the decision whether or not to release the Tridentine Mass lay with the Pope. Can he, dare he, has he the strength, to override a strong majority of his own cardinals? We are told that he himself strongly wishes to get the SSPX "back into the Church." Is he being moved by grace? Is he afraid, as he approaches death, of coming before the judgment seat of God with the 12 year condemnation of Archbishop Lefebvre and of Catholic Tradition weighing upon his soul? Or is he merely continuing to promote that all-round ecumenism to which the 12 year "excommunication" constitutes such a disconcerting exception? We may never know.

Howsoever that be, it does seem sure that to bring the SSPX "back into the Church," about one year ago he gave a personal mandate and wide-ranging powers to Cardinal Castrillón. And of course for many decent Romans and decent Catholics throughout the world, such a "reconciliation" between Catholic Tradition and the Church authorities is a consummation devoutly to be wished. But as the proverb from England says, "A fact is stronger than the Lord Mayor." What the SSPX's new book does is merely to recall that fact which many "decent" people would prefer to forget, namely that what is going on today inside the Church is a war between two religions, which it will take much more than mere "decency" or a bit of negotiating to bring to an end.

The fact of its being a war between religions that is going on inside the Church is also the reason why the SSPX is right to have said that even if the Romans do undeclare the "excommunication" and release the Tridentine Mass, still that will only mean that the SSPX will sit down to begin negotiating. For indeed those two gestures would prove serious good will on Rome's part, but they could only be a beginning of the dismantling of the false religion presently occupying the Church.

Now those who would like to see Rome–SSPX negotiations taking place are apt to raise the objection that in Church history many crises of the Faith have only been solved gradually, so the SSPX is being unrealistic if it demands today that all cardinals tomorrow suddenly declare that Archbishop Lefebvre was right. But the SSPX is only demanding that the cardinals begin to realize what a problem they have on their hands. When Mother Church has a mega-problem, what truly loving son proposes mini-solutions? The false new Mass is the major symptom of an entire false new religion. Sooner or later both must go.

That is the clear implication of *The Problem of the Liturgical Reform*. The book is in three parts: it shows firstly that the New Mass is a liturgical break, or breakdown; secondly, that that break proceeds from a new theology of basics such as sin and Redemption; thirdly, that this new theology is condemned by Catholic doctrine.

The first part proving that the 1969 reform of the Mass represents not a harmonious development of the Catholic liturgy but a liturgical break with the Church's whole past subdivides again into three chapters: in place of the "Mass" offering satisfaction and propitiation for sin, the 1969 reform gave us mainly a "Eucharist" or thanksgiving for nice things; Chapter Two, whereas Christ in the old missal is sacrificer (through his priest ordained for sacrifice) and sacrificial victim (through transubstantiation), in the new missal He is mainly the talking Lord of the meeting; finally whereas the old missal was structured as a sacrifice, the new missal is structured as a memorial meal.

To these obvious changes from the old to the new missal corresponds in the second part of the book a likewise threefold presentation of the coherent and in-depth new theology behind these changes. Clearly, the Cardinal Ratzingers of this world have thought out their new religion, and as we saw on March 22, they are not about to let go of it!

Richard N. Williamson

Firstly, upon a new concept of sin follows a new concept of Redemption. Instead of sin primarily offending God and requiring satisfaction to be made to Him, modern people pretend sin cannot offend God that much, so it primarily hurts ourselves and requires our own restoration. Accordingly the Redemption is no longer primarily the Cross satisfying God's justice, it becomes the "PASCHAL MYSTERY" revealing God's unbreakable love for us, especially in the Resurrection (hence of course the risen-Christ crucifixes). Secondly, Mass then ceases to be a true and proper sacrifice renewing the Cross, becoming instead the "Eucharist," or thanksgiving, commemorating the Paschal Mystery from Passion to Resurrection. Thirdly, the Holy Sacrament ceases to be the "ex opere operato" producer of grace objectively sanctifying the soul, instead it becomes the revealing experience of mystery, subjectively feeding faith. Correspondingly the priesthood of Christ's minister offering Christ in the Real Presence to the Father, makes way for the priesthood of the people offering themselves with faith in Christ.

The third part of *The Problem of the Liturgical Reform* measures against Church doctrine this gigantic and coherent shift in the way of conceiving the Church's central act of worship, and it judges that the shift is dogmatically condemned! Firstly, that the Mass propitiates God and satisfies His justice is dogma of the Council of Trent (and of Vatican I, had the latter been able to conclude). Secondly, Trent also defined the Mass to be a true and proper sacrifice, not just some memorial, however objective, as commemorated by the new missal (e.g., words of Consecration printed in narrative form). Lastly to extend the word "sacrament" from the seven objective producers of grace to any sign or symbol apt to arouse a subjective experience of things divine is virtual modernism, as condemned by Pius X.

Of course such a brief summary cannot do justice to the documented and close-knit argumentation of the book, so readers can only be urged to read it for themselves as soon as the Angelus Press will publish it in English.

Meanwhile the recent series of Rome–SSPX negotiations have at least shown so far that the SSPX, by insisting on the Mass, is looking out firstly for the interests of the Universal Church, that the SSPX is far from having a schismatic mentality, and that Rome is not yet ready to let go of its new religion. We can also be grateful for the measure of protection of the Truth that Rome has unintentionally given us by the "excommunication" sealing us off for 12 years so far from much of the Newchurch's contamination.

Patience. With, if necessary without, the dear SSPX, the Truth will prevail. Only the timing and mechanics of its prevailing are uncertain.

Britain's Decadence

PRODDED BY A venerable American priest who admires the SSPX but finds it rather anti-American, I just read a recently appeared book castigating my own country: *The Abolition of Britain* by Peter Hitchens. To console Fr. Pablo, and to take the heat for at least one month off the dear United States of America, let us take a good look at Hitchens' devastating criticism of modern Britain. But then to console and enlighten Catholics, especially in England, let us see how his perspective on our poor country needs to be corrected and completed by a Catholic understanding of history. For I love my homeland as none of us can love any other, and I love the USA as the land where Providence has brought me to work, but I measure both countries by Catholicism, and not the reverse.

A journalist from Oxford, Peter Hitchens has not only the good reporter's familiarity with the contemporary scene, but also a deep and patriotic sense of the last three centuries of British history, enough to give him a clear view of the degradation of that scene. His book has been a surprise bestseller in Britain, no doubt because it gives voice to the deep concern of many Britons at the turn our country is taking. As Hitchens sees it, "A great civilization, whose greatest possession is liberty, is on the edge of extinction and we have very little time to save it." (p. 11)

In this respect a decisive event for Hitchens was the 1997 General Election in Britain which brought to power the Labour Party with Tony Blair at their head, much as the USA 1992 election brought in the Democrats and Clinton. Of that 1997 Election Hitchens says that it was "a historic choice between two utterly different ideas of Britain, a choice that had little to do with economics and even politics, and everything to do with what kind *of people we are*" (Hitchens' italics). In other words, that election was merely the political manifestation of the cultural sea change of modern times. In place of the old Britain's crumbling patriotism, faith, morality and literature, came the new Britain personified by Tony Blair, whom Hitchens quotes as saying about himself, "I am a modern man. I am part of the rock and roll generation – the Beatles, colour TV, that's the generation I come from." (p.1)

That is why, after the introduction devoted to Tony Blair ("A Modern Man"), nearly all of Hitchens' book deals with cultural issues: the rewriting of British history books, education, the countryside, the (Anglican) Church, television, satire, unwed mothers, the debasement of language, family and divorce, pornography, soap operas, contraception, homosexuality, the death penalty and the turn to Europe. Hitchens' conclusion is named "Chainsaw Massacre" after the American film, to suggest how the new Britons have, as it were, taken chainsaws to cut down the entire forest of noble trees that made up the old Britain.

However, Hitchens is rather more anxious for the future than he is nostalgic for the past, so he is angry at the present degradation of Britain with a sharpness giving rise to hundreds of quotable quotes. Alas, there is room here for only a handful of them:

Richard N. Williamson

On the 1997 election:

> The two Britains which faced each other . . . were ut-
> terly alien to one another and unfairly matched. One
> was old and dying, treasuring values and ideas which
> stretched back into a misty past. One was new and
> hardly born, clinging just as fiercely to its new values
> of classlessness, anti-racism, sexual inclusiveness and
> license, contempt for the nation-state, dislike of defer-
> ence, scorn for restraint, and incomprehension for the
> web of traditions and prejudices which were revered by
> the other side.

The English countryside, source of national identity and
consolation,

> has largely disappeared, digested by urban sprawl, lev-
> eled by new roads... English rural, urban and subur-
> ban life has been strangely denatured. People live in
> places, but are not of them. Communal activities . . .
> have died away. Front gardens . . . are increasingly con-
> creted over and turned into car parks.

Children between two and three, watching up to 18
hours of TV a week with little to no adult supervision,
have been

> abandoned in a way only the late 20th century could
> invent . . . it is frightening to think what kind of ad-
> olescents, what kind of adults, they will become and
> almost unbearable to imagine what kind of parents
> they will be.

On television: "In this medium, a conservative message
will always look foolish" (like a grandfather in a T-shirt).

On the "millennium generation", shown by a November 1998 survey to be less Conservative than ever:

This does not record a mere change in political loyalty, which is not specially important in itself. It shows that, for the first time this century, the young are not inheriting prejudices, opinions, values, morals and habits from their parents. The continuity that once ensured that most people followed their parents in such things, has been broken. The post-revolutionary generation, whose families have often disintegrated and are usually weak, whose schools do not uphold authority or tradition, whose religious experience and understanding often do not exist, has also grown up with several immensely strong outside influences, all of them radical enemies of existing culture. The same generation has had little chance to develop its own critical, personal imagination through reading, and so has been a blank page on which the revolutionaries have been able to scrawl their own slogans.

On a country which ploughs under its own culture without violence or open suppression: "The objects of attack are unaware that they are under attack, and there are no martyrs or persecution to bring resistance into being." Elsewhere: "What an achievement – the power of totalitarianism without the need to imprison, torture or exile." On State "protection" of the unmarried: "It is in fact a theft of privileges from the married." On modern old age: "The old have become unpersons, long before they die." On modern young men: "They failed to grow up because they no longer needed to. The old disciplines of marriage, fatherhood and work had gone."

These quotes and many others demonstrate Hitchens' admirable grasp of the symptoms of the new Britain's malady. A number of American readers may recognize the same symptoms in the USA, but let anyone who thinks I am anti-American believe that I am delighted for a change to point them out in my own country. The problem is international. However, in

Great Britain, what are Peter Hitchens' diagnosis and proposals for a cure? By way of diagnosis, he says two profound things, each in several places in his book, but neither is profound enough to give him, apparently, any idea of a cure.

Firstly, he says that the leaders of the old Britain had ceased to believe in the old values, and this was why the new Britain has swept all before it: "On almost all fronts there has been no coherent, organized resistance to the cultural revolution. *The other side has lost its nerve, and no longer really believes in itself*" (my italics). On the death penalty: "Once again . . . the reactionaries lost because they did not really believe in their case." But the deeper question, why the old leaders ceased to believe in the old values, Hitchens does not ask, let alone answer. He merely quotes a key Labour politician from the 1960's declaring, more or less, that the old values are "puritanical restriction, petty-minded disapproval, hypocrisy and a dreary, ugly pattern of life." Where the purpose of discipline is lost, pleasure is always there to take over. But why was the old purpose lost?

The second profound truth that Hitchens tells concerning today's cultural radicals is that they are the distant but direct descendants of England's religious radicals of the 17th century, the Puritans. He says that Britain's cultural revolution of the last 30 years represents "a long-buried radical strain" in England climbing out of its tomb and finishing "a revolution which first threatened this country during England's Civil War (1640's), was defeated by the royalist Restoration (1660) and headed off by the historic compromise of 1688 (the "Glorious Whig Revolution"). It rose again in the aftermath of the French and American Revolutions but was defeated by Church, King, law, patriotism and tradition," those noble trees that the revolutionaries are at last cutting down.

But, Mr. Hitchens, that Whig Revolution of 1688 which you glorify as the basis of three glorious British centuries, was, more than half, the achievement of the same radicals you hate! You have no cure for new Britain's poisoning because you more than half believe in swallowing the poison yourself! Take your diagnosis one century further back! For where do you think those Puritans came from? You think the Reformation rendered England a service by cutting her off from all those unhappy and unreliable peoples on the European continent. But Protestantism so split Catholic England that Elizabeth I, to stamp out Catholicism, established the semi-Catholic Anglican Church, which the pure Protestants, or Puritans, naturally found too Catholic by half. Hence the Civil War of the 1640's. But Cromwell's triumph in turn caused the anti-Puritan reaction of the Restoration of King Charles II in 1660, which, when King James II converted to Catholicism, had to be again dethroned by the Puritans mutated into Whigs, in their so-called "Glorious Revolution" of 1688 (compare the Puritans of America's New England mutating into rationalists and materialists).

Thus Hitchens is right that today's cultural revolution is the final triumph of a centuries-old crusade to cut down everything noble in England. He is right that 1688 still partly embodied that nobility, which sort of lasted for another 300 years. He is right that its believers have finally lost belief in it, that Whiggery is at last dead. Where he is wrong, what he cannot see, is that Whigs were semi-revolutionaries from the very beginning, who sooner or later were bound to have no way of standing up to full-blooded revolutionaries. And that is why Peter Hitchens has no remedy for Tony Blair, who is presently polled to win Britain's upcoming General Election.

Who does have a remedy? Only that Church which England abandoned at the Reformation, the real Catholic Church, and not the one semi-revolutionized by Vatican II! And this Church can only be presented to men in her full saving force by Catholics whose minds and hearts are not contaminated by Whiggery, nor half-seduced by the modern world. Dear readers, let us lead Catholic, and not semi-Catholic, lives, despite all our surroundings, so that the Whigs and radicals around us are bound to see the only answer to all of their real problems. And let us ask the Mother of God, for her month of May, to obtain mercy for the remains of what was once her dowry, dear England.

Rome: Stick or Carrot

A NUMBER OF you may have been alarmed recently at news that negotiations to bring the SSPX into line with the Conciliar Church are continuing. Do not worry. The news is false!

One must admit, the Romans are clever! The SSPX makes a pious Jubilee Year pilgrimage to the Roman basilicas in August. The Church authorities seize upon the Society's Roman excursion – which they made possible, let us not forget – to re-open contacts with the SSPX that had been officially nullified since the Episcopal Consecrations of 1988. By mid-March of this year, for fundamentally the same reasons as in 1988, the Society announces that the contacts – not negotiations – are again nullified. In May, last month, Rome has the media pretend that the negotiations – not just contacts – are continuing! To reverse the famous comment of the French General on the charge of the Light Brigade: it is not magnificent but it is war.

Thus on May 11, Zenit.org reported on the Internet that Cardinal Castrillón Hoyos was engaging in talks with Bishop Fellay in Germany and/or Switzerland. On May 14 a normally reputable Catholic news agency based in Fribourg, Switzerland, APIC, likewise reported that on May 11 and 12 Cardinal Castrillón was in Germany and Switzerland to meet the leaders of the SSPX and the Fraternity of St. Peter. When APIC was told as from SSPX headquarters in Switzerland that there was no such meeting with SSPX leaders, it persisted in its story at first, but apologized a few days later to Menzingen – they had been so sure of their story, because it came from "a source in Rome." (Immediate moral of the story, dear readers: do not believe everything you read on the Internet. At least check out the SSPX HQ website at www.fsspx.org).

Of course it is remotely possible that the "Roman source" was in good faith when it told this tale to APIC, but it is rather more likely that the disinformation was deliberate, to maintain the illusion of ongoing negotiations. What for? To attempt to divide and destabilize the SSPX and its lay supporters, and to keep them in a state of agitation, as certainly happened for a number of our friends in Europe. "All is fair in love and war" goes the saying, which includes pretending that there is no war!

Yet we are at war, whether we like it or not. Today the war is total between the one true religion which can alone save souls for all eternity, and the universal anti-religion which has taken effective control in Rome, and which is putting and keeping millions and millions of souls on the road to eternal Hell-fire. In this war the little SSPX has played for the last 30 years an honorable part in helping to prevent the total success of the anti-religion, so last summer, to overcome the SSPX's resistance, Rome changed strategy. This change is very well presented in the May 31 issue of *The Remnant*, valiant bi-weekly journal edited by Michael Matt, and known to many of our readers in the USA.

Starting out from the Internet's news report that SSPX-Rome negotiations were continuing, Mr. Matt presents four possible explanations. It is the third that

I will here summarize and slightly adapt, as being the most likely to be true.

Let us assume, he says, that Rome is losing the Faith, and that the Revolution that has engulfed the world also succeeded with Vatican II in taking effective control of the Catholic Church in Rome. With all such Revolutions there comes a time to take out the last pockets of resistance which might otherwise evolve into fully-fledged enclaves, capable of taking down the Revolution itself. Mr. Matt interestingly quotes an example from history, how Napoleon Bonaparte at the height of his fame and power nevertheless went after and executed one little journalist in Belgium, because Napoleon knew how just one little journal could, given time, bring him down.

Now by its almost complete triumph at Vatican II, the Revolution succeeded in crippling soon afterwards every approved order of priests, so that none of them could effectively resist any longer the New Mass, the Council or the novel teachings of the new style popes. Only the SSPX, founded for that purpose in 1970 by Archbishop Lefebvre, managed the feat of resisting the Newchurch while remaining inside the Catholic Church.

The Revolution had to put an end to that! They began with the stick: "dissolution" of the SSPX in 1975, and "suspension" of the Archbishop and his new priests in 1976. That did not work, so in 1988 they used the big stick of "excommunication," but that still did not work. It succeeded neither in bringing the SSPX to heel, nor – as Mr. Matt admirably recognizes – in driving it into schism. By maintaining not only its resistance to Vatican II and the New Mass, but also its allegiance to the Pope, the SSPX, with its steadily increasing numbers of priests, nuns and layfolk, threw into the Revolution's works a serious monkey-wrench. The time had come to try the carrot.

The carrot is Rome's offer to the SSPX of "legitimacy" after so many years of "illegitimacy." Mr. Matt accurately imagines and eloquently describes the temptation for SSPX bishops and priests to become once more "real" bishops and "real" priests. Rome is here dealing not just in words but in emotions. Catholic hearts ache to be united with the Pope and with Rome: "Come back," Mr. Matt can hear Rome saying, "Keep your organization and keep your property! No more exile, no more excommunication, come back inside and help us, with everything you have! An end to the war!"

Of course hardliners within the SSPX might resist any deal, but then Mr. Matt imagines how such hardliners could be resented by all the Roman hearts within the SSPX beating high for Rome once more. Thus Rome's offer could split the SSPX from within, like Rome split the Fraternity of St. Peter from within. And as for any bishops or priests who might accept a deal, asks Mr. Matt, how could they then bite the hand that fed them by continuing thereafter to resist the Revolution?

Mr. Matt imagines how difficult it might be for himself as editor of *The Remnant* to resist a similar seduction if one came from Cardinal Ratzinger, and he can see how much more pressure might be now being brought to bear on the SSPX by the present flattery and kind words than ever was by any previous intimidation or threats. The routine is as old as the hills: carrot or stick, stick or carrot! Americans call it the "good cop, bad cop routine"!

Well done, Michael Matt!

Not that he agrees with everything that the SSPX does or says (any more than the SSPX may agree with everything that he does or says), and he goes on to mention what seem to him to be some failings of the SSPX. Regular readers of this Letter will understand me if I say I have no objection to his doing so, but for the sake of readers who can be puzzled by this apparent disloyalty to the SSPX, let me open a parenthesis.

God forbid that I should be guilty of real disloyalty to the Society. From the time that by His grace I arrived at Catholic Tradition, it is from the Society that I received everything. If I do not mind human failings being mentioned of the Society, which I am convinced has a divine mission, that is for at least three reasons:

Firstly, to highlight our human weakness may help to keep us humble. Humble we must never cease to be if we wish to continue serving God. He gives His grace to the humble. He resists the proud; it is with human nothings and nobodies that it pleases God to wreak His mighty works (I Cor. 1: 25–29).

Secondly, the reminder of our human frailty may help to prepare us for an eventual possible worst, e.g., a betrayal by the Society, although I never say that such a worst will necessarily happen. In February I gave reasons why I thought it would not now happen. But, as Jeremiah says, woe to whoever puts his trust in man (Jer. 17: 5). The Catholic Church has a divine guarantee of indefectibility, the SSPX has not. The difference needs to be remembered.

Thirdly and mainly, to evoke any failings of the SSPX is to recall that this cosmic spiritual war in which we are all engaged at this beginning of the 21st century, is NOT about the insignificant SSPX, it is about the one true religion fighting for survival against the greatest anti-religion that the world has ever seen. As Michael Matt says, he writes what he writes in his editorial "not as an apologist for the SSPX, but rather as someone who is interested in the big picture." Exactly. And that is why I for one do not mind Mr. Matt (or anyone else) criticizing failings of the SSPX, so long as God is served. End of parenthesis.

Meanwhile let us make sure to thank God for the Society, because, for reasons mentioned, it has been for 30 years now an immense gift to the Church. It has stayed on track. Despite false news items, it is not yet (not yet? – Jer. 17: 5) going off track. And let us also thank God for the prospect still of seven new priests being ordained here at Winona on Saturday, June 23 at 9 am, Vigil of the Feast of St. John the Baptist. Pray to Padre Pio for good weather so that, amongst other delights, the seminary lawns will be full of your children playing. There are still places on the Men's Retreats here from July 16 to 21 and July 23 to 28. Sign up!

May the Sacred Heart of Jesus have mercy on us through his month of June.

Deadly Ambiguity

FROM FOREGROUND AND background, good news. The good news in the foreground is that we have seven new priests from North America. Five Americans and two Canadians were ordained in ideal weather on June 23, in the ceremony of ordinations as glorious as ever, and in front of a congregation larger than ever. It was a fitting climax to another peaceful school year. To all of you who have supported and continue to support the Seminary, our ongoing thanks. Details and pictures as usual in next month's *Verbum*.

The two Canadians return to Canada, while three of the five Americans are due to stay in the USA. This must mean further consolidation of the SSPX's work for Catholic Tradition in North America.

The good news from the background is the continuing fulfillment of Archbishop Lefebvre's wish for books to appear, analyzing the disaster of Vatican II. When the Catholic Church struck that iceberg, the urgent need was to man the lifeboats to save Catholic Tradition, in particular the true sacrifice of the Mass and the true sacrificing priesthood. But the Archbishop saw that once that immediate problem was solved, then calm in-depth analyses would be required to see how and why that iceberg was struck.

This letter is accompanied by flyers presenting two such books. *The Problem of the Liturgical Reform*, from the Angelus Press in Kansas City, is the English translation of the book by the SSPX priests which was announced in the April letter from the seminary. This book is not strictly about the Council, but it goes to the heart of the liturgical consequences of the Council, the Novus Ordo Mass. Readers may remember how the book argues, from a mass of quotations from the fabricators themselves of the "renovated" liturgy, that this Liturgy represents in fact a new religion. The Resurrection instead of the Passion of Our Lord, "resurrexifixes" to replace crucifixes, swiftly sums up the difference between Catholicism and this new religion. *Luv* and happiness with no penance or pain. I might wish it were true, but I know it is false!

The second flyer presents the first two volumes to have appeared in what is due to be a massive eleven-volume analysis, this time directly of the Second Vatican Council itself, by a Brazilian layman now living in the USA, Mr. Attila Sinke Guimarães.

The series is entitled *Eli, Eli, Lamma Sabacthani*, which is Our Lord's cry of distress from the cross, "My God, my God, why hast thou forsaken me?" Clearly, the series will say that the Second Vatican Council was like another crucifying of Our Lord. Volume I, *In the Murky Waters of Vatican II*, appeared in 1997. Volume IV, *Animus Delendi* (Desire to Destroy), appeared last year. Mr Guimarães hopes to publish the remaining nine volumes one a year for the next nine years, which is a major undertaking and "a consummation devoutly to be wished."

Mr. Guimarães describes in Volume I how he was a disciple of Dr. Plinio Correa de Oliveira, the founder of TFP (Tradition, Family, Property) a major post-war lay

Catholic movement launched in Brazil and now spread through many countries. It was Dr. Plinio who in 1982 asked Mr. Guimarães to undertake his analysis of Vatican II. For 16 years Mr. Guimarães plunged into the study of a mass of sermons, speeches, writings, books by the master spirits of the Council. His conclusions, Traditional rather than conservative, have caused a separation between himself and TFP, so that now he is publishing on his own. Nevertheless, at the beginning of Volume I he pays handsome tribute to the late Dr. Plinio and to TFP, because he received so much from them both.

Now the SSPX has serious problems with Dr. Plinio as a Catholic leader, especially towards the end of his days, and with the TFP, mainly because of the insufficient role it seems to attribute to the Catholic priesthood in its planned rescue of Christian civilization. Given the left-wing decadence of the Brazilian clergy in the years just before Vatican II when TFP was launched, this contradictory plan is understandable, but it is no less contradictory. It may help to explain how the leadership of TFP has now swung to the opposite excess, an implicit acceptance of Vatican II. (Truly, when the shepherd is struck in Rome, the Catholic sheep are scattered.)

As for the SSPX, it can only approve of Mr. Guimarães' no longer being with the TFP leaders because of their implicit acceptance of the Council. However, that does not mean that the SSPX necessarily approves of everything he says, any more than he must agree with everything said and done by the SSPX. In fact in these first two volumes to appear, there is no trace of the SSPX and little trace of Archbishop Lefebvre. No matter. As Othello says, "It is the cause, my soul, it is the cause," and Mr. Guimarães renders great service to the cause of Catholic Tradition.

In the first volume he presents the plan of all eleven volumes: Vol. I, the "letter" of Vatican II; volumes II to V,

the "spirit of the Council"; volumes VI to XI the thinking and fruits of the Council.

In Volume I, he declares that the hallmark of Vatican
II is ambiguity. In the General Introduction he writes,
"After some time of analysis and reflection, we reached
the conclusion that it is difficult to harmonize the conciliar texts amongst themselves. They present a fundamental dichotomy (split) of language – Conciliar language appeared to us to have been designed to be able to
be interpreted from the standpoint either of sound and
traditional Catholic doctrine, or, surprisingly enough, of
the teachings of the neo-modernist current which has
installed itself in many key positions in today's Church.
Such language appears to be a masterpiece of sustained
doubletalk. Woven like precious Flemish lace out of the
precious threads of the vocabulary of Tradition, it nevertheless appears to reveal the specter of a quite different
mentality. Thus progressivism entered the official documents of the Magisterium with its head decorously cov-
ered by the laced veil of the old Traditional language."
(pp. 35, 36, translation slightly adapted)

Here Mr. Guimarães is right on target. The Vatican
II documents are a continual mixture of two things that
will not mix: Catholicism and the Revolution. As long as
one insists that these unmixables will mix, one is affirming that contradictories do not contradict, one is sus-
pending in one's head the law of non-contradiction, and
one is destroying one's ability to think. Divine Wisdom
says, "I hate a mouth with a double tongue." (Prov. 8: 13)
Amongst other things, a double tongue rots the brain.

For instance, how can a Cardinal write, as he did
recently, that there was no doctrinal problem between
(Conciliar) Rome and Archbishop Lefebvre? Because
resolute adherence to Vatican II has dissolved his idea
of doctrine. How can he write, as he did recently, that
in 2001 there are no longer such "difficulties" between

(Conciliar) Rome and the SSPX as there were in Archbishop Lefebvre's time, because since then the Church has been "purified"? Because persistent doublethink has destroyed in his head the meaning of notions like "purity." How can he write as he did recently that there are today no such heresies as there were in Athanasius' time? Because unrelenting Conciliarism has blinded the Cardinal to the triumph all around him of what St. Pius X called "the synthesis of all heresies," modernism, or, as renovated by Vatican II, neo-modernism. For the Cardinal to say that Catholics today hold no particular heresy like that of Arius, when their (and his) minds are washed out by neo-modernism, is like somebody saying there are no puddles in a field when the field is totally flooded!

Ambiguity is indeed the key to Vatican II, and it is the key to Mr. Guimarães' presentation of Vatican II in the rest of his Volume I. He ends with two chapters on the destruction, by this ambiguity, of the Church's faith and unity, of her clergy and laity. That stands to reason. Documents designed to satisfy at one and the same time conservatives and progressivists were bound to justify contradiction, which was in turn bound to generate contradiction, civil war and mutual destruction inside the Church.

The other volume of Mr. Guimarães presented in the enclosed flyer is not actually Vol. II but Vol. IV, the first part of *Desire to Destroy*, and he means next to publish the second part, Vol. V. This is because he wishes to lay bare the directly destructive element at work in Vatican II, a.k.a. the Revolution. With a mass of direct quotations from the masterminds who directed Vatican II intellectually and politically, he shows how it was their deliberate intention to destroy the hierarchical, sacred and militant Catholic Church. These progressivists had a design (chapter 1) to empty out the Church (ch.2), a clear plan (ch.3) to level down the Church as a monarchy (ch.4), to discredit her as a teacher of Truth (ch.5), to dissolve her holy and Roman character (ch.6), and by these means to fabricate a total Newchurch (ch.7).

Interestingly, Mr. Guimarães' *Desire to Destroy* (I) shows clearly that in the villains' own writings, they have not hidden that which they still felt the need to disguise by ambiguity at Vatican II, in order to gain control of the Church. So the disguise at the Council may have been good, but the Council's churchmen should have known better. (Some bishops did). Conclusion – "Watch and pray." And read *Eli, Eli, Lamma Sabacthani*.

Dear readers, it is a glorious war, and we now have seven new warriors from Winona in the frontlines. As St. Thomas the Apostle said of his beloved Master, "Let us also go, that we may die with him." (Jn. 11: 16)

Are There Nice Liberals?

IN ALL THE series of contacts between Rome and the
SSPX since June of last year, we had hardly heard in
public from the SSPX bishop residing in Spain, Bishop Alfonso de Galarreta, until there began circulating
recently the text of a sermon he gave at the SSPX's main
seminary in Switzerland on June 3.

When "nice" liberals make a "practical" offer, he says,
it will still be a nasty offer. That is why the SSPX was
right to refuse Rome's recent offer, even if not all contacts with Rome need be cut off. Let me translate his text
for you, while abbreviating and adapting certain parts
to bring out his interesting analysis. Bishop de Galarreta
speaks:

> From the beginning of these contacts with Rome,
> the SSPX wished to get into the major questions of
> doctrine and theology, faith and apostasy, while Rome
> wanted to give the contacts a purely practical charac-
> ter. We then somewhat lost interest because we knew
> where that would end up . . . Sure enough. To the two
> pre-conditions laid down by the SSPX for the resump-
> tion of SSPX-Rome discussions (liberation of the Tri-
> dentine Mass, nullification of the 1998 "excommunica-
> tions"), Rome at last replied officially a few weeks ago

Richard N. Williamson

by implicitly laying down its same old condition for
the SSPX's "re-integration", namely acceptance of Vatican II, the New Mass, etc. In other words Rome would
accept the SSPX as it stands, so long as it stopped opposing the Conciliar Revolution.

But the SSPX as it stands is bound to oppose the
Council. So Rome would be granting everything to the
SSPX while taking it all away. Truly a fool's bargain!
For Rome began by saying, "Let us be practical and not
doctrinal. Come in!" The SSPX replied, "Fine! To be
practical and not doctrinal, let us come in as we are,
opposing the Council." To which Rome replied, "To be
practical and not doctrinal, come in as you are but do
not oppose the Council." We had, of course, run right
back into the problem of Catholic doctrine against
Conciliar doctrine. "Practicality" was a mirage.

It was only to be expected. Today's modernists in
Rome divide broadly into two groups: on the one hand
the theoretical modernists, more logical and more
consistently liberal and so less friendly to ourselves; on
the other hand the pragmatic or practical modernists,
closer to real life and so more friendly to ourselves, but
correspondingly less consistent with their liberal principles and therefore objectively (I do not speak about
personal sincerity or intentions) more false and two-
faced in their dealings with ourselves.

So when last year one of Rome's practical modernists made us an apparently golden offer, the danger was
not of the SSPX giving way in theory or in doctrine,
because for all of us the doctrine of Tradition is beyond
doubt or question. The great danger was rather of our
giving way in practice by taking our desires for reality, by thinking that liberals (modernists) really can be
nice, by believing that Rome was offering us what it
really was not offering us, namely their acceptance of
us on our own terms. In fact, as this official answer at
last made clear, they will accept Tradition only on the
Council's terms. Rome having said it, at last things are
now clear. It's a shame, but that's how it is.

As for Rome's offer being merely "practical", remember that it was by mere "practicality" that modernism was foisted upon the Catholic Church in the 1960's and 1970's. Take for example the New Mass. It was a select group of theologians and liturgists who concocted it almost out of thin air, and when Msgr. Bugnini presented it to Catholic bishops in 1967, it was rejected by a large majority. Yet it was the selfsame rite of Mass that Paul VI forced upon the Church in 1969, because a select few had constructed their new liturgy to fit their new religion, unwanted in theory by the mass of faithful, priests and bishops. But as this mass of Catholics out of obedience then practiced the new liturgy, so they came to accept and to believe in the new religion. Doctrinal Modernism had triumphed by "practicality." Crammer used exactly the same "practicality" to enable Protestant doctrine to take over the Church in England in the 16th century.

Now Rome is trying to do the same thing again. The SSPX is to be granted everything in theory, so long as it accepts the Council in practice. That is like saying to policemen, "Talk as much as you like in theory against theft and crime, but do not lay a finger on any thief or criminal. They have their rights, and in practice they must be left to do what they want." It is like telling the SSPX, "Play Don Quixote to your heart's content, tilt at all the theoretical windmills you wish, but do not touch the practical realities."

But the SSPX cannot accept such a "practical" deal. In practice, modernist Rome is destroying the Faith. It is not a problem of persons or obedience or charity or discipline or respect or whatever. IT IS A PRACTICAL PROBLEM OF THE FAITH. We can accept no "practical agreement" which would mean silencing the voice of Tradition, the voice of the Catholic Faith. We can only defend the Truth, yet the Truth is what Rome is asking us to keep quiet. That is why we can only refuse Rome's "practical" offer.

However, we are not slamming the door on Rome,

Richard N. Williamson

because we want to be able to keep presenting our doctrinal objections to the destruction of the Faith. So if anyone says to me we should cut off all contacts with Rome, I reply "No", or "It depends." That is a judgment to be made in each succeeding situation. In general, we should maintain contacts with the Romans because God alone knows when He will give them grace to recognize that we are right. In any case, our duty is to bear witness to the Truth, and to explain our stand, in Rome or wherever, but especially in Rome.

Thus far Bishop de Galarreta. Three points seem to me to be particularly worth elaborating on: Why is it in the nature of liberalism (of which modernism is one virulent species) for liberals to divide into nasty doctrinalists and nice pragmatists? Why must the nice pragmatists – unless they renounce their liberalism – always prove nasty in the end? Why will the nice liberals frequently appeal to "practicality" when dealing with opponents of liberalism?

Firstly, liberals are bound to divide into nasty doctrinalists and nice pragmatists (and all shades in between) because liberalism is always two things at once: primarily the rejection or negation of absolute Truth, secondarily the affirmation of absolute liberty. Note that, as clearing ground must precede rebuilding, so liberalism's negation of Truth is prior to its affirmation of liberty. I cannot romp freely unless I am first unshackled. The negation is basic to liberalism.

Note next that liberalism's negation of Truth and affirmation of liberty are always in tension because each pushed to its extreme has to override the other. For instance, if I absolutely reject Truth, I will not allow even liberty freely to consent to it – "No liberty for the enemies of liberty." Such are the nasty doctrinal liberals who push liberalism's primary negation of Truth to its logical conclusion. On the other hand, if I absolutely affirm liberty, then I will affirm liberty even to accept the Truth – "Liberty even for Catholic Tradition." Such are the nice conciliatory liberals who turn liberalism's secondary affirmation back against its primary negation. (With this tension and contradiction and instability inside every liberal, compare and contrast the unification and stability wrought within a Catholic by his submission to uncontradictory and unchanging Truth).

This tension between negation and affirmation, this contradiction intrinsic to liberalism, is why liberalism is constantly throwing up liberals both as nasty as possible and as nice as possible, and all shades in between, according as each liberal cleaves more to the primary negation or to the secondary affirmation. But even the nicest of liberals will never completely abandon the basic negation, otherwise he would cease to be a liberal, and that is the answer to our second question, as to why even nice liberals must turn out nasty in the end, as Rome's nice liberals have just done.

For indeed the nice liberal's affirmation of truth is quite different from the Truth-teller's affirmation of Truth. The liberal's affirmation of truth rests upon his own consent to "truth," whereas the Truth-teller's affirmation of Truth rests upon Truth's absolute demands and one's natural submission to those demands. In other words, even if a nice liberal accepts "truth," he is still negating Truth's absolute demands, he is still holding to the negation of absolute Truth and so he is still sharing the nasty liberal's basic principle. On the surface, your nice liberal may look like a Truth-teller, but deep down he is operating on the same basis as the nasty liberal.

That is why, when your nice liberal is challenged by a truth-teller (e.g., a Catholic), unless he gives up the basic negation making him a liberal, he must side with the nasty liberal. What nice liberal Rome just showed to the SSPX was its preference for liberalism's basic nastiness. Kyrie eleison!

The answer to our third question follows in turn. Why will your nice liberal frequently appeal to the Truth-teller to be "practical," as just did Rome? Because your nice liberal knows that he and the Truth-teller have a basic disagreement on principles (Truth demanding, or "truth" consented to), so he brackets out basic principles and appeals to being nice, having lunch together, using the same taxi, simple practical things. This he does in the hope that shared action will lead to shared beliefs.

It is a well-known technique of Communists and Freemasons in their dealings with Catholics: let the Catholics just join them in a common action and they will get the Catholics to end up by believing as their enemies do. How many Catholics have, for instance, lost the Faith by behaving, for instance in the Knights of Columbus like, or with, Freemasons?

The SSPX has therefore rightly turned down modernist Rome's invitation to behave like, or with, modernists. However, as Bishop de Galarreta wisely concludes, the SSPX does not therefore refuse any and all contact with Rome, where more than anywhere else the Truth must be told. We pray for these Romans, because "Great is the Lord, and His mercy endureth for ever."

Girls at University – Emancipation's Mess of Pottage (Gen. 25: 29–34)

ANADIANS STRIKE ME as a gentle people, but "strike" is the word! Ten years ago I was innocently asked in Canada whether women should wear trousers. Some ten weeks ago, also in Canada, I was asked whether a girl should go to a conservative Novus Ordo university. The answer now to the second question may be as stormy as the answer to the first: because of all kinds of natural reasons, almost no girl should go to any university!

The deep-down reason is the same as for the wrongness of women's trousers: the unwomaning of woman. The deep-down cause in both cases is that Revolutionary man has betrayed modern woman; since she is not respected and loved for being a woman, she tries to make herself a man. Since modern man does not want her to do what God meant her to do, namely to have children, she takes her revenge by invading all kinds of things that man is meant to do. What else was to be expected? Modern man has only himself to blame.

In fact, only in modern times have women dreamt of going to university, but the idea has now become so normal that even Catholics, whose Faith guards Nature, may have difficulty in seeing the problem. However, here is a pointer in the direction of normalcy: any Catholic with the least respect for Tradition recognizes that women should not be priests – can he deny that if few women went to university, almost none would wish to be priests? Alas, women going to university is part of the whole massive onslaught on God's Nature which characterizes our times. That girls should not be in universities flows from the nature of universities and from the nature of girls: true universities are for ideas, ideas are not for true girls, so true universities are not for true girls.

NATURE OF UNIVERSITIES

Let us begin with the true university. As defined by Cardinal Newman in his famous *Idea of a University*, it is "a place of teaching universal knowledge." Universities in this sense were a creation of the Catholic Church in the Middle Ages, and, as the Cardinal splendidly recalls, theology held pride of place there because, as science of the Supreme Being, it is the supreme science which alone can appoint to all other sciences their proper place. So a true university is a place for all-round learning of reality beneath the queenship of Catholic theology. The value of sciences and this need of theirs for theology is why the Catholic Church is always tending to create universities, and why she alone can create true universities, directing all study ultimately to the glory of God and the salvation of souls.

From which, one must question what kind of queenship can be exercised by Novus Ordo theologians, even conservative. Normally, "conservative" Catholics who have left Tradition are in bad faith, so will be bad teachers, while those who have never known Tradition will be ignorant, and so bad teachers. Both will make a point of "rescuing" a damsel in "schismatic" or "excommunicated" distress. Therefore a Traditional girl putting herself under "conservative" teachers will, to keep her Faith, require a special effort to resist the menfolk whom God designed (and her parents paid) her to follow. She will then be voluntarily so setting her true Catholic Faith against her true feminine nature that one or the other is almost bound to suffer.

It also follows from the queenship of Theology that a democratic age like ours, rejecting God and dethroning Theology, will make a nonsense of universities. Sure enough. All around us we see "universities" which are much worse than brothels, because not only does democratic "equality" indiscriminately herd there together all kinds of boys and girls with little or no interest in ideas so that they should not be studying in the first place, but also, by silencing Theology and rendering Philosophy ridiculous, these "universities" corrupt the highest part of the youngsters' nature, their minds, leaving their lower nature with little or no means of resisting the aided and abetted promiscuity of the two young sexes. Survey the waste on any "university" campus today – feckless unmen and trashy unwomen whose noblest activity is throwing frisbees at one another!

Such "universities" dedicated to the defiance of God and Nature, make mincemeat of the youngsters' Faith (if they had any), of their morals and of their common sense. Poor parents. But they have mocked God, and God is not mocked. Obviously no boy, let alone any girl, should be sent to such a "university." What needs to be proved is that even to a decent university, if such could be found, few or no girls should be sent. This is because of the God-given nature of girls. Which, despite today's massive propaganda to the contrary, is quite different from the God-given nature of boys!

NATURE OF GIRLS

For a sane grasp of woman's nature, let me appeal to the Church's Common Doctor, St. Thomas Aquinas, distant now by three-quarters of a millennium from our own disturbed times. The three reasons he gives in his Summa Theologiae (2a, 2ae, 177, 2) why woman should not teach in Church in public can all be applied to why she should not teach or learn in a public university. Firstly, he says, teaching is for superiors, and women are not to be superior, but subject, to their men (Gen 3: 16). Secondly, women stepping up to teach in public can easily inflame men's lust (Ecclus. 9: 11). Thirdly, "Women are not usually (in Latin, "communiter") perfect in wisdom."

To grasp these three reasons, let us back up another five millennia, to Adam and Eve. Since the word "nature" comes from the Latin word for "being born," then to study a thing's nature one goes back to its birth. Eve was created by God to be a "help" to Adam (Gen. 2: 18). She was to help him, says St Thomas Aquinas elsewhere (1a, 92, 1), not for any other work than that of generation (or reproduction), because for any other work man could be more suitably helped by another man. It follows that woman's nature is intrinsically geared to motherhood, so that in all things pertaining to motherhood she is man's superior, in all else she is his inferior, and in none of all the things in which the two sexes are complementary are they equal.

Now to attract a man so that she can marry and become a mother, to nurture and rear children and to retain their father, she needs superior gifts of feeling and instinct, e.g., sensitivity, delicacy, tact, perspicacity, tenderness, etc. by which her mind will correspondingly be swayed, which is why no husband can understand how the mind of his wife works! For to do the work of generation, i.e., to ensure nothing less than the survival and continuation of mankind, <u>God designed her mind to run on a complementary and different basis from her man's</u>. His mind is designed not to be swayed by feelings but on the contrary to control them, so that while his feelings may be inferior to hers, his reason is superior. And reason being meant to rule in rational beings, then he is natured to rule over her (Gen. 3: 16), as can be seen for example whenever she needs to resort to him for her feelings not to get out of control.

Correspondingly, while she senses family (and loves to talk about it), he responds to the world around and wants to master it (Gen 2: 15, 19, 20). While she is people-oriented, he is reality-oriented. (How often will a woman pull an idea or a question of reality back to family! – "You're against drink? You're attacking my husband!" This is in woman's nature. One does not mock her for it.) So while she is queen of feeling within the home, he must be king of reason over the home. So while he must love her and listen to her, at the end of the day she must obey him, because he is natured to take the broader view and to be the more reasonable (Eph. 5: 22, 25; Col. 3: 18,19).

FIRST REASON

Now what does a university call for? Whereas in modern "universities" the males all believe in "If it feels good, do it," which is why they are, as they wish, overrun by feeling females, on the contrary in a true university one thinks about universal reality, which is the prerogative of men. A woman can think in this way, or do a good imitation of handling ideas, but then she will not be properly thinking as woman. The dilemma is inescapable: she cannot do what is properly men's thinking or work without cutting across her deepest nature. Did this lawyeress check her hairdo just before coming into court? If she did, she is one distracted lawyer. If she did not, she is one distorted woman.

Moreover, true university thinking tends to produce leaders because true students have pondered on more or less universal reality. Cardinal Newman may argue that the cultivated mind is an end in itself, but if Mother Church has always raised universities, is it not because an elite of all-round minds will in any society powerfully help many souls to get to Heaven, if those minds' studying has been governed over all by the true Faith? But women are neither meant, nor normally gifted, to be leaders! Therefore girls should not be at university. As for a Queen Isabella the Catholic, Spain was her family and she never went to university! Nor did Teresa of Avila, Catherine of Sienna or Joan of Arc.

Concretely, if a girl devotes several years of her youth and much money of her parents to acquiring a university education, especially a decent one, how easily will she submit to her husband, especially if he has not had that education? And how may she not argue with him if he has had it? And if she has a "degree," how will she not think herself above the multiple humiliations of being "barefoot and pregnant"? And if she is a "graduate", how will she not hold herself superior to being a "vegetable at the kitchen sink"? And if making a family makes her forget in the right kind of way all about "graduating," "degrees" and "university," why go there in the first place? The dilemma is inescapable: in doing manly things like going to a university, either she is merely going through the motions or she is damaging her potential for motherhood – conclusion: she should not go there.

SECOND REASON

We come to St Thomas' second reason: the inflaming of lust. Enough said about today's unibrothels. What will happen if heaps of boys and girls are thrown together with mention of God even forbidden, is massive common sense, but that is not the whole story!

Just suppose that a decent girl can find a decent university which is cultivating on a broad front minds of an elite of boys who will provide tomorrow's world with its leaders. If she is smart enough to study, will she not be smart enough to know that even if she does not wish to distract the boys, she will still be a distraction? To this reason there is no exception. So if she is that decent, will she not prefer to hang back from distracting the future leaders that she and all her society tomorrow will need? Then the more decent the university, will she not the more keep away? What woman can be imagined taking part in Plato's Dialogues? Not even the Blessed Virgin Mary took part in the Last Supper. Girls at university are a double source of confusion, both doing what girls were not created to do, and distracting the boys from doing what the boys were created to do.

At any true university, the worthwhile students do not want to be distracted by girls. Those are exactly the potential husbands that the really intelligent girls will go after. That is why even really intelligent girls should not be at university.

THIRD REASON

For indeed – St. Thomas's third reason – "women are not usually perfect in wisdom." This is because woman's family wisdom is priceless, it comes straight from God, but it is imperfect as wisdom, because it orders only a part of reality. Woman's thinking is subjective, inward, intuitive, concrete, small-scale, with a gift for loving details. University thinking needs to be objective, outward, rational, abstract, large-scale, with a drive towards the grand principles. Her thinking follows her heart. University thinking can only follow the head. While a university professor is teaching, the boy will be listening to and learning from the words, but the girl will naturally be listening to the man and learning by osmosis. Only by an effort will she listen to the words, because her heart is elsewhere – usually on the boys. Naturally docile and possibly possessed of more than sufficient brains, she can always do a good imitation of a good student, especially if she wishes to please a particular male professor. Nor, again, should she be mocked for that, insofar as God designed her to please and to attract – a husband. Rarely, however, will the impressive studentess be a really good student, because the Lord God simply designed her heart and mind for a quite other task. Girls, do you really want to spend so much of your time and of your parents' money on doing something God almost for sure did not mean you to be doing?

OBJECTIONS

But Pius XII encouraged women to make the best of being forced out into the world?

Maybe he was making the best of an already bad situation in the 1940's and 1950's, when he hoped women would bring to bear their femininity on the public domain. However, by the definitions of "feminine" and "public," that is a contradiction in terms. Fifty years later, who can deny that the public domain has de-feminized woman? As a friend said, "Women used to have careers open to them only in nursing and teaching, which they did well. Now they no longer know how to do either!"

It is high time for Catholics to buck the current and to buck the world! Europe, center of Christendom, is collapsing, because European girls are all being taught to go to "university" and to "put off" having babies! Woman and family are in desperate crisis – do we want to follow the swine over the cliff?

But men today are unfit to lead, so women have to go to university to take their place?

Women cannot take their place!!!! (The exception proves the rule). Today women are merely following them into "universities," tomorrow they will be following them out. By hook or by crook, girls do something motherly, play the part as God meant you to play, and God can give you back from above the manly leaders and the husband that you pray for and need, but that you cannot by the nature of things wrest to yourselves from below. You cannot restore God's order by breaking it. Get behind your men! <u>Behind, you have an enormous power to inspire and guide</u>. In front, you will merely make them more irresponsible than ever...

But what about the Dominicans' school for girls in Idaho?

As much as St Thomas Aquinas disapproves women teaching in public, he approves their teaching in private, in other words at home, "or in a home-like setting." A <u>university</u> cannot resemble a home, but wise Mothers can keep a girls' <u>secondary school</u> like a home.

But where will girls' secondary schools find women teachers if no girls go to university?

One needs no university to learn most of what secondary schoolgirls need to be taught, for instance "domestic economy, setting up home, running a house, the care and education of children, the spiritual and social preparation for marriage" – Pius XII's timeless list, to the Union of Catholic Women, June 24, 1949. Of course if the law of the land, as now in France, demands "university" "diplomas" for women to teach or to open girls' schools, then some women's "university" attendance becomes, for the duration of that law, an exceptional necessity. However, exceptions make bad rules!

But what about the co-educational college of the Society of St Pius X at St. Mary's in Kansas?

It is still a family-scale operation, typical of the true Church's drive to teach the true Faith in as much depth as possible amidst difficult circumstances, but according as it may expand and rise in the future to a truly university level of teaching, I for one piously hope that the boys will by then be giving such a lead and example, creating such a new world, that the girls will no longer feel any need to attend.

But what are girls in the meantime to do, who have a brain and are not ready to get married?

Let them use their brain: firstly, to grasp how God designed them, and for what role; secondly, to pray God He grant us all some men; thirdly, to read at home on their own (for instance Jane Austen, a classic example of how much domestic woman can do); fourthly, to devise with their parents a feminine place and function where they can mature towards marriage. Or – for Heaven's sakes – let them think of a vocation! Old saying: "A woman is once a woman, a nun is twice a woman"!

CONCLUSION

For all these reasons, domestic girls are not by nature for public universities. Where did modern man go wrong?

As man puts himself in the place of God, so this life on earth blocks out of view any afterlife in God's Heaven or Hell. Man's pride unchains his inclination to pleasure here below. Self comes first. But children – however unconsciously – demand and reward selflessness in their parents. Therefore the children, and the demand, and the reward, must go. But woman's life is natured to center around children. Therefore woman's life in particular becomes empty, as does her home, especially if working conditions take her husband also away. She will inevitably follow him into his domains, e.g., university, where she is liable to impose female patterns that do not belong, but that are frustrated at home. She will not let her being remain meaningless!

As this letter has often argued, such a breaking of family, home and woman is too deep a violation of Nature for the modern way of life to be able to survive. With men in the lead, Catholics, whose Faith should give them a handle on Nature, will be wise, according to circumstances, to take remedial action now. The journey of a thousand miles begins with the first step.

Men, think! Give substance to the home! Girls, I bless you, your parents and all dear readers.

WTC – The Scourge of Sin

I F EVER THERE was a sign of the times, surely it was
the cloud of smoke choking Manhattan after the terrorist attack of September 11th, and rising slowly into
the New York sky from the ruins of the World Trade
Center. Everything modern man believes in – capital-
ism, materialism, globalism – struck down and reduced
to a lethal pile of smoking rubble! We pray for the souls
suddenly appearing before God, and for their bereaved
families. But there is every chance modern man will roll
on into World War III.

That is a religious and not a political calculation. Man
proposes, God disposes. On the political level, we can be
virtually certain that the vile media will not tell us the
full story. There is serious reason to believe that in 1898,
it was not the Spaniards who sank the "USS Maine"; that
in 1917, it was not the Germans who set up the "Lusitania" as a target; that in 1941 it was not the Japanese who
set up Pearl Harbor for attack; that in 1963 it was not Lee
Harvey Oswald who killed President Kennedy. In 1990
it was certainly not Saddam Hussein who promised not
to react if he invaded Kuwait. In 1994 it was certainly
not Timothy McVeigh's van exploding outside the Al-
fred Murrah building in Oklahoma City which brought

— 224 —

the front of the building down. In 2001…? Saddam Hussein, Slobodan Milosevic, now Osama bin Laden, from CIA-assets to personal enemies of the American people – how many more times will the trick work?

Politically, behind the Arab terrorists are most likely the would-be architects of the New World Order, who have long been using the United States as an instrument to achieve their control of the world. Long ago they planned three World Wars to achieve their aim. It is they who provoked the sinking of the "Lusitania" and the attack on Pearl Harbor to bring the USA into the first two. Now they seem to be using the Arabs also. Humanly, they are clever. They are even diabolically clever. But little do they realize that they are in turn mere instruments of God who uses them for the salvation of souls.

For the last fourteen hundred years Mohammedans, whether Saracens or Arabs or Moors or Turks, have served God as a scourge to punish faithless Christians, or slack Christendom. When Catholics are fervent, God can grant them miraculous victories over the Mohammedans, as at the sea battle of Lepanto in 1571. When Catholics are slack, God can allow the very survival of their nations to be threatened, as now, by birth rates in Europe, by terrorism in the USA. When Spanish Catholics were slack in the 700's, God allowed the Jews to betray Spain to the Arabs. When Spanish Catholics were truly Catholic, God granted them by 1492 to reconquer Spain from the Arabs, and then granted them to create a Catholic empire in the Americas. Either way, God writes straight with crooked lines for the salvation of souls.

The Jews are a similar case. As early as 200 the Church author Tertullian remarked that as Catholic faith goes up, so Jewish power goes down, while as Catholic faith goes down, so Jewish power goes up. In the Catholic Middle Ages the Jews were relatively impotent to harm Christendom, but as Catholics have grown over the centuries since then weaker and weaker in the faith, especially since Vatican II, so the Jews have come closer and closer to fulfilling their substitute-Messianic drive towards world dominion.

If we return for a moment to politics, the United States is now caught precisely between these two scourges of God. Unquestionably one main grievance of Arabs against the United States, provoking their terrorists to lash out as we have seen, is the United States' one-sided favoring of Israel over the Arabs for the last forty years. But each time the United States attempts to act even-handedly towards the Arabs, Jewish power inside the United States – e.g., virtual control of finance and the media – blocks the attempt, and the United States returns to oppressing the Arabs.

This problem of the United States is politically insoluble, because it is a religious problem! The United States is caught between these two scourges of God, because it has turned away from God. God chastises those whom He loves (Heb. 12: 6), so that if God were not now chastising the United States, it would be the proof not that He loved, but that He did not love the United States! Let us be grateful that God is using Arab and Jew to chastise us! And let us therefore, with no thought of hating Arab or Jew, because they are NOT the real problem, turn to the real problem, which is the sins by which we offend God. Let us take the Ten Commandments in reverse order, culminating in the first.

10 By our materialism, the exciting of envy and love of money in all hearts. 9 By our internetted pornography, the rousing of mortally sinful desires of impurity on a global scale. 8 By our vile media, the lying and deceiving of north, south, east and west. 7 By our vicious financial system, the enriching of the hidden manipulators and the stripping the people of their land, inside and outside the United States. 6 By our national glorification of the

"alternative lifestyle" (amongst multiple other crimes of impurity), our screaming to God for vengeance. 5 By our nationalized abortion, the slaughtering of innocents in life's sanctuary, the mother's womb. 4 By our incestuous individualism, the ruining of the family. 3 By our sport and supermarket Sundays, our scorning of the Sabbath. 2 By our Disneyland projection of God, our utter mockery of His holy name. And finally 1, worst of all, by our all-round liberalism, our setting up of man as God, our committing of total idolatry.

In truth, another main reason for the Arabs' hatred of the United States and of everything represented by the World Trade Center, is that with all their false religion, Arabs still have enough sense of the dignity of human life to scorn and loathe the cheap food, music and clothing, the culture of materialism, that has been spread all over the world – from the United States. Does such a loathing of trash justify suicidal terrorism? No, but it goes some way to explaining it. Man does not live by bread alone, still less by McDonald's, MTV and jeans.

But is the United States to blame for the rest of the world taking in its trash? Certainly not, and that is why God's punishment has surely started, but will surely not finish, with the September 11 attack on the United States. Abortion, to take an obvious case, is a worldwide crime, and that is why, short of a miraculous turning around on the part of mankind, God will surely allow all men to carry out what will be His chastisement of them by their own third World War. Actually the crimes of mankind are so great that not even a third World War may be enough for His purposes, which is why He has warned us of even worse. Let me remind you of what His Mother told us on Fatima Day, October 13th, 1973, in Akita, in northern Japan, through a humble lay sister, in a locution officially approved by the competent Catholic diocesan authority:

Richard N. Williamson

My dear daughter, listen well to what I have to say to you. You will inform your superior. (A short silence). As I told you, if men do not repent and better themselves, the Father will inflict a terrible punishment on all humanity. It will be a punishment greater than the Flood in Noah's time, a punishment such as will never have been seen before. Fire will fall from the sky and will wipe out a great part of humanity, the good as well as the bad, sparing neither priests nor faithful. The survivors will find themselves so desolate that they will envy the dead. The only weapons which will remain for you will be the Rosary and the Sign left by my Son (It is not certain what that sign is). Each day recite the prayers of the Rosary. With the Rosary, pray for the pope, the bishops and the priests.

The work of the Devil will seep into the Church in such a way that one will see cardinals oppose cardinals, bishops against other bishops. The priests who venerate me will be scorned and opposed by their fellow-priests... Churches and altars will be ransacked; the Church will be full of those who accept compromises and the Devil will press many priests and consecrated souls to leave the service of the Lord. The Devil will be especially merciless against souls consecrated to God. The thought of the loss of so many souls is the cause of my sadness (Her wooden statue in Akita wept real tears 101 times). If sins increase in number and gravity, there will be no longer pardon for them (no more access to the sacrament of Confession?). With courage speak to your superior. He will know how to encourage each one of you to pray and to perform works of reparation.

Dear readers, let us take the destruction of the World Trade Center as a great sign from God. It is not merely a human affair. If God wishes to punish, no human system of counter-terrorism, however ingenious, will succeed. If God wishes to protect, no terrorist will succeed.

Of Fr. Wickens' two Traditionalist parishioners who worked in the WTC, one ran down some 70 flights of stairs and escaped from the North Tower eight minutes before it collapsed, while the other did not go to work high up the South Tower that day, because he had a doctor's appointment!

The 6,000 who died, as Our Lord says, were not specially guilty, but we must all do penance, or we will perish likewise (Lk. 13: 4,5). Modern cities are fragile, as the terrorists have shown. Life is always fragile. Any of us can die at any time. "The readiness is all," the readiness of the state of grace to step into eternity. A great event like the fall of the WTC is a God-given warning. Let us pray steadily and constantly, and as Our Lady asked, perform above all our duty of state in reparation for the overwhelming sins of our poor, poor world.

Nor forget the seminary in your prayers. Fourteen new seminarians for the moment, although some may not stay long. But that is still fourteen good hearts, ten of them from the United States. God bless America!

And may He bless you also, dear readers.

Hamlet – Alien Amidst Apostates

TODAY'S ANTI-CHRISTENDOM HAS so untaught history and literature that even Catholics who have the Faith can think that engineering and chemistry are more important. But let such readers allow a recent book from Germany, claiming Shakespeare was an underground Catholic, to give them a keen insight into many troubled souls of today.

The life of William Shakespeare, 1564–1616, is a major crossroads of literature, history and religion. He towers over English literature, because no other poet or writer in the English language comes near him for the varied and rich use that he makes of our mother tongue. He is a giant of world literature, as hardly another dramatist in the world can rival the breadth and depth of his stage dramas. History explains the depth. He wrote for the stage of Elizabethan England, poised between the Middle Ages and the modern world, when Elizabeth I and James I were finally wrenching England away from Rome, with enormous consequences for world history. And at the heart of that disastrous wrench was of course the question of religion: England was apostatizing. The

Reformation so-called had wrought an earthquake in English souls. Faithful Catholics were in real pain, and many were being martyred for their pains. It makes sense that Shakespeare was wrestling in depth with the meaning of life. It makes particular sense of the turmoil of "Hamlet."

However, if Shakespeare was shaken, he did not go as far as to be martyred like a number of his canonized contemporaries. From 1592 when he began his brilliant career on the London stage, until 1612 (or 1613) when he retired to his home-town of Stratford-upon-Avon, in all his 37 or 38 plays one can find the traces of Catholicism only if one knows what one is looking for. They are there, but so well concealed that if the Protestant government knew Shakespeare was a Catholic, as they most likely did, they must have felt no need to make a martyr of him. He was a superb propagandist for the Tudors, a most popular entertainer of Court and people, and as a Catholic he was keeping a sufficiently low profile...

In fact Shakespeare in his plays and in his life so cleverly disguised his Catholic Faith that it needs to be proved that he had it at all. Scraps of evidence have for a long time pointed in that direction, for instance the known Catholicism of his parents, wife and daughter; the Catholicism of fellow-actors; his purchase of an important Blackfriars building as a haven for Catholic recusants just before he finally left London. However, not only did Shakespeare so paint himself out of the picture that he has been absurdly identified with a variety of more famous Elizabethans by modern critics unable to accept that such significant works could have come from such an apparently insignificant personage, but also all England since Shakespeare's time, proud of its greatest writer but repudiating his religion, has not sought to tear away the disguise. And the plays let them get away with it...

But research is being done today, a Shakespeare scholar tells me, by which the truth is coming out. That much is certainly indicated by the book which appeared earlier this year in Germany, *The Hidden Existence of William Shakespeare*, by Mrs. Hildegard Hammer-schmidt-Hummel. She has assembled all known pointers towards Shakespeare's Catholicism, studied them with a Germanic thoroughness, added the fruits of her own research, and succeeded by the concordance of all this circumstantial evidence in making what looks (at least to a non-Shakespeare scholar) like a conclusive case that he was a "rebel in the Catholic underground" of Elizabethan and Jacobean England. Not all the details need concern us here, because we are more interested in her conclusion for the light which it throws on "Hamlet" in particular, and on the ways of God in the modern world in general. So two examples of the kind of evidence she adduces will have to suffice.

She begins with the previously known fact that a 1966 X-ray of the 1608 Flower-Portrait of Shakespeare showed that it had been painted over a picture of the Madonna with Child and St. John. She speculates that the over-painting was not from a shortage of canvas but from a desire to hide from anti-Catholic authorities a possession they made so dangerous. She concludes with her own discovery of three entries in the guest register of the English College (England's priestly seminary) in Rome: from April 1585, "Arthurus Stratfordus Wigorniensis"; from 1587, "Shfordus Cestriensis"; and from 1589, "Gulielmus Clerkue Stratfordiensis." The three entries are easily decipherable as pseudonyms of Shakespeare: (King) Arthur's (compatriot) from Stratford (in the diocese) of Worcester, Shakespeare from Stratford (in the diocese) of Chester (where he spent two years), and William clerk-secretary from Stratford, respectively. All three entries fall within the – for Shakespeare biographers – "missing years" between early 1585 when he is known to have left Stratford, and 1592 when he began his career as playwright in London. From a close knowledge of Italy shown especially in Shakespeare's early comedies, Mrs. Hammerschmidt-Hummel speculates that he spent in Italy these years, which were among the fiercest of the anti-Catholic persecution in England. For some 60 mentions of London in the 37 or 38 plays, she says there are 290 mentions of Rome!

But let us assume, from her wealth of detail not to be quoted here, that Mrs. Hammerschmidt-Hummel has made her case. What follows for a Catholic today? Almost final light, I would venture to say, on Shakespeare's fascinating but puzzling presentation in "Hamlet" of the predicament of many a modern soul. The "medieval solution" presented in one of these Letters four years ago to Hamlet's famous riddle ("To be or not to be"), by the highlighting of the clash between the Catholic and modern elements in the play, was good as far as it went, but to suppose that Shakespeare was driven to be an underground Catholic takes the solution further. Let us see the Prince of Denmark's story by numbers, to make clear the parallel both with Shakespeare's own case as a consciously disguised Catholic, and with many a spiritual young man's case ever since, as an unconsciously smothered Catholic. Here goes:

1 Hamlet is Prince of Denmark and rightful heir to Denmark's throne. 2 But his villainous uncle murdered his father, the king, incestuously married his mother, usurped the throne and is corrupting and rotting Denmark. 3 Hamlet is an exile at home. His world has crumbled about him. He is virtually isolated. He is all but overcome by his death-wish. 4 Finally, he lashes out. Of course his uncle resists. Hence a blood-bath. 5 He was <u>right</u> to resist, because Denmark was rotten, but he was

<u>wrong</u> to resist, because of the blood-bath. "To be or not to be?"

Next, the parallel with Shakespeare's own case, as illuminated by the assumption that he was an underground Catholic:

1 Shakespeare is Catholic, and rightful heir to a Catholic England. 2 But Protestant heretics have virtually murdered the Catholic Church in England, turning it incestuously into the Church of England. They have hijacked England in the process, and are spiritually ruining it in depth. 3 Shakespeare has been made a stranger in his own land. Catholic England has collapsed. Nearly all people around him are going along with Protestantism. Shakespeare is tempted to despair (in "Hamlet" as in no other of his plays). 4 A handful of fellow-Catholics (some relatives and possibly friends of Shakespeare) lash out, for instance in the Gunpowder Plot (1605). The Protestants trap, torture and execute all the plotters. 5 Shakespeare was <u>right</u> to dream of killing off the Protestants (they were rotten heretics), but he was <u>wrong</u> to do so (his friends merely got killed). "To be or not to be?"

And now the application to the case of any young man with no Catholic Faith but with any spiritual awareness that something is deep down wrong in the dazzling modern world:

1 As a human being, he is, since the Incarnation, rightful heir to Christendom ("Going, teach all nations" said Our Lord). 2 But the modern world has virtually extinguished Christendom, and is replacing it incestuously with secular humanism. Mankind has been taken over and is being deeply corrupted, from some, to him, unknown cause. 3 But the young man well knows that he is surrounded by hollow men, and he feels very much alone. His world is unlivable, yet everybody seems to be going along with it. He is all but overcome – or he is overcome – by Rock, drugs, immorality, etc. 4 Or he takes

whatever arms are at hand against his sea of troubles and lashes out. Of course the world around him resists, so he too is physically – or psychiatrically – crushed. 5 He was <u>right</u> to resist (he was affirming some divine spark). But he was <u>wrong</u> to resist (it all turned out to be pointless). "To be or not to be?"

According to this reading of "Hamlet" as the conscious but disguised cry of agony of a Catholic seeing his country drive itself into a tunnel of darkness, Shakespeare has caught the unconscious and undisguised cry of agony of numberless souls who would follow him at all stages further down the tunnel, where they would be buried in a world of spiritual darkness. Shakespeare could only have such a clear view down the centuries because he was Catholic, but was it because he was a disguised Catholic that he lost at least for a moment the clearness of his Catholic sight and lashed out in "Hamlet"? Let us blame Shakespeare if we wish, but let us admire the ways of God.

As for blaming Shakespeare for hiding his Faith and perhaps for that very reason momentarily wavering in it, let him who has never in any way disguised his Faith in public cast the first stone. Late Elizabethan England persecuted unto blood, by torture, hanging, drawing and quartering. Today's "Western civilization" may be strongly anti-Catholic, but it is not yet persecuting unto blood. Let us pray now for the strength of martyrs if – or when – the blood does flow.

As for the ways of Providence, let us admire how it works with the weakness of men. Let us suppose that Shakespeare was not as brave as he could have been. Let us suppose that he was not a full hero like St. Edmund Campion, whom he may easily have met in Lancashire in 1580 when he was 16 years old. Let us suppose he was only a half-hero who wrote only implicitly Catholic plays. Do not two things follow? Firstly, that we have any

Shakespeare plays at all. Had he run straight into the martyr's death when he came back to London, perhaps from Italy, in 1592, we would have none of them. Common sense says that that would be an enormous loss to the human race. Because secondly, even if the plays are not explicitly Catholic, they are implicitly Catholic, by for instance the accusation of spiritual darkness in "Hamlet." Now if "Hamlet" were explicitly Catholic, could it have got through to numberless young men in the darkness since? No, because a large part of that darkness consists, precisely, in the automatic rejection of anything that is explicitly Catholic. And so Providence, knowing from eternity into what a tunnel mankind was plunging itself at the time of the Reformation, arranged for this dark sign post to point towards the light. Modern moles cannot bear sign posts that are too bright...

Thank you, Shakespeare! Thank you, Providence! "O the depths of the riches of the wisdom and of the knowledge of God! How incomprehensible are His judgments and how unsearchable His ways!" (Rom. 11: 33).

Please pray for the new school year at the seminary, where we need a houseful of full heroes! And order from the seminary any number of new Seminary Christmas cards, at no cost other than your contribution enabling addressees to be included in a Christmas Novena of Masses at the seminary.

Dialogue at the Crib

A S ADVENT COMES again, leading to Christmas, it
is easy to imagine an anxious father and mother
praying by the side of a crib with the Christ-Child.
Many worries run through their minds. Since this child
is God, even as a baby He can reply within their minds,
so His replies can be imagined as well:—

Child Jesus: Dear father, dear mother, you need not be
so anxious. Here I am, a defenseless little baby with only
two animals and a mother and a foster-father around
me, and yet this sheep-stall is a corner of Heaven.

Parents: Yes, Lord, but you were God, so of course the
help of God was with you, and any number of angels as
well. We are just ordinary people, almost lost in a wicked world.

Child Jesus: But why are you here to pray? If you pray,
do you not have God with you? And if you pray to the
angels, do you not have them with you? You may not be
able to see them, but your Faith tells you that they are
there. Tell me one thing: have you abandoned Me?

Parents: Oh no, Lord!

Child Jesus: Then how do you think I could abandon
you? And if I am with you by your staying with me, do
you think you are that much more defenseless than I

was? When the two of you were babies, did either of you have a Herod coming after you to murder you like I did? You remember how Joseph and Mary had to pick me up in the middle of the night, and we had to flee to Egypt. This crib may be a corner of Heaven, but it is not free of tribulations!

Parents: Lord, why do you let your friends have so many tribulations? Why do you let it be so hard for us to be Catholics? Why don't you make the whole world Catholic?

Child Jesus: Did the two of you come here to pray of your own free will? Of course you did. But what would your prayer be worth if as God I had used some kind of force to bring you here? All of you human beings were created through me, and I know and love every single one of you, but I did not love you in order to force your love for me. As a baby, I may tug at the heartstrings of men, but I still do not force them.

Parents: Yes, Lord, but still, why do there seem to be so many extra tribulations for us Catholics?

Child Jesus: There are tribulations, open or hidden, for all of you, and every one of them goes back to sin. Guilty souls must suffer tribulations for their own sins, but the weight of sin in the world is such that less guilty souls also need to suffer. I was for the whole of my life on earth as innocent as the baby you now see in the crib, yet I took all the weight of all sins on me, to redeem you. I did it gladly. Would you like to help me?

Parents: Oh Lord, we are poor creatures. We will help as best as we can. But our children! We have managed to keep the Faith, but do you know the massive difficulties for youngsters today if they are not to lose hold of you?

Child Jesus: I know in every single detail every snare and trap being laid for their feet, every ambush being prepared for their souls. How I can be choosing to allow this corruption so to surround and close in on young souls is a mystery which you may not be able to understand now. You must trust me that I allow no evil out of which I will not draw a greater good. As for the criminals responsible for this corruption, you must not hate them. Only I can judge them. Leave them to me. If they refuse all my appeals from the crib to promote the holiness of families like you see here, then better if a millstone were hung around their necks and they were cast into the sea, but that is not your problem – vengeance is mine, and I will repay. Pray for them, to prevent the Devil from slipping bitterness and poison into your own souls. Trust me, and pray.

Parents: Lord, what else can we do to protect our children?

Child Jesus: Look after their souls as well as you look after their bodies. Neglect neither what is supernatural nor what is natural in their formation. Enlighten their minds by instruction, strengthen their wills by discipline. Teach them self-sacrifice from a young age. Above all, give good example. And use in the home as relatively few machines as possible. In many ways electric machines in particular can replace the real world with a virtual world which can give only a virtual formation. Ban television absolutely, and if to earn your living the Internet must be in the house, keep it strictly under lock and key, with the only key always in father's pocket. Did Joseph or Mary need one single machine for my own human formation? Yet was my formation lacking in anything from the crib onwards? Children to become human need human care and human guidance which come best from their very own father and mother, and which can come from no machine.

Parents: But, Lord, we have growing and grown children, sinking and sunk in sin!

Richard N. Williamson

Child Jesus: Father, make the right use of any degree of control still remaining to you. To that degree you are still responsible, and you cannot do less. Mother, trust me to listen to the prayers of a mother. Imagine how I loved the Mother whom you see cradling me in her arms. Imagine the power of her least wish over my divine Heart. Go through her, and be ready for your children to break your heart, as my Mother from this crib onwards foresaw and accepted for her heart to be broken when I would be crucified. Someone must pay. Often that someone is mother. That is her glory, and will be her crown.

Father: I will do my best for my family, but the economic situation does not look good. I fear losing my job.

Child Jesus: Sufficient for the day is the evil thereof, but if you are afraid, start trusting St. Joseph now. The outlook for the three of us in front of you was soon to be grim, as we fled for my life to Egypt, but did God let us lack for anything we truly needed? I allow many an economic recession or depression in order to separate souls from too much prosperity and comfort when these get in the way of their eternal salvation. Countless souls are now plunged in a materialism which does not really make them happy. Rejoice if a return to sheep-stalls will put a number of souls back on the path to true happiness.

Parents: We are being threatened also with a third World War.

Child Jesus: My peace I give you, not peace as the world gives, but my peace I give you. Let not your hearts be troubled, nor let them be afraid. As long as there is sin in the world, there are going to be wars. Men today have let loose a deluge of sin, which you must trust in my wisdom for having permitted. True, my justice will have to punish at the moment I will know to be best, but trust me still that that punishment will be an act of divine mercy towards souls. And if you yourselves are in the grace of God, at peace with God, what does it matter who else makes war on you? With the three of us here is true peace. Concentrate on staying in my grace.

Parents: Lord of Lords, that is all we wish to do, but what a state your Catholic Church is in! May grace not be cut off?

Child Jesus: In all these recent years, have you ever wanted to reach me through true sacraments with a true priest, and been unable to do so, at least at intervals?

Parents: No, come to think of it, you were there when we looked for you.

Child Jesus: And if you meet other souls looking for me, what do you do?

Parents: We tell them where to find you, in the crib of Tradition.

Child Jesus: Then if you see that I did not lose you in the past, why should I lose you in the future?

Parents: But what about a mass of souls in the mainstream Church, only half-looking for you?

Child Jesus: They half-find me. They may have half-abandoned me, but I have not abandoned them. They find me as much as they want to find me, and that is true also for the leaders of my Church.

Parents: But, Lord, how can they possibly still be true leaders of your Church as they lead so many souls astray?

Child Jesus: Leave judgment to me, who alone have all the elements on which to judge. Be thankful for the good around you. Avoid the evil. Tell good and evil apart by the fruits. Pray for all gone astray, especially for the leaders. And pray for yourselves, that you never lose your present sense of where to find the Truth. Here is indeed the Incarnate Word of God, hidden beneath the appearance of a mere human baby. And trust me. I have overcome the world, and I am with you all days, until the world comes to an end.

Richard N. Williamson

Ladies, I am sorry we will offer no retreats for you this year, but send your menfolk instead. They are the ones who most need it!

And many blessings upon all of you for Advent and for Christmas.

"...Old Time Is Still a'Flying"

S O THE GREAT and good God has given to all of us to begin another calendar year. How quickly the years go by! As the Psalmist says (89: 6), "In the morning man shall grow up like grass . . . in the evening he shall fall, grow dry, and wither."

Life speeds by, and its swiftness can be a heartbreak. We can live long enough to get to know and to long for all there can be of goodness and beauty in this life on earth, but if death cuts off everything, then how can this short life fulfil the longing it has awakened? As the unbelieving poet said, "We learn to love, only to die." Then the disproportion between the light of love and the darkness of death looms so large, the tension becomes so unbearable and the heartbreak so senseless, that men must either defile the love or disbelieve in the death. But nothing is surer than death at the end of this life, so whoever refuses to defile love is bound to believe in further life after death.

That is why many souls that may not believe in God still believe in a life after death. Or they arrange some kind of deity in their minds to sustain on their own terms whatever life after death they want – how easily we human beings come to believe what we want to believe! Catholics on the other hand know the truth. Nor can they unknow it for as long as they do not lose the Faith. This life is a mere trampoline on which we jump a few times in order to spring into eternal life – upon the terms of the living God! Here at full length is how the same Psalm 89 frames our earthly existence (translation from the Revised Standard Version, with headings added in italics):

The greatness of the Everlasting God.

1–2 | Lord thou hast been our refuge in all generations. Before the mountains were brought forth, or even thou hadst formed the earth and the world, from everlasting to everlasting thou art God.

The smallness of man and the nothingness of time.

3–4 | Thou turnest man back to the dust, and sayest, 'Turn back, o children of men!' For a thousand years in thy sight are but as yesterday when it is past, or as a watch in the night.

The brevity of man's life on earth.

5–6 | Thou dost sweep men away; they are like a dream, like grass which is renewed in the morning: in the morning it flourishes and is renewed; in the evening it fades and withers.

The sinfulness of men before God.

7–8 | For we are consumed by thy anger; by thy wrath we are overwhelmed. Thou hast set our iniquities before thee, our secret sins in the light of thy countenance.

The fewness of years beneath an angered God.

9–11 | For all our days pass away under thy wrath, our years come to an end like a sigh. The years of our life are threescore years and ten, or even by reason of strength fourscore; yet their span is but toil and trouble; they are soon gone and we fly away. Who considers the power of thy anger, and thy wrath according to the fear of thee?

Concluding appeal for God's light and mercy.

12–14 | So teach us to number our days that we may get a heart of wisdom. Return, O Lord! How long? Have pity on thy servants! Satisfy us in the morning with thy steadfast love, that we may rejoice and be glad all our days.

Coming from God to go before God, in a time-frame determined by God, we are to flee the sins that incur His anger, begging mercy for the sins we still commit, so as to live and die in His love, for all of which, as He determines, 70 or 80 years are enough. And then eternity.

Eternity! The thought to overwhelm all other thoughts! A thought that will not get into our little heads. Unending life, life without end, upon God's terms, which exclude mediocrity – no mediocre hell or heaven, but, for all who have reached the age of reason, an eternal horror or bliss, each beyond all powers of imagination! The thought MUST get into our heads! "So teach us," O Lord, to number the days of AD 2002 "that we may get a heart of wisdom"!

An eternity to depend on how we spend these brief days of ours on earth. Then – a first consequence – what is – or what is not? – each single day? Each moment of our lives moves, in a time frame appointed by God, towards that moment when we come before His judgment seat, by when He has mysteriously determined that we have lived long enough to make our choice between living for ever with Him or without Him. Moment of death, in which no soul will be able to accuse God of not having given it enough chance to make that choice; moment of God in which every soul will see the simultaneous justice and mercy of God in the fixing of that moment.

Then certainly God gives to no soul any moment of its life for any other purpose than its building of that choice. Yet looking around us today and seeing the mass of souls leading their lives heedless of God, we might wonder how this can be so. How can such souls be building a choice of which they appear to be so completely unaware?

We come to a second consequence of an eternity depending on our brief stay on earth – souls cannot be as unaware of God as they may like to appear. God is just, and cannot possibly consign a soul to eternal Heaven or Hell for a choice of which that soul is unaware. Therefore deep down, the soul is aware. And since life is so short, then, logically, at each moment of their fleeting lives souls must be aware. If God is apparently nowhere in their lives, they must be continually shutting him out. Then where is He?

He is infinite Goodness. He dearly wishes all souls in Heaven. He came down from Heaven to die on a Cross to take us all back with Him to Heaven. But He created us with free will, and as St. Augustine says, He who created us without us, will not save us without us. So he will not save us unless we freely want to be saved, and if we do not want it, He will not take away our free will, nor will He disconnect the eternal consequences from our free choice, however evil.

But to each of the souls refusing Him it is logical that with a divine tact and delicacy He will be appealing each day with graces to draw them towards Him, graces occasionally heavy but often so light as to be almost unnoticeable, because otherwise they would serve merely to increase the damnation of the souls refusing them. Therefore with what wisdom and care for each individual God must dose these graces, and down what a variety of unexpected channels He must send them to us, we poor mortals can only imagine. But the justice and goodness of God, the brevity of life and the length of eternity together make this conclusion inescapable: even in today's world, souls know what they are doing. If they fall into Hell, it will only be because they wanted to!

And this is because our loving of God or our refusing of God is taking place at a level deeper than meets the human eye. Obviously mere words are not enough to prove that we love God – "Not every one that saith to me 'Lord, Lord' shall enter into the kingdom of Heaven" (Mt. 7: 21), is Our Lord's own warning. And even actions seeming outwardly good to others or to ourselves may not seem so before God. As again St. Augustine remarked, how many souls are in the Church that are not of it, of it that are not in it. Catholics can turn into Pharisees. Catholics can make the worst of Pharisees.

For "The heart of man is perverse above all things, and unsearchable, who can know it? I am the Lord who search the mind and try the heart, to give to every man according to his ways, according to the fruit of his doings" (Jer. 17: 9, 10). That is why, since even if we wish to see our sins we may not see them all, the Psalmist prays to God to uncover to us our own souls – "My iniquities have overtaken me, and I was not able to see" (Ps. 39: 13). And "Who can understand sins? From my secret ones cleanse me, O Lord" (Ps. 18: 13).

But, as the Irish proverb says, "The help of God is closer than the door." And for every two verses from the Psalms declaring our perversity, there are two dozen declaring the mercy of God.

Divine Lord, you have brought us to the start of a new year, which is already slipping away. Each moment of it will be a gift from Your hand. At each moment You will be offering Your help for me to save my soul. But my heart is perverse above all things, by Your wrath I am overwhelmed. Soon I fade and wither, soon I am gone and fly away. Teach me to number the days of this year so that I may get a heart of wisdom. Have mercy upon us, O Lord, have mercy! Let Your mercy be upon us, as we have hoped in you! In You, O Lord, have we hoped. Let us not be confounded for ever!

Many thanks, dear friends, for all your generous support of the Seminary, both at Christmas and throughout the last calendar year. We are always grateful, even if not every letter says so. May every moment of your New Year be fruitful for God!

Campos is Fallen

S O CAMPOS IS fallen. The two dozen priests with
their own bishop who for 20 years from distant
Brazil were the reassuring comrades in arms of the
SSPX in its lone stand for Catholic Tradition, have gone
back in with Conciliar Rome. What happened? What
will happen? What does it mean?

What happened can be briefly told: in Shakespeare's
phrase, the Campos priests had greatness thrust upon
them. They laid the burden to one side.

The story of how the diocese of Campos came into
the limelight of Catholic Tradition after the Second Vatican Council is known to many readers from the book
The Mouth of the Lion by Dr. David White. Before the
Council, the Brazilian country diocese of the seaside city
of Campos, lying three hours by car to the north of Rio
de Janeiro, was gifted with a truly Catholic bishop, An-
tonio de Castro Mayer. As is clear from his marvelous
*Catechism of Opportune Truths Opposed to Contempo-
rary Errors*, written for his diocese in the 1950's, Bishop
de Castro Mayer thoroughly understood the danger of
the heresy of modernism. All the pernicious errors then
and since devastating the Catholic Church are laid out
in all their deadly charm. Opposite, the bishop presents

the Catholic truth, less charming but free of poison. Beneath, he explains where the poison lay hidden and why the Church's teaching on the matter is the truth.

This bishop, whether or not he was conscious of the impending disaster of Vatican II, in any case by his insistence on true doctrine, as Dr. White expresses it, earthquake-proofed his diocese in advance of the earthquake. When the Council happened (1962 to 1965), his priests and people were prepared, so that the bulk of them kept the true Faith, and when the New Mass was introduced (1969), while a few of his priests took it up and left for another diocese, most of his priests made use of his permission to continue saying the old Mass.

Not that the bishop was defiant of Pope Paul VI, or heedless of the Pope's pressure to introduce the New Mass. But he had written to the Pope a most respectful letter, asking for doctrinal problems that he had with the new rite of Mass to be cleared up, and when he received absolutely no answer from the Pope, he acted upon what he knew to be good doctrine, and gave his priests the permission to stay with the rite that was safe and sure.

So his diocese, priests and laity, in large part followed him until his mandatory retirement at age 75 in 1981. The official Church appointed to succeed him a bishop who would by force and violence wrench the diocese away from the old religion and establish it as a "normal" part of the Newchurch. But the priests formed by Bishop de Castro Mayer resisted, almost to a man, and the laity followed their good priests, with the result that when these priests were – of course – thrown out of their parishes, the best of Campos' laity rallied behind them and built – this is not a wealthy diocese! – ten brand-new churches in which to continue the brand-old religion. I can hardly believe my ears when I hear that none of the Campos laity (or priests) are protesting the putting back under Rome of these churches expressly and expensively built to resist that very Rome, but this is what we are told has happened! Have the priests been up front with their laity?

But back to the story. When Bishop de Castro Mayer had to resign and the Newchurch put in a wrecker to replace him, for ten years the resistance movement flourished in the form of the St. John Mary Vianney Union of Priests. But in 1991, one month to the day after Archbishop Lefebvre died, Bishop de Castro Mayer died. At the Union's request, three SSPX bishops consecrated a successor, Bishop Licinio Rangel, so that the Campos Catholics would continue to receive Confirmations and Ordinations. However, as we know now, replacing Bishop de Castro Mayer as Confirmer and Ordainer was the easy part. The hard part was to replace the anti-liberal leader. And we are back into the mystery of neo-modernism, this incredible mind-rot capable of rotting apparently the most Catholic of minds.

For there can be no doubt of the Catholic orthodoxy of the Campos priests and laity that Bishop de Castro Mayer left behind him. Nor, at least until the summer of 2000, was there any trace (as far as I know) of deviation from the line of defense of Catholic Tradition laid down by the two great bishops (Lefebvre and de Castro Mayer) in the 1970's and 1980's. But from the time of Tradition's pilgrimage to Rome in August of 2000, maybe discrete contacts between Campos and Rome were re-established (or fortified?). In any case there emerged last year the recent agreement, proclaimed all over the Newchurch media in the middle of last month (January, 2002).

This agreement whereby the Campos Traditionalists are "welcomed back into the Church" looks like a sweetheart deal for the priests and laity of Catholic Tradition. In return for putting an end to their resistance to the Newchurch, they are granted what is called an "apos-

Richard N. Williamson

tolic administration," meaning, more or less, a personal diocese coming directly under the Pope, and depending only upon the person of their own bishop, presently Bishop Rangel. They are allowed to keep the Tridentine liturgy, in other words they may continue to say the true Mass. It looks too good to be true!

And it is of course too good to be true. For instance, as everybody knows, Rome better than anybody, Bishop Rangel is stricken with cancer, and his days are numbered. The Campos priests must believe that he will be replaced, but if Rome is in control when he dies, what will stop Rome either from choosing the most liberal priest in the group, or from declaring that the mainstream bishop in Campos is sufficient for all Catholics, mainstream or Traditional, now that they are all in together again? Already the Pope's theologian in Rome, Fr. Cottier, is re-assuring any conciliarists alarmed by the apparent concessions to Tradition in Campos: "Little by little we must expect other steps, for example that they (the Campos priests) also participate in concelebrations in the reformed rite. However, we must not be in a hurry. What is important is that in their hearts there should no longer be rejection. Communion found again in the Church has an internal dynamism of its own that will mature" (Interview, Jan. 20).

Indeed. Indeed. Another classic example of the "internal dynamism" of "communion maturing" in the Vatican II Church was provided recently by the appearance in Rome last November of a little book entitled "The Jewish people and the Holy Scriptures in the Christian Bible," written by Rome's Biblical Commission and prefaced by Cardinal Ratzinger, no less. This book's thesis is that "The Jewish wait for the Messiah is not in vain," a typically ambiguous statement, capable of meaning that the Messiah will come at the end of the world either a second time (perfectly true), or for the first time (horrendously false).

When questioned about the ambiguity, the Pope's (Opus Dei) spokesman, Dr. Navarro Valls, replied: "It means that it would be wrong for a Catholic to wait for the Messiah, but not for a Jew"! In other words Jesus of Nazareth truly was, and truly was not, the Messiah promised in the Old Testament! In other words, there is no objective truth. Truth all depends on who you are!

So the Campos priests are also losing their minds. They are putting their trust in Romans to protect the absolute truth of Catholic Tradition when these Romans believe in no such thing. What do the Romans believe in? In making us all feel good. And that is what the Campos priests are switching over to. The Campos priests claim they will continue their fight for Tradition from inside the mainstream Church. But what chance do they have up against the insanity of Rome, as continued for instance in another Assisi meeting, clearly condemned by Bishop Fellay on the sheet enclosed?

The poor Campos priests! Having given away the store (the sanity of their minds) in order to come in from the cold (the marginalisation of their hearts), they will almost certainly from now on go along with anything the Romans say, rather than have to go back out into the cold of being "excommunicated," "schismatic," etc. Like St. Peter's Fraternity, they will have paid so dearly (with their sanity and integrity) for acceptance by Rome, that they will pay anything further in order not to lose that acceptance. Which Rome well knows, and will exploit to the full, but "little by little," as the Pope's theologian says.

Incredible. But let us throw no stones. Today's confusion is universal, and it is coming from the top – "the shepherd is struck, and the sheep are scattered" (Zach. 13: 7; Mt. 26: 31). In war, bullets fly, comrades go down. One spends half a minute with one's handkerchief to

Richard N. Williamson

wipe away a disfigurement, or to wipe away a tear, and then the war goes on. Rather than throw stones, let us take thought for ourselves. The Campos priests presently falling in with the insanity and betrayal of Rome HAVE HAD THE TRUE MASS, BREVIARY AND TRADI-TIONAL PRAYERS FOR THE LAST 20 YEARS, yet still they have fallen. Who then is safe?

I might say that the Campos priests fell because under Bishop de Castro Mayer they had too easy a passage from pre- to post-Council, so that theirs is just a belated case of Fiftiesism. But as recalled above, they were earthquake-proofed before the Council, and had to rebuild from ground zero afterwards. Was that still not enough to vaccinate them against neo-modernist mind-rot? Apparently not. Truly, if these days are not shortened by God intervening, we all of us risk losing our minds. Kyrie eleison. "But when these things begin to come to pass," says Our Lord, "look up, and lift up your heads, because your redemption is at hand" (Lk. 21: 28).

Dear readers, God has thrust upon us the greatness of not falling in with the madness all around us. For love of Our Lord and his Mother of Sorrows, let us not lay the burden to one side: "He that shall persevere to the end, he shall be saved" (Mt. 10: 22).

Teachers of Our Lord – Judas and the Newchurch

RECENT EVENTS IN Catholic Tradition have reminded us how easy it is to fall away from the truth, and how especially seductive is the corruption presently devastating the Catholic Church. We can hardly come back too often to take its measure.

In *The Keys of This Blood* (1990), the late Malachi Martin wrote a fascinating chapter entitled "The Judas Complex," in which he compared the fall of the Catholic churchmen into the Newchurch of Vatican II with the fall of Judas Iscariot. The comparison may seem violent at first sight. Surely even the Newchurchmen are not as wicked as that? But then Judas did not start out that wicked either . . . Let us, for Lent, reflect on the terrible figure of the Apostle who betrayed, in the hope of course that such reflection will help ourselves not to betray. Let us begin with what is of Faith in the Gospels, fill out the picture with a 20th century elaboration of the Gospels, and conclude with a brief application to the Newchurchmen, along the lines laid out by Malachi Martin.

Understandably, the Gospels tell us little of the Apostle who turned traitor. Before the Passion, they tell us almost nothing of the Apostle listed twelfth (e.g., Mt. 10: 4), except that he had betrayed his function as bursar of the Apostles by stealing, a detail mentioned by St. John to help explain Judas' begrudging the expensive ointment poured out on Our Lord by Mary Magdalene a few days before the Passion (Jn. 12: 2–6). Perhaps Our Lord's gentle rebuke on this occasion (Mt. 26: 10–13) was what finally drove Judas to hand Our Lord over to the chief priests for 30 pieces of silver (Mt. 6: 14–16). Then Judas' pretended innocence at the Last Supper, and early departure; the treacherous kiss in the Garden of Gethsemane, and his subsequent despair; his flinging back the blood-money at the contemptuous chief priests, and his terrible suicide – all these details are well-known from the Gospel narrative. But how did Judas come to this? The Gospels hardly say.

However, from the moment we begin to reflect on the drama of Judas, one shattering truth breaks through: the reality of free will. Jesus, foreknowing infallibly and from eternity that Judas would betray him, could not possibly have accepted him amongst the Apostles with their correspondingly huger graces and responsibilities unless Judas had been genuinely free for all three years of his apostleship to convert, <u>had he wanted to</u> – But he did not, finally, want to.

This great truth is underlined again and again in the full-length portrait of Judas given in Maria Valtorta's *Poem of the Man-God*. This – in English – five-volume life of Our Lord, based on visions supposedly given by Our Lord himself to a bed-ridden Italian woman during the Second World War, is much controverted. But in our time of all-round and on-going betrayal of the Catholic Church, who can dispute the reasonableness of the last of the seven reasons given supposedly by Our Lord for his granting this panorama of his life to mankind in mid-20th century? – "To acquaint you with the mystery of the fall of a soul upon which God had bestowed extraordinary benefits . . . to acquaint you with the process by which servants and sons of God fall, changing into devils and deicides, killing the God who is within them by killing grace . . . Apply yourselves to studying the horrible but all too common figure of Judas, a knot tying together, like twisting snakes, all seven capital vices . . . how many people, in all walks of life, imitate Judas by giving themselves over to Satan and hurtling to their eternal death!" Judge for yourselves the authenticity of the portrait of Judas Iscariot as presented in the *Poem of the Man-God*:

He is presented as an intelligent and talented young man, but proud, complicated, sensual and worldly. He recognizes Jesus' outstanding qualities, correctly discerns in Him Israel's King and Messiah, and begs repeatedly to be accepted as an Apostle so that he will share in the triumph of Christ the King. Again and again Jesus warns Judas that this kingdom will be spiritual and not political. Outwardly Judas accepts this disclaimer, but inwardly he <u>never renounces his own ideas</u>. Jesus, knowing that the Apostleship may be Judas's best – or only – hope of conversion and salvation, gives way to Judas' insistence on becoming an Apostle.

Through the following three years, Judas is by no means always evil. Patiently instructed by Our Lord, there are moments when he sees himself as he really is, weeps over his own hardness of heart and genuinely tries to be better. Alas, these moments pass, and by shameless lying in particular, he works his way regularly back to the world, the flesh – and the Devil.

His falls get progressively worse. Finally he has himself convinced that Jesus is a mere man, and that the Temple authorities are right to want Him out of the way. Our Lord leaves him free to make his own appalling choice, but in the hope of preventing Judas' terrible damnation, covers for him to the very last moment, in Gethsemane, a moment known to us from the Gospels: "Friend" (friend!!), "whereto art thou come?" To the traitor on the very brink of the abyss, the Sacred Heart still gently appeals!

The portrait in the "Poem" of Judas from Gethsemane to his death, is truly harrowing, but corresponds to what we know with certainty from Scripture – Mt. 27: 3–10, and Acts 1:16–20. Still we ask, how could somebody so close to Jesus for so long have come to such an end? Malachi Martin makes a fascinating analysis when he compares Judas with the Newchurchmen in *The Keys of This Blood* (pp. 660–676). Here is how:

Judas began serving Our Lord with the best of intentions, and received great graces. He had no desire to leave Jesus, in fact he resolutely stayed with Him each time Our Lord left him perfectly free to depart. Similarly Newchurchmen no doubt began their vocations well, received many graces and loved Our Lord. Nor, like Judas, do they mean to leave Him or to destroy His Church – they only want to fit Our Lord to the world according to their own ideas.

For indeed Judas truly hoped for the kingship of Jesus, with a major role for himself in the future kingdom. But Jesus would keep on refusing political power, He would insist on clashing with the Temple authorities, He would not stop acting in an unworldly way. Now if only He would listen to Judas who got along with those authorities and understood the ways of the world, then a decent compromise could have lead to an enormous success of Jesus' kingdom, powered jointly by Jesus' extraordinary gifts and the Temple's worldly clout.

Similarly the Newchurchmen really wish for the Catholic Church to triumph, with a major part for themselves to play in the New World Order. But Catholic Tradition is uninterested, in fact it insists on condemning the modern world and its Judeo-masonic masters. If only Catholics would listen to the Newchurchmen who understand the modern world, if only all Catholics would agree to an updating of Tradition, then a decent compromise could lead to the Church's worldwide success, powered jointly by the force of Tradition and the ideals of the Revolution.

Finally Judas is so disillusioned with Jesus' unworldliness that he ceases to believe Jesus is God. And since Jesus insists on wasting His gifts on an unreal kingdom highly disturbing to the normal, and practical, Temple authorities, then best let them deal with Him. Similarly the pre-Council Churchmen were so tired of the failure of the pre-Conciliar Church to get through to the modern world that they ceased to believe in the divine origin of Catholic Tradition. And since that Tradition was nothing but an obstacle in the way of the admirable modern world, then best if an ecumenical Council would turn Tradition over to the world. Hence the historic compromise of Vatican II, a Judas betrayal, a tissue of ambiguities mixing Our Lord with His enemies who run the modern world, and putting Him into their power.

Therefore the Newchurchmen are, objectively, Judases, however sincere or well-intentioned they may be. In fact they are crusading Judases, because they have themselves convinced that their Newchurch will save both Church and world. That is why they not only firmly believe in compromising Catholic Tradition with the world, but also they are set upon pulling what remains of Tradition into their compromise. That is why the SSPX both refused the recent approaches of "Rome" to draw it into the Newchurch, and must prepare to resist any more such approaches.

This situation is bound to continue until the Newchurchmen abandon their (objective) Judas compromise with the world, and return to Catholic Tradition. On that day they will have once more a huge problem with the same old wicked world, but at least they will be true churchmen again. And a clear sign of their return to sanity will be that they have no more problem.with Catholic Tradition, not even with the SSPX!

May God grant us all to be faithful until that day. Meanwhile, may you all have a holy remainder of Lent, and a happy Easter, and may you find something useful in the enclosed Seminary tape flyer.

Resurrection of the Arts

THE ARTS TODAY are dying or dead. What will it take to resurrect them? Eastertide may be the right time of year to consider a sequence of three museums in Pittsburgh, Pennsylvania, which by presenting respectively art of past, present and future, may put us on the track of an answer.

The first of the three is the Frick Museum, a classical museum containing painting, sculpture and decorative arts by famous artists of past centuries. Completed in 1969 by Helen Frick, daughter of Pittsburgh coal millionaire Henry Clay Frick, it contains her collection of masterpieces, now bequeathed to her city and nation.

The second is the Andy Warhol Museum, a museum of a different style which might be called a "factory," because that is the name that the famous American "Pop" artist of the 1960's, Andy Warhol, gave to his New York studio, out of which came the exhibits now filling the museum named after him in his home town of Pittsburgh.

The third museum is not called a museum at all, but goes by the name of the "Mattress Factory." It contains a series of exhibits – if one can call them that – put together by contemporary artists – if one can call them that – from various nations, but living and working in Pittsburgh to produce, as the publicity material calls it, "art that you can get into" (we will see what that means). Indeed the exhibits in the "Mattress Factory" are so different from those in the Frick museum that even to mention them in the same breath raises instantly the great question, what is art?

If to answer we start out from the exhibits, nobody would deny the name of "art" to the religious pictures, five to six hundred years old, which are the glory of the Frick Museum. Painted originally for purely religious purposes, they present Our Lord or Our Lady or Catholic Saints with a visual beauty springing from their spiritual depth. With no houses, buildings or landscapes in view (at least prior to the Renaissance), they offer almost no visualization of the outer world of matter, but there is, through the painters' pursuit of the spirit, a huge presentation of the inner world of the soul, or, a deep and noble vision of life. So if for the moment we define the artist as a man with an eye and a hand, then when souls were full of God, an eye saw and a hand moved to generate art of the highest kind.

We skid down half a millennium to the second museum, of Andy Warhol (1928–1987), who was certainly a man with an eye and a hand. He had no gigantic talent, like that in modern times of a Pablo Picasso, but he did have a real talent with which he achieved in the 1950's a very successful career as a commercial graphic artist. However in 1960 at age 32 he shed commercial work as such, and set out to conquer the prestigious art world of New York. He believed in making money but he also believed in Art, so he would from now produce artifacts fit to be shown in museums.

Notwithstanding, the modern world with its commerce and consumer products was by now well into his bloodstream, besides surrounding him on all sides, as it surrounds all of us. So what would make him famous would be his resorting to an old-style medium to express a contemporary message, for instance a meticulous oil-on-canvas painting in black and white – of the front page of a newspaper! Or a screen made fit to hang on a museum wall, portraying a Campbell's soup can. Or, to hold up the mirror to our industrialization and mass-production, a screen-print of one hundred such soup-cans in mechanical rows.

The interest of Warhol – and he does continue to interest people, as on-going exhibitions of his work prove – thus consists in his combining prestige with trash, or high-class presentation with low-class content, or, the noble art-in-a-museum framework from the past with the ignoble artifacts of our mechanized and throwaway present. Each time the prestige medium jars with the trash content, there is a little electric shock – the prestige gilds the trashy message even while the trash besmirches the prestigious medium.

In the case of Warhol, there can still be seen in his use of color and line the eye and hand of an artist at work, but are there spirit, or soul, or vision? Only just enough to enable him to hold up the mirror to our fragmentary and dislocated world which Warhol does not basically criticize, but accepts. In brief, the artist who believed in Art generates museums – Warhol produced enough product to fill dozens of them!

Finally we come to the third "museum," or the "Mattress Factory." Andy Warhol had called his New York studio the "factory," no doubt because he wished, instead of being scorned by our materialistic society as an "artist," to be admired by it as a "manufacturer." In this too he holds up the mirror to his age. So I would guess it was following Warhol's example that super-modern artists of Pittsburgh kept on the functional name of a disused mattress factory when they look it over to display their wares.

But how were they to out-Warhol Warhol? Go and see. On three or four floors, with a few rooms to each floor, most of the rooms are virtually empty! In one room, some wires run across the floor between little upturned loud-speaker dishes which gently fizzle. In another room there is at one end a false window lit with blue light from behind. Another long room is actually filled, with a jungle of barbed wire festooned with scraps of popped balloons. The title of this art work is "Beautiful Violence." Get it? Barbed wire = violence, balloons = beautiful. Wow! In another room, three shop display mannequins dressed in wigs and red paint blotches stand on a correspondingly blotched floor amidst four mirror walls and beneath a mirror ceiling, so that if you get into the mirror room (remember? – "art you can get into"), you see yourself amidst the mannequins multiplied for mirror-miles around!

In brief, when men believed in God, they produced the highest art. When they ceased to believe in God but still believed in Art (with a capital letter) as a spin-off from God, substituting for Him, then they produced imitation temples to house that Art, namely colonnaded museums (and concert-halls) to enshrine their substitute-religion. But when men moved so far from God as to lose all sense of what art is about ("Honey, you look at the pictures, and I'll read out the catalogue"), then Museums (by now with capital letter) became a shell game, and they fill themselves with substitute art, in fact with anything that goes, until the whole shell game will collapse.

But do not think that the shell game is yet collapsing! Fabulous "installation museums" (or whatever one cares to call them) are being built all over the world. Pittsburgh's "Mattress Factory" is famous amongst them, and has recently obtained funding to the tune of three quarters of a million dollars for its "in-residence" artists and its 27,500 annual visitors! Wow! Where's the nearest mattress? Perhaps if I scattered a bunch of Seminary Letters over it, and called it "I Rest My Case," somebody would grant me $ 100,000? Can't wait! I sure no longer need an eye or a hand to be an "artist" – just plenty of B. Sc., without the c.

So what is art? Most broadly defined so as to include the exhibits of the "Mattress Factory", we might say it is the manipulation of more or less manipulable materials to express for others what is in the manipulator's soul. The more finely manipulable the material, the finer the art, which is why oil-on-canvas has had such a long and honorable career. However if barbed wire and balloons express something either for their manipulator, or for any visitor to the "Mattress Factory", then "Beautiful Violence" is also art in this broadest sense. The whole question comes back to what is in men's souls.

For some will deny that the soul even exists, but the sequence of our three museums, located in Pittsburgh but parallelable anywhere, demonstrates that the message (or soul) governs the medium. As the message ebbs or flows, so rises or falls the medium. God as message generated art as medium; Art as message generated museums as medium; museums as message generate barbed wire and balloons as medium – anything to get somebody to visit a Museum.

Coming as he does between the Frick Museum and the "Mattress Factory", Andy Warhol is especially valuable to illustrate this process. Between prestige and trash, he was pivotal. As he trashed prestige, so he gave prestige to trash. Filling the then prestige medium of museums with a trash message, he signaled the end of museums and their replacement by "factories," the end of Art and the arrival of Anything Visual Goes. He is as clearly the end of the Frick line as he is the beginning of the "Factory" line. Judged by the prestige standards preceding him, he is trash. Judged by the trash standards which he did much to establish, he is the prestigious Prince of Pop Art. When his work first gained admittance to a prestigious New York art gallery, the abstract artists previously shown there walked out as one man to demonstrate their disgust with his "Pop Art." Yet Warhol's "Pop" is high art compared with much that has followed.

And the future of art? Clearly it depends on what will be in men's souls. If there is order, harmony and beauty in the souls, there will be order, harmony and beauty in the arts. If there is only ugliness and disharmony in the souls, there will only be ugliness and disharmony in the manipulation of materials, with medium to match.

And from where do uplift and beauty come into the souls of men, weighted always downwards by original sin? From God alone. And in a world and a civilization that has known Jesus Christ, Son of God, whom to hate is to hate the Father (Jn. 15: 23), from Jesus Christ alone. Ever since the coming of Jesus Christ, His Catholic Church has been a magnificent mother of the arts, and a just judgment upon the arts of the last half millennium must recognize that even artists in more or less rebellion against God have only been great as artists by what they were continuing of the Catholic heritage, and not by their rebellion, which fed on what it was destroying and destroyed what it fed on. Interestingly, Andy Warhol was a Catholic son of devout Czech immigrants, and a regular Mass-goer. Say what one will about the shallowness of his art (he himself said, "I am a deeply superficial person"), would he have any of the interest he has without that Catholic perspective?

Therefore only from the true Mass of the one Man-God has Western art any future. From loss of God the museums and concert halls are dead or dying. But in, for instance, SSPX Mass centers, the "Traditionalists" want music and decoration worthy of the great God they humbly worship. They start a choir. Then the fights start! But art is on the move again. Mother Church is once more mothering the arts. Thank you, great God! Let us only adore and worship and love You at Mass, and You will raise our arts from their graves.

Notice from the enclosed summer schedule that men could attend an Ignatian retreat and then a week of the Literature Camp, or a week of Literature and then a Session on Encyclicals. This summer offers unusual possibilities. Ladies, send your menfolk, and then draw out of them what you need when they get home!

The NewChurch
Against Nature

FOR MONTHS NOW, the mass media in the United States have been hammering the Catholic Church for the grave misbehavior of a certain number of her priests, over the last 30 to 40 years, towards young people in their congregations. Therefore much has been written and said on the problem, much more than I myself know or have read. However, some important truths which bear on the question I have seen mentioned little, or not at all. Let them surface here.

By way of preliminary, let us say where the blame does not essentially belong. It does not essentially belong with the media. This letter frequently calls the media "vile," and their vileness shows up in this case in their using the word "pedophilia" rather than "homosexuality" to name the problem. The word "pedophilia" refers properly to the molestation and abuse of children, let us say under the age of 10, whereas according to numerous reports the overwhelming majority of the crimes of which the priests are being accused involve adolescent boys, over 10 years old, activity which would normally be called by the h- word.

But for years now the media in their vileness have been conducting a consistent and persistent campaign to legitimize in the popular mind the sin of h-, also called the sin against nature, one of the four sins crying to Heaven for vengeance. How then could the media have glorified h- activity for so long, and then turn around and condemn it in priests? Hence their pretence that the problem is pedophilia, because most people are – still – horrified by the molestation and abuse of small children, whereas they are being – in large part by the media – desensitized to the horror of that sin against nature, crying to Heaven.

The media can also be blamed for coordinating what is surely a worldwide campaign to exploit to the full this present weakness of the Church. Having been taken largely into the hands of Mother Church's enemies, by the lack of vigilance or care on the part of Mother Church's friends, the media are no friends of the Church, and so they are naturally using to the full this opportunity to pull the Church down. However, there is no smoke without fire, says the proverb. How could the media make smoke unless there was some fire within the Church? If there was no such widespread misbehavior amongst churchmen, and known to the people, what could the worst of media do? Essentially, the churchmen committing or covering for the sins cannot blame the media.

Nor can they blame the people for being unreasonable, because in at least two respects popular reaction within the United States is seeming to be reasonable.

Firstly, while every Catholic priest should at all times and in all places, by the sublimity of his calling, behave like an angel, nevertheless he carries the treasure of his priesthood in that weak vessel of clay which is fallen human nature (II Cor. 4: 7), so that none of us who knows human weakness is entirely surprised to find even its worst outbreaks recurring within the priesthood, alas. Reasonably, the American people today are showing themselves less shocked by the lower clergy committing the sins than by the higher clergy covering for them, which is no longer a weakness (however grave) of the flesh.

And secondly, to the people's credit, when they blame the higher clergy for covering for the sins of the lower, they do seem to some extent to be recognizing a prior right of the Church over the State to discipline men of the Church. The people seem to be saying less that priestly crimes are a matter for the State, than that the Church should keep order in her own house, which, as long as the Church does so, is ancient good sense.

Therefore neither media nor people are essentially to blame. We come back to the churchmen. And if, as said, men who are Catholic priests have in all times and places given proof of their human weakness, then what is special about today's problem is its scale. The sin of h- amongst priests seems to be no longer scattershot but rather systemic. And, what angers so many people, it seems to have been systematically swept under the carpet by the higher clergy.

Alas, it is notorious that for tens of years now the Catholic Church has been infiltrated in the USA by h-s. Back in the 1980's, Fr. Enrique Rueda published his book *The H- Network* to document this fact with a mass of evidence. Today one learns that the mainstream seminaries are riddled with h- professors and h- seminarians. As one bishop recently commented, a first step in cleaning up the present mess would be to "de-lavenderise" the seminaries. Another bishop commented how apprehensive are normal (i.e., "straight") young men of entering the US seminaries today, for fear of being harassed by these perverts who are protected by the system!

But how can the system have reached this point? Here is where two systemic answers arise, neither of which is mentioned much today, if at all, and neither of which will be pleasing to today's Catholic hierarchy. That is exactly why there is a systemic problem. The first of these answers concerns the Mass, the second, still more generally, concerns the Ten Commandments.

As for the Mass, Archbishop Lefebvre always used to say that he could not have operated any of his seminaries with the Novus Ordo Mass (NOM). Everything possible was done by Rome in the 1970's and 1980's to make him introduce the NOM into his seminaries, but he said that had he done so, he might as well have put the keys in the seminary doors, and walked away! He himself never put it this way, but as far as he was concerned, a Catholic seminary without the true (Tridentine) Mass is like an atomic reactor without the uranium. There was no way he could make real priests with a dummy Mass.

For, he always said, priest and sacrifice are intimately related. There can be no ritual sacrifice without priest, no priest without sacrifice. The sacrifice is at the heart of the priest, and if you take away his sacrifice, you tear out the heart of the priest. So if you dumbify the Mass, which is of course the Catholic priest's sacrifice, then you dumbify the priest. And if you dumbify the Catholic priest, then he is liable to turn in all kinds of dumb directions for substitute purposes and satisfactions, which will include h- activity. I think if Archbishop Lefebvre were alive today, he would say that, given that the Novus Ordo Mass has now been imposed on Catholic priests for 30 plus years, the astonishing thing is not how much h- activity there is amongst priests, but how little!

However, as in the whole of today's crisis of the Church, while the problem of the Mass is the outstanding symptom, the malady is broader and deeper. What the NOM is essentially tending towards is to put man in

Richard N. Williamson

the place of God, direct violation of the First Commandment, "I am the Lord thy God, and thou shalt not have
strange gods before me" (Ex. 20: 2,3). In fact the whole
Newchurch's essential drift and aim is the idolatrous
putting of man in the place of God. Now what does St.
Paul (word of God) say are the consequences of idolatry?
See Romans 1: 18–31. "Men who detain the truth of God
in injustice (18) . . . changed the glory of the incorrupt-
ible God into the likeness of the image of a corruptible
man (23), <u>wherefore</u> [*I underline*] God gave them up to
the desires of their heart, unto uncleanness, to dishon-
our their bodies among themselves (24)."

St. Paul goes on to repeat this <u>cause and effect</u> connection between breaking the First and the Sixth Commandments with <u>specific reference to the sin against
nature</u>: "Who changed the truth of God into a lie; and
worshipped and served the creature rather than the Creator.... (24). <u>For this cause</u> [*I underline*] God delivered
them up to shameful affections. For their women have
changed the natural use into that use which is against
nature (26). And, in like manner, the men also, leaving the natural use of the women, have burned in their
lusts one towards another, men with men working that
which is filthy, and receiving in themselves the recom-
pense which was due to their error (27)." And in case we
have still not understood that idolatry is at the heart of
the problem, St. Paul says it a third time! – "<u>And as they
liked not to have God in their knowledge</u> [*I underline*],
God delivered them up to a reprobate sense, to do those
things which are not convenient (28)," and there follows
a list of grave sins.

God forbid "Traditionalists" should throw stones at
the weakness of mainstream priests, because we could be
punished by His allowing us to fall into the same traps.
But it is not Traditionalists who made two times two
equal four. It is St. Paul, speaking for God, who puts his

finger here on the systemic problem of the Newchurch. God uses this sin to highlight idolatry, and He seems now to be resorting to the secular authority to clean this sin out of His Church. Both moves are acts of mercy on His part. May He have mercy upon us all!

More positively, if I know a h-, and wish to get him (or her) out of it, let me do all I can to bring him back towards the <u>true love and worship of the true God</u>. It was when Augustine found the true God and began obeying the First Commandment, that he found the strength to obey the Sixth!

Campos – What Went Wrong?

IN FEBRUARY THIS letter presented the fall, finalized in January, of the Traditional bishop and priests of Campos back into the clutches of neo-modernist Rome. That fall was a disappointment for the SSPX, whose lone stand for Truth they had shared for 20 years. To explain that fall, I think it is worth further presenting to you an analysis sent to me recently by a priest stationed in Brazil, who is a friend of the SSPX, and who was for a long time a friend of those Campos priests. Here is what he wrote to me:

> I had already prepared to put in the post an essay by one of our priests on Campos, or rather on the last statements coming out of Campos as compared with what they used to teach. However, this comparison does not go to the heart of the problem. In my opinion, the heart of the problem is to be found in the lofty vision of Archbishop Lefebvre, a lofty vision lacking in Campos.
>
> The Archbishop achieved a well-balanced overview of the whole problem in the Church, which was the fruit of his experience and spirit of prayer, his virtues

and gifts received from God. Bishop de Castro Mayer drew closer to the Archbishop in his last years, but it seems that the Campos priests did not have their own bishop's wisdom or, perhaps, his humility. In my opinion the Campos priests have gone backwards because they had a different way of looking at the crisis of the Church.

Let me explain: up until the consecrations of 1988 Bishop de Castro Mayer's reaction to the crisis was curious. On the one hand he was legalistic, tending to stick to the letter of the law. For instance after ceasing to be the diocesan bishop of Campos, he ordained no more priests except one that he ordained after the 1988 Consecrations. On the other hand he had a tendency towards sedevacantism, as when he would say of John Paul II, "Whoever does not belong to the body of the Church cannot be its head."

Archbishop Lefebvre was aware of this twofold tendency in Bishop de Castro Mayer, which is why he would say concerning the bishop's legalism, "Bishop de Castro Mayer must understand that today we have to "go illegal", if necessary" (a remark to be understood, obviously, in the present context), and concerning his sedevacantism, Archbishop Lefebvre said, "Were it not for me, Bishop de Castro Mayer would be sedevacantist, but in order not to separate from us, he holds back from sedevacantism."

I think the Archbishop was right. There were in Bishop de Castro Mayer the two tendencies of legalism and sedevacantism. The bishop's friendship with Archbishop Lefebvre moderated these two tendencies and enabled Bishop de Castro Mayer to take courageous and well-founded positions. However the Campos priests seem never to have completely shaken off these two false ways of posing today's problem, because they seem to me to argue like the sedevacantists: "If John Paul II is Pope, we must obey him. If we do not obey him, we must declare that he is not Pope"...

The Campos priests, in my opinion, are lacking in

vision. They are taking too simple a view of this crisis. What is the cause of this turning back of theirs? Either they never judged the crisis in the way that the Archbishop did, or, under the influence of some of their own number, they slipped back, and left the good road on which Bishop de Castro Mayer had set out before he died... For sure and certain they always kept a certain distance between themselves and the Society.

End of analysis of the fall of Tradition in Campos by the Society's priest friend in Brazil. It is an analysis rich in lessons, or in reminders, of how this 40 year old crisis of the Church does its damage.

Firstly, let us relativize the criticism of Bishop de Castro Mayer implicit in this analysis by recalling his enormous achievement which the analysis was not designed to bring out. Catholic Tradition has few enough heroes today, and this bishop is certainly one of them.

He was 56 years old, and the normal Catholic bishop of the little diocese of Campos, three hours by car north of Rio de Janeiro, when the Second Vatican Council opened in 1962. During the Council he was a steady opponent of the neo-modernists' Revolution overthrowing the Church, and after the Council he would not let his diocese follow the new religion. When Pope Paul VI imposed the New Mass in 1969, Bishop de Castro Mayer most respectfully resisted him to his face, and allowed his own priests to continue celebrating the true Mass. The good bishop was followed in this faithfulness to the old religion by the large majority of his priests and people, so that amidst the thousands of Church dioceses throughout the world which were (at least objectively) letting themselves be led into apostasy, his diocese alone stayed essentially Catholic.

In 1981 at age 75 he had to retire. For his successor, the Newchurch sent in a chain-and-wrecking-ball bishop to smash the Traditional diocese. That is when Bishop de Castro Mayer and his faithful priests began publicly to associate with the SSPX in its policy of rebuilding alongside the mainstream church, but not outside the Catholic Church. Under his leadership, his priests built for the true Mass a series of brand-new churches alongside their former parish churches, now hijacked for the new religion.

And so Bishop de Castro Mayer's heroic defence of the Faith continued in Campos until he died in April of 1991, with his faithful priests clustered around his deathbed. Had he lived longer, there can be no doubt that he would have stayed on the course he had set between 1981 and 1991, and there can be little to no doubt that his priests would have continued to surround him. As it was, it took ten years for them to fall back into the powerful magnetic field of "obedience to Rome."

It was necessary to recall this unique fidelity and achievement of Bishop de Castro Mayer lest anyone should think that the priest's analysis, quoted above, was meant to pull him down. Not at all. But what the analysis does is to remind us of the incredible power of the apostasy of the 1960's, which had even an excellent bishop wavering between the twin false solutions of legalism and sedevacantism through the 1970's, until thanks to a still greater archbishop he steadied his Catholic balance through the 1980's.

That an apostasy should carry away millions of Catholics, thousands of priests and hundreds of bishops, well, that is what apostasies do. But that – as the analysis quoted above suggests, and I think it is right – even a churchman of the quality of Bishop de Castro Mayer tottered in the wake of Vatican II is testimony both to the volcanic force of all that was behind that Council and – here again I think the analysis is correct – to the extraordinary gifts and wisdom of Archbishop Lefebvre.

Richard N. Williamson

Far be it from me to indulge in a cult of personality, or to declare that the Archbishop was infallible or impeccable. However, the fruits are there to tell us how much God gave us in him, or, what a gift of God to us he was: the guidance of his example enabled a wise fellow bishop to keep the heads above water of the Campos priests around him, but now that both bishops are dead, those priests slip back beneath the waters of apostasy – may they rest in peace!

But they cannot. Already they are taking positions that contradict everything they said and did for the last 20 years. They will soon be bearing little more Catholic fruit than the rest of the Conciliar Church, and meanwhile they have scandalized and alienated all Catholics of Tradition.

Whereas the Society, continuing along the lines of Archbishop Lefebvre, continues to bear Catholic fruit, as I have been able to see from recent journeys to the Philippines and to Germany. In the Philippines, we now have a dozen Mass centers, all well attended by Catholics joyfully picking up, or picking up again, on the true Faith, while in our German centers families are at last re-appearing with large numbers of children. It has taken Germany time, because the anti-birth "culture" has been so strong, but the Faith wins out in the end. In death-dedicated Europe this flourishing of children is like a miracle, but nobody who knows the power of the Faith can be surprised.

And so death-dedicated Rome continues to harass the Society, and will cripple it, if it can. To the Italian press Cardinal Castrillón Hoyos recently spoke of the Society as being composed of a majority of reasonable bishops, priests, laity, etc., who want to rejoin Rome, while a "difficult and fanatical" minority will perhaps continue "in schism, believing that they possess the truth, and forgetting that where there is Peter, there there is the Church."

And then the Cardinal denies that he is trying to split the Society!

One may pray for the Cardinal, as for the priests of Campos, but humanly speaking, one may fear they will only increase in blindness. Lord, have mercy – upon us all!

At the Seminary's Doctrinal Session from July 30 to August 3 these Encyclicals will be studied – From TAN's *The Popes Against Modern Errors*, "Diuturnum Illud," "Rerum Novarum," "The Sillon," "Lamentabili" and the Anti-Modernist oath; from TAN's *A Light in the Heavens*, "Satis Cognitum." Sign up, men, to see that the SSPX is only standing for what the Catholic Church has always stood for.

Priestly ordinations take place here at Winona on Saturday, June 22. The more numerous you are, to come and show your joy and appreciation of four new "Lefebvrist" priests, the more vocations God will surely incline to awaken. Come, and fill our meadows with your children, so as to fill your seminary with seminarians!

Well Done, Young Parents

S O ONE MORE school year at the seminary came to a glorious end, with the ordination of four new priests, three Americans and a Canadian, at Winona on June 22. On the day before, a violent storm and wind had begun to tear apart the tent erected for the occasion, and a large part had to be replaced, as you will read in the August Verbum, but everything was repaired in time for the ceremony which took place in lovely weather.

Some two thousand souls attended, from all over North America and beyond. How many familiar faces! People come back now year after year for the special graces that go with the birth of new priests, and with the celebration of their first Masses. Colleagues at the seminary commented on how the congregation this year seemed especially recollected and joyful.

There were plenty of little children, as I had hoped for, and a corresponding number of young parents. What a delight it always is to see the young mothers, truly fulfilled by doing God's will in the home, and rewarded with a gracious femininity which the feminism of worldlings quite destroys! In support of these young mothers and their children and their homes, let me quote at length from an article by a colleague in France who runs a retreat house, and who must then have every year many young fathers and mothers coming through his hands.

Fr. Delagneau begins by lamenting how many households he sees, either breaking up or preparing to break up, with spouses destabilized and placed in great spiritual danger, with children disturbed for life. Such breaking up may seem no problem to worldlings, but it must give Catholics pause to reflect: these breakups do not happen overnight – so what am I doing in my own home now which may be leading in that direction?

Following St. Paul, his article is divided into two parts: "Husbands, love your wife" (as Christ loved the Church, giving himself up for her – Eph. 5: 25), and "Wives, be submitted to your husband" (as to the Lord, for the husband is the head of the wife, as Christ is the Head of the Church, his Body Eph. – 5: 22). The complementarity of man and woman, the understanding of which is the key to understanding marriage, and the living of which is the key to living a happy marriage, is a marvel of nature built by God into the design of the two sexes. Notice, however, the reference to Christ and his Church in the two quotes above, taken from the Epistle for the Catholic Church's Wedding Mass. This reference means that only grace, or supernatural Faith in Christ and his Bride, the Church, can take the full measure of, and if need be protect, the natural marvel.

Fr. Delagneau notes that whereas in the old days the wife could and would endure a great deal in order to save the home, today it is often she who initiates the process of separation because life at home has come to seem unlivable. Yet separation is a non-solution, so Fr. Delagneau begins by addressing the husbands:

> Remember firstly that by nature the wife is more sensitive, more emotional, which is why certain worries or

problems in the home weigh on her more heavily. And if she stays at home, she has little by way of conversation or activity outside the home to take her mind off these upsets which thereby take on an importance her husband can hardly understand, which wears on her nerves.

The sensitive side of woman likewise explains how, once she has lost trust in her husband, everything weighs upon her. She becomes tense and withdrawn, and goes on the defensive, increasing her nervous fatigue.

To regain her trust is a long process and the husband will need to show great delicacy to prove that he really means to change. But that is the price he must pay, because without trust the marriage is going nowhere. Without trust, decisions are never taken together and relations become heavy and superficial while flare-ups and unkind words become more frequent.

Realize also that, by her nature, woman can for a long time take things upon herself and endure difficulties without showing it, but if one day she cracks, it can be very difficult to repair. She then goes into a nervous depression, or she gets fixated on some problem.

Finally, realize just how wearying work in the home can be. Many husbands think that keeping house and rearing children is no heavy burden. But while house keeping may not seem much, it requires time, effort and organization. Rearing children requires in addition a mother's full attention, self-control, and readiness to put everything else aside. Such obligations also give rise to a real nervous fatigue. Mother has not the same authority as father to settle problems. Fortunately she has more gentleness, patience and understanding, so she is more selfless. But all of that wears on her nerves.

Bearing children, especially when they follow closely on one another, while still having to keep house, is for mother an extra burden on her health that must be taken into account. If the husband bears all this in mind and much else besides, he will love his wife with a quite different love, and he will exercise his authority as head of the house with more care and gentleness. Here are a few suggestions:

Firstly, he will make a real effort not to let his work take over his life so that he is never at home to take any active part in family life (children's homework, games, conversation, helping around the house or with the washing up to make life more pleasant for his wife).

Next he will make time to talk with her, to listen to the major events of her day, to encourage and congratulate her and make a few suggestions. Forgetting his own weariness he will also speak of his own day and of current events, remembering that she has often had no adult conversation all day long, and needs something to open her mind.

He will keep an eye open for his wife's nervous fatigue, and he will be realistic. That way he can advise her how to organize things better, and to stick to essentials. With his manly authority he will help in the education of their children, so that she is not swamped by their running wild. He will also watch over her rest and health, and sometimes even change his own schedule to enable her to take a few necessary days off.

The wife is sensitive and delicate, so she knows how to please. But she expects something of the sort in return. A little gesture, a little kindness, a little display of affection will make her forget many pains and much weariness, and will give her renewed energy for her work. What may cost him little effort can mean a great deal to her, so let him find out those little things that mean so much to her.

The trust on her part which makes her gladly fall in with her husband's way of thinking, comes from two things; firstly, from her respect for his good qualities and for his success in what he undertakes, and secondly from his readiness to heed her wishes and her judicious advice, so that when he takes decisions, he does so in view of the welfare of the family as a whole.

This trust is acquired at the beginning of a marriage, but it continues to be earned thereafter. Of course the husband is the head of the family, but he must learn how to exercise his authority firmly but gently. Clashes should always be avoided. Giving way need not mean he loses his authority, on the contrary it can show that he knows how to adapt it to circumstances. Authority can be undermined by his never making up his mind, or by his giving way every time.

In fact, as St. Paul says so well, it is love for one's spouse that will discover the happy medium between being firm and being gentle.

Under certain circumstances, one must know how to kneel down and pray for light to God, our Father.

To conclude, let me point out that family problems do not arise only in other people's homes. Let the husband keep watch to preserve the union of harmony in his own.

Thus far Fr. Delagneau's recommendations to husbands. There is no space left for much to be quoted from his presentation of the need and way for wives to submit to their husbands. Here then are brief extracts:

By becoming a wife, woman enters into a hierarchical society, the family, in which by the will of God man is the head. Just as Christ as man submitted to his Father, so the woman as wife submits to her husband. Neither did Christ lose in dignity by submitting to his Father, nor does the wife by submitting to her husband. On the contrary, obedience makes the soul noble because it makes the greatest sacrifice of self for God, the sacrifice of one's own will . . .

Wives, do not listen to the vile propaganda of the anti-culture all around us, which is deliberately anti-Christian and is trampling upon the law of God. Listen to Pope Pius XII, addressing women in 1941: "Numerous voices will make out to you that submission is in some way unjust. They will suggest that you be more proudly independent, that you are in all respects the equal of your husbands and that you are in many ways their superior. Watch out for such words of the serpent, temptations, lies. Do not follow in Eve's footsteps, but keep to the only path that can lead to happiness, even here below. . ."

In practice, the wife collaborates in all family decisions by her judicious advice, and then she falls in with her husband's opinion in view of the family welfare, God's will for each and all. She learns how to use the power that her looks and words have over her husband so to enter into his soul as to bring him round to the good of the family. And he learns to take decisions gently influenced by his wife, without losing authority, but also without being weak or giving way to her charm when she is not seeking the common good. There is a whole art in the wife's influencing her husband for the good. What a misfortune for some wives to have no idea of that art! They openly oppose their husbands' will, and the result can only be a head on clash. At that point two self-wills compete, and only brute force or blackmail can win out. How far we are then from close collaboration in charity.

I add my own conclusion to Fr. Delagneau's good sense: let a husband and wife, who both want to make their marriage work, never despair, despite everything the modern world throws at them. A happy home can be achieved. It is an incomparable strength for the children, an edification as on June 22 for one's fellow men, and it must be a joy for the angels and God to behold. May He bless all of you husbands and wives, young or old, who keep trying!

SSPX in Distant Lands

AY WHAT ONE will about monster machines, there
is no denying that today's gigantic aeroplanes make
possible, as I can remember Archbishop Lefebvre
once remarking, long and accurate apostolic journeys.
Between the end of June and mid-July they enabled me
for the third time to travel around the world for the SSPX.

First stop was for the priestly ordinations at the end of
the school year in the Society's main seminary in Ecône,
Switzerland, where 15 new priests were ordained, mostly
French, for postings all over the world. Since the first major ordination of priests by Archbishop Lefebvre for the
Society in June of 1976, this made the 27th ordination in 27
years in the tent erected each year in the meadow beneath
the seminary. For a canvas cathedral, that is a remarkable
stability and source of strength for the Faith!

The event being now annual routine, the crowd attending the ordinations in Ecône was less than double
the crowd attending ordinations in Winona five days
beforehand, but in Ecône no fewer than 159 priests
helped Bishop Tissier to lay hands on the ordinands. Of
the many priestly friends I can remember that used to
come from outside the Society to lay on hands in the
early days, few are still living. To replace them, each year

now more and more of the Society's own priests come to the ordinations for this purpose, and it is interesting to watch these men swiftly growing older, or maturing, under the steady pressure of the priesthood. With each year that passes, the Society's priests become less and less a mere collection of youngsters, as one can have thought of them a little while back. They are becoming with God's grace a formidable phalanx in defense of the Faith. Pray we never betray!

Second stop was Holland, to provide a Sunday Mass and two Confirmations in the Society's one and only floating chapel, which is in The Hague. Property is so expensive in this city of Europe's International Court that years ago Fr. De Mérode (now based in St. Louis, serving Cincinnati) purchased a retired barge moored by the side of one of Holland's multiple canals. Here he established an attractive and perfectly workable chapel. It may be faintly disconcerting for the preacher to watch the chandeliers gently swinging over the congregation's heads during Mass, but after all Our Lord Himself used a boat for a pulpit (Lk. 5: 3)!

Holland is very liberal, and it is a difficult country for Catholic Tradition today (see Verbum # 77). But the Society priest who looks after The Hague, Fr. Robert Schmitt from neighbouring Germany, is a happy young man nevertheless. To celebrate the tenth anniversary of his priesthood, amongst other things we visited an exhibition in Amsterdam's renowned Rijksmuseum of a 17th century Dutch artist from Holland's golden age, Aelbert Cuyp. What a contrast between his Holland of sailing ships in golden sunsets, and today's Holland of six-lane freeways! Yet even from the freeway one recognizes by moments Cuyp's landscape, and, truth to tell, even Cuyp could idealize with his paint brush what he saw with his eyes. Is the camera then more truthful than the artist? Not necessarily...

Richard N. Williamson

Another aerial monster lifted me for the third stop
to Malaysia, former British Malaya, where I had never
been before, and where I wanted to visit in particular
a historic town of lesser importance today, but made
famous amongst Catholics for having been made by St.
Francis Xavier one of the bases of his Far Eastern missionary journeys in the mid-1500's: Malacca. However,
today's important city of Malaysia where the aerial mon-
sters land is Kuala Lumpur, modernized capital of one
of those nations known as the "Asian tigers" for their recent material prosperity. One may wonder for how much
longer the United States' huge imports from Asia will
continue to found this prosperity, but in the meantime
Kuala Lumpur boasts a pair of towers taller than the
Twin Towers that were dynamited in New York.

Malaysia is not a Catholic country, and never has
been, yet still Catholic Tradition has a footing there.
The coordinator and his family are English speakers of
Chinese extraction. With Fr. Daniel Couture, Asian District Superior from French Canada, they showed me the
Society's handsome chapel hewn out of a commercial
building, with delightful stained glass windows of Asian
coloring painted by the coordinator. Some 30 souls attend Mass celebrated twice a month by a Society priest
coming up by bus from Singapore. A rest, three Confirmations, and then the visit to Malacca, two hours south
by car on a splendid freeway.

Malacca, strategically located on a Strait shielded
by the Island of Sumatra opposite, midway between
the East (India) and the Far East (China and Japan),
achieved prominence as a major center of shipping and
commerce well before it was conquered in the early 16th
century by the Portuguese to act as a major base for their
own running of the lucrative spice trade. To establish
their rule of Malacca, the Portuguese (1511 to 1641)
built a stone fortress around the hill dominating the

port, which the Dutch (1641–1795) strengthened, and the British (1795–1957) destroyed, except for one gateway, now a delight of tourists. How empires come and go! Presently, the "Asian tigers" are part of the American Empire's comings and Boeings, but these too will one day be gone with the wind....

St. Francis Xavier's five stays in Malacca belong to the time of the Portuguese. Readers of his life will remember how he attempted to convert those he found there, so that their bad example would cease to alienate from the Faith so many "natives," a word politically incorrect but saying what it needs to say. One ponders on the ways of Providence: why did God send a Xavier to the pagan East and Far East in the 16th century, and not before? And why is Asia not now converted? Men are to blame. Today, the museums in Malacca reflect a scorn for the Europeans who once brought the Catholic Faith. Alas, if in the streets of Malacca one sees someone sloppily dressed and lacking all dignity, sure enough, it will be a Westerner. If I was today an Easterner, I would despise these moneyed tramps and their past colonialism and their supposed Faith. How we need an army of Xaviers, if souls are to be saved!

Little trace remains of Xavier in today's Malacca. There is a statue of him outside the walls of St. Paul's church still standing atop the fortified hill, where Xavier would stay on his visits, and there is the vault beneath ground within the church where his body rested for a few month's between Shangchuan Island off China, where Xavier died his mysteriously cold and lonely death in 1552, and Goa, the then Portuguese enclave in India where it rests to this day. But Xavier would never have cared for physical monuments. His true monument is the implanting of the Faith all over the East and Far East, and hundreds of thousands of souls safely garnered for Heaven then and since. And his dazzling example!

Richard N. Williamson

St. Francis Xavier, pray that Westerners come to their Catholic senses! Pray that your Company of Jesus generate once more Jesuit conquerors of the world for Heaven and God!

Fourth stop was Australia, actually the main destination of the entire journey, for the purpose of ordaining at home amongst his own large family Winona's Australian seminarian for the last three years, Rev. Mr. Brendan – now Father Brendan – Arthur. For pictures from his ordination and first Mass in Melbourne, see the enclosed "Verbum."

In Melbourne the question of the camera came up again when Fr. Kevin Robinson (known to many of you) took two of us to see a film which he highly recommended on the ministry and death among Hawaii's lepers in the mid-19th century of Fr. Damien. Indeed the film was well done as films go, especially on a Catholic subject, but still it left one with a dissatisfaction. Why? Surely because just as the cinema has such power to make the unreal seem real, so it is bound to make the real seem unreal, including Fr. Damien. Surely it would be truer to say that the camera always lies than that it never lies. But that is another story.

Last stop on this on-Boeing world tour was Japan, a small island or collection of islands, but a world giant, economically speaking, not by its physical resources but by the ancient natural virtues of its people. These virtues are today being eroded, as everywhere, by the modern uprooting from a natural way of life, yet the Japanese people remain those that Xavier came to love in his brief but decisive missionary visit in the 1540's. Here as in other Asian countries, the Society has a foothold significant not by numbers but by Truth.

My host was Fr. Thomas Onoda, himself Japanese, another young Society priest with a lonely ministry when he visits his homeland each month, but with a happy heart. Into a tiny tenth-floor apartment serving as Society Chapel in downtown Osaka, Japan's second city after Tokyo, two dozen souls crowded for nine of them to receive Confirmation, and in Tokyo itself a similar number attended Sunday Mass in surroundings more spacious but still without chairs. These are replaced by prayer mats and one's own haunches!

Praise be to God for the gift and survival of the Catholic Faith in these distant lands! Honor and prayers for the isolated priests in their far flung ministry! May Our Lord send more workers into his harvest! They have a happy life if they are faithful.

State of the Nations:
Three Layers of Lies

ALL AROUND US today, things are not what they seem. By a just punishment of God, the Devil is in virtual (only virtual) control of the world, and the Devil is the Father of Lies (Jn. 8: 44). So in politics, in the arts, in the law, in education, in the media and – worst of all – in religion, we are today smothered in lies. For the sake of truth and for the sake of our temporal and eternal survival, we should attempt to discern what is, from what seems.

In the domain of economics, here in the USA, we are being told that the economic recession is only temporary, that the fundamentals are sound, that things will soon take an upturn, that the good times will continue to roll. Holders of stocks and shares need only sit tight, and they will soon see Wall Street rising again. Here is a first major layer of lies. To establish what is true in economics, let us turn to two writers on matters financial who have their heads on straight, and then let us climb to the corresponding political and religious layers of lies.

FIRST LAYER: ECONOMICS

View From USA

The first of these writers is James Cook, based in Minne-
apolis, MN, who lays out what he foresees for the American economy in his *Market Update* of last month, August 2002. With an old-fashioned common sense he explains in general economic terms why hard times must
–normally – lie ahead:

Booms are followed by busts . . . It's an economic
premise generally accepted by every historical economist. The boom couldn't get started without artificially low interest rates, easy money and credit. A
boom comes from businesses expanding in a way that
wouldn't have happened if the market wasn't sending
them false signals caused by rapidly expanding levels
of money and credit. Low interest rates make it attractive to borrow excessively and to build up overcapacity.
When this process ends and contraction begins, then
comes a bust. The greater the boom, the greater the extent of the bust. We had (in the 1980's and 1990's) the
greatest boom in decades. The bust will be a humding-
er and, for a number of reasons, it could turn into a
severe depression. In fact, I believe it will alter America
like nothing since the Civil War.

A runaway expansion of money and credit has ruined our economy. Savings are at the worst level ever.
Profits and capital spending are in the tank. Deep-seated structural problems in the economy preclude better times. The loosest monetary policies in US history
have failed to work. There are terrible days ahead. Consumer spending must collapse. The dollar's sure failure
spells doom for stocks and bonds. Credit will seize up
and paralyze the capital markets, followed by a raging
epidemic of bankruptcies and a collapsing housing
market. Governments across the nation will see bankruptcy and defaults on their bonds, which will turn

this last bastion of security into financial quicksand. Then, in the depths of depression, inflation will rage . . . Blame will become the national pastime.

View From South Africa

Possibly James Cook is taking too dark a view of the near future, but his general position is substantiated with many facts and statistics by our second writer, author of the lead article in the *Aida Parker Newsletter* of June, 2002. This newsletter comes out of Johannesburg, South Africa. If I give these details, it is because in a world of lies, Aida Parker is a gallant teller of the truth, and her newsletter tells more truth about what is happening within the USA than the mass of the American media. I have shortened and edited the June lead article, "Armageddon Approaches," only very slightly. Any underlinings are my own:

"Armageddon"

We saw it coming: but the US financial and corporate blow-out is now right on top of the bloodiest smash-up in history, far more damaging than anyone could have foreseen. And it becomes evermore critical: already in certain sectors worse than the Great Depression of fearsome memory. The façade of US financial impregnability built up over the past decade is *kaput*. Its much-delayed recession is here.

US Stock Market

Of most immediate danger is the staggering stock market debacle. That alone guarantees catastrophe. Total investor losses on the Wall Street meltdown now exceed $6 trillion, all of it from investors' pockets. This crash has destroyed up to half of people's life savings and scrambled the retirement nest eggs of more than 45.7 million "baby boomers" due to retire over the next five years. It has vaporized the prosperity, financial security and retirement dreams of millions.

In sheer $ terms, the collapse since March, 2000, has brought the largest loss of wealth in the history of humanity, dwarfing the great 1929 stock market crash by a factor of 29 to 1. The resources, financial and otherwise, squandered in a vain attempt to keep the Dow between 10,000 and 11,000 "forever" don't bear thinking about.

The Dow and the S&P are still both grossly over-valued. Historically, investors invariably overreact to such a threat, driving stocks well below their historical valuations. Yet not in the US today. As the market moves into its third full year of stock losses, despite everything more than 50% of shareholders remain in it, ensnared by the despicable lies and manipulation of the US Government, Wall Street, Federal Reserve, all aided by the general media.

The picture gets worse: much worse. With zero savings, householders hold $7.6 trillion in debt. Such debt is at its highest level in US history, with consumers holding $1 trillion in new home mortgages acquired in the last year. Personal bankruptcies last year were more than double those 1990/91. 2002 will be even worse.

The Dollar

The US Government insists that its "Strong $ Policy" remains intact. Unfortunately the $ does not remain intact. Today it crumbles before the eyes of the world. The $ as a currency is bankrupt. We all know that the US $ is dropping against all other currencies: in some cases, very hard. The US trade deficit is huge and growing.

Morgan Stanley recently wrote that the trade deficit is now 4.3% of US trade. If the trade deficit of a developed nation reaches as high as 5% of GDP [Gross Domestic Product], there is usually a drop of 20% in that

Richard N. Williamson

nation's currency within three years. Morgan Stanley projects that the US trade deficit could reach 6% by next year, which means a deficit of $2 billion a day. Net real investment in the US is now nil. Further, the US has been importing far more than it exports.

US Corporations

Much of corporate America is in deep trouble. There have been five consecutive quarters of declining corporate profit. US companies now owe a record $4.7 trillion to banks, venture capitalists, bondholders, money funds and other institutions. The Fed says this debt is growing almost three times faster than GDP.

In 2001, more than 40,000 businesses filed for bankruptcy. Estimates are that 652 big companies will have a tough job surviving another year. Xerox has $162 billion in debt, exponentially more than it has in assets. Nextel had $16.7 billion of debt, only $4.2 billion in cash reserves. Both could fall into bankruptcy. Del Monte, General Mill, Trump Hotels & Casinos, Ford, Kellogg, Campbell Soup, 7-Eleven, all are in trouble.

Boeing's orders dropped 45% last year. Hotel chains are plagued with very high vacancy rates; steel makers have a ±50% in excess capacity, and the worst earnings in 40 years. The Ford Motor Co. is closing five plants in North America, and has chalked up 35,000 job cuts over the past year.

Levi Strauss is closing another six plants in the US, laying off 3,600 workers. This means the company will have shut 29 plants in the US, while opening lower wage plants overseas. Sears is closing 89 stores; drugstore chain CVS is closing 200 pharmacies; Toys "R" Us, 64 stores. Heavy truck sales, a measure of US transportation, shipping of raw and finished goods, are down 25% over the past year, Mack trucks down 19.3%.

Many of America's largest public companies are so weak that they could go bankrupt at any time. As company earnings decline, companies are cutting dividends, adding still further to investor woes. Martin Weiss of *Safe Money Report*, recently reported: "<u>Corporate America is swamped with debt to the tune of 156% of GDP</u>. That's more than 44% a year ago. It's also bigger than the debt load Japan faced before its stock market bubble burst back in 1990."

As hundreds of thousands of homeowners are laid off, <u>so the recent real estate bubble bursts</u>. Sales of existing homes dropped 8.3% in March, and continued down in April and May. There's over-capacity and dwindling demand for new office space and shopping malls.

US Banking

All of the above is devastating news for the US banks, <u>themselves their nation's curse</u>. The US Government estimates that 9% of banks are "very vulnerable" to a real estate turndown, another 16% "somewhat vulnerable." In other words, on top of all else, it is a banking catastrophe. A reported 4,913 banks suffered an increase in bad loans in the first nine months of 2001.

The final nail in the banks' coffin is derivatives: high-risk bets on stocks, bonds and foreign currencies that now stand at truly staggering levels. In 1998 US banks held about $27 trillion in derivative contracts. Today, according to the US General Accounting Office (GAO), US banks are exposed to more than $40.5 trillion in derivatives. All told, more than 400 commercial banks are in financial derivatives.

Government Spending

Financially, the US Federal government stands with a deficit budget, with deficit spending blowing out while tax revenues fall. The US needs to import $1.6 billion of capital a day just to fill the deficit. That's no longer happening. Just as the fertilizer hits the fan, so the international community has decided to take its money away from the US.

Richard N. Williamson

According to the US Treasury, foreigners sold a net $16.9 million of US securities in the first two months of this year. Japanese banks are already dumping the $447 billion in US stocks and bonds they hold.

Federal Reserve

The raw economic facts are terrifying. The physical US economy is cluttered with massive over-investment, malinvestment and horrendous mismanagement, all of it held up by minuscule investment rates and very fancy bookkeeping. The Fed lowered interest rates eight times before the Great Depression: without effect. Alan Greenspan has cut interest rates eleven times, till rates now are very near zero. Still with no effect.

Dr. Kurt Richebacher, in his *Richebacher Letter*, writes: "While the Bank of Japan deliberately pricked its bubble in the late 1980's with tight money, the Fed has tried to sustain the US bubble with ultra-loose money policies. Such an effort has no precedent in history. Such madness was bound to fail. On the other hand, the unsustainable excesses are of such preposterous magnitude that in any case they would come too late to avoid disastrous consequences."

US Prospects

Summing up: What we are seeing is the troubled homecoming of ALL the US economic chickens. US financial powers are now embattled on all fronts. The US $, the US stock market, the entire US economy stand with their collective backs to the wall. Result? The US economy has entered a period of observable decline. And the real economic problems have not even begun to be tackled yet.

Indeed, prospects are that the position will continue to get much worse, not better. In the face of worldwide economic recession; escalating geopolitical tensions, with Israel on the boil and Mr. Bush threatening war against Iraq's Saddam Hussein and the US market now in its 35ᵗʰ month of bear market decline, US recovery prospects appear nil.

Former World Bank chief Economist and Nobel Prize winner, Joseph Stiglitz, is advising Asian economies to pool their vast foreign reserves as a step towards a re-shaped monetary system that would be less of a tool for US interests, the IMF and other agencies . . .

Many hearts elsewhere will probably not bleed too much for the US and its dire calamities. To quote Bill Buckler of *The Privateer* newsletter: "<u>America has im-posed a draconian clampdown on the freedom and liberties of its own citizens</u>. It has dived headlong into deficits. <u>It has lost control of government spending</u>. It has antagonized its friends and allies with import tar-iffs, demands for military alliances and ultimatums that you are with us or against us. No neutrality is al-lowed.

Again, it is possible that the *Aida Parker Newsletter* is taking too dark a view of events, but it is not likely. Those are too many hard facts and statistics. The truth is that for some years now American "prosperity" has been upheld by smoke and mirrors, of which "fancy bookkeeping" (as the APN calls it) is merely one now notorious example. There is a whole house of cards to come crashing down, and the longer the crash is delayed, the harder the crash will be. The interesting thing is the deeper layers of lies in politics and religion which make such fantasy possible in economics.

SECOND LAYER: POLITICS

A First Lie

The first political lie is that economics is independent of politics. It is true that there are laws of econom-ics, like the law of supply and demand, which oper-ate independently of the politicians, but how a nation

Richard N. Williamson

will navigate in amongst those economic laws is still a political decision. For instance, in the 19th Century, selfish capitalists pretended to justify their selfishness by the inexorable working of economic laws, but all the time they were choosing which of those laws to set in motion, and how, so that labor would be cheap. President F.D. Roosevelt is famous for saying, "If something happens in politics, you can be sure it was planned that way," and that will include economic booms and busts.

A Second Lie

So the second political lie is that the present threat of a severe economic crash was not planned. The foolishness of a people (not only in the USA) believing in a free lunch, or loving a party and wanting the party to go on for ever, has been skillfully exploited to create either the threat or the reality (it little matters which) of a severe crash, to drive the nations into a Third World War. Well over a century ago Judeo-Masonry is known to have been envisaging three World Wars to achieve its unified global domination.

By lies, Judeo-Masonry brought about the first two World Wars. To get Americans to enter the First World War, President Woodrow Wilson told them that it would be the "war to end all wars." In fact, WWI established the Masonic League of Nations in Geneva and the Communist Revolution in Russia, and crushed numerous Christian monarchies, in particular the Catholic Austro-Hungarian Empire. And the Masonic Treaty of Versailles ending WWI deliberately paved the way for WWII, of which President F.D. Roosevelt promised it would "make the world safe for democracy." In fact, WWII established the Masonic United Nations, hugely promoted socialism in the USA and in the Western "democracies," and crushed the Eastern "democracies" under Communism.

World War III

By lies, Judeo-Masonry is preparing for the Third World War. As the Depression of the 1930's necessitated WWII, triggered for the US by the supposed treachery of the Japanese at Pearl Harbor, so we see all the conditions created for another much worse Depression in the US, with the supposed treachery of Arabs last year against the Twin Towers in New York already igniting American public opinion to go to war against Afghanistan and now Iraq. And as we now in 2002 know with certainty that our governments and media told us far from the complete truth in 1941 as to who was truly responsible for the attack on Pearl Harbor, so we will eventually know that those truly responsible for the attack on the Twin Towers were certainly not those primarily held up as being responsible by our governments and media.

And if some decent men in the US and Western governments wish to resist this insane drive towards World War III in the form of an overpowering drumbeat for an attack upon Iraq, then their hands will be forced by the economic crisis which will cause such troubles at home that they will be virtually forced to fight a war abroad. As Shakespeare's dying Henry IV said to the imminent Henry V (who successfully acted upon the advice): "Busy giddy minds with foreign quarrels."

A Third Lie

However, let none of us think that minds are giddy only under monarchies. Pearl Harbor and the Twin Towers are classic examples of how modern democracies must be led with lies, and we come to a third great political lie behind today's economic crisis, and that is the lie that only "democracy" is an acceptable form of government.

In either a monarchy or an aristocracy where there is an authority recognized above the people, the people could be told, with authority, "There is no such thing as a free lunch. The party is over. These and these are the measures which all of us must take to get over the crisis." As it is, if in Western democracies today a politician dares to breathe a word, for instance, against welfare or against the Jews, he knows he will be shouted down and voted out at the next election. In other words, the politicians are virtually controlled by public opinion, which is fabricated by the media, which are tightly controlled by a handful of Judeo-masons, the people who also control finance and the governments.

A Fourth Lie

Therefore, a fourth great political lie making possible today's economic crisis is the lie that modern "democracies" are government of the people, by the people, for the people. The truth is that they are secret oligarchies, i.e., government by the few, and those few are hidden.

Catholic Truth

What the Catholic Church teaches about democracy, aristocracy and monarchy (rule by all, by a few or by one) is that all three are acceptable and all three are corruptible. So God leaves any nation free to choose whichever of the three forms of government it prefers, so long as all authority is recognized to come from Him. In other words, contrary to what most people think today, the choice of democracy or aristocracy or monarchy matters much less than the godliness or godlessness of the people involved. A bad system with good people is much preferable to a good system with bad people.

THIRD LAYER: RELIGION

Democracy Idolized

This priority of goodness over systems leads by itself to the third and by far the most important layer of lies: the religious lies which make possible the political and economic lies. For when all common sense says that the people of a nation cannot lead themselves, how can it be that the mass of people, as in the West today, hold the quasi-religious belief that only rule by the people, or "democracy," is acceptable? Democracy for the Catholic Church means not that the people rule themselves, but that the people choose the ruler upon whom authority to rule the people descends from God (see Leo XIII's "Diuturum Illud"). "Democracy" for the modern world means on the contrary the sovereignty of the people. Then how did the West come not only to believe in sovereignty of the people, but also to make out of it a quasi-religion, a worldwide crusade?

A Religious Problem

The answer lies in the last 500 years of the history of the West. Before the so-called Reformation, the Catholic Church possessed the total Truth with certainty, and taught it with a divine authority to all the nations. "Woe is unto me if I preach not the Gospel," says St. Paul (I Cor. 9: 16). Woe to the Catholic Church if it does not authoritatively teach God's truth to the nations! (Mt. 28: 19)

But then came Protestantism which disputed that Truth and denied that authority, whereupon Truth at least appeared to be disputable and authority questionable. Then came the liberals – secretly led by the Freemasons – who said that since Truth is unknowable and there is no divine authority, then there only remains for the people to decide for themselves, i.e., sovereignty of the people. (And indeed if truth were unknowable and if no authority were more than human, then sovereignty of the people would be reasonable. But Catholic Truth is not made questionable merely because Protestants question it!)

It should now be clear why sovereignty of the people, like liberalism, has a quasi-religious status in so many minds today. Since Protestantism, to this day, replaces Catholicism wherever it can, it sets itself up as a replacement religion, and since liberalism unceasingly pretends to resolve all religious clashes, then it too presents itself as a substitute religion. That is why Freemasonry claims both that it is not a religion and that it is, because it is not a religion like Catholicism or (supposedly) Protestantism, but it claims to take the place of both of them, and of all other "religions," so that it serves an entirely religious function. That is why Masons and liberals push sovereignty of the people with a religious fervor. And all people who believe in no Truth or Authority are ready to follow them.

Thus the deep-seated problem of modern politics is religious, and it began with the apostasy of the West from the Catholic Church, from Our Divine Lord, and from God. That this God, His Son and His One True Church are in fact sovereign is the reason why – in reverse order of the political lies listed above – sovereignty of the people is necessarily a lie, "democracy" is not the only acceptable form of government, this economic crisis was planned to promote the interests of the enemies of God's sovereignty, and nations do not drift on self-moving economic currents but are either led towards God by His friends or are led away from Him by His enemies.

Thus as economics is directed by politics, so politics is directed by religion. So economics is directed by religion? Our Lord says so: "Seek ye first the Kingdom of God, and His justice, and all these things (food and clothing, etc.) will be added unto you" (Mt. 6: 33). Food and clothing are, after all, the basics of economics.

Bishops' Lie

That economists, politicians, Freemasons and Jews should miss out on these truths is progressively graver, but when Catholic bishops miss out on them, we have a problem far graver still, because it is then the highest ministers of God, appointed by Him to guard the religious Truth, who are betraying it. Yet what do we hear of in the last few days? The American Conference of Bishops has issued a declaration of policy that no attempt should be made any longer to convert Jews to Catholicism, because they have a still valid Covenant of their own with Almighty God!

Poor dear American Jews! You may not think it, and you may hate me for saying so, but you are being horribly betrayed! The Old Covenant between the Israelites and God came to an end with the death of Our Lord upon the Cross. From that moment on, a soul can be saved only within the New Covenant, sealed by the Blood of Our Lord flowing from the Cross. Howsoever it be with your interests in this world, which are comparatively of no importance, the eternal salvation of your souls can be secured only by your becoming members of the one true Church. And if you wanted to martyr me or anyone else for saying so, I pray we would have the courage to give you that Catholic witness!

Dear Catholics, let us, as Our Lord commands us to do, love for their eternal salvation the agents of our poor world's corruption, which is our own fault. Wars come from our own evil desires, says St. James (4: 1). Let us, as Our Lord commands us to do, respect the lawful authorities and governments over us, but let us not always believe them. Let us put no trust in the media. Let us get out of debt, as far and as soon as possible, or at least get into no new debt. Let us pray the Rosary, and let us put our trust in God and in His Blessed Mother alone.

He seems to be bringing to Winona this year some 18 new seminarians. Never despair. May He bless you.

A Congress on Vatican II

A S THE SSPX strives not to lose its Catholic footing in its on-going diplomatic war-dance with the churchmen presently in Rome, it could be helped by a Congress taking place in Paris early this month to examine the documents and fruits of the Second Vatican Council (1962 to 1965).

The reason for the Congress taking place this autumn is that October 11, 2002, is the 40th anniversary of the solemn opening in St. Peter's Basilica of that Council, which was by any reckoning a momentous event in the history of the Catholic Church. And so a number of interested priests and layfolk, drawn mainly from within the ranks of the SSPX and its followers, are meeting on October 4, 5 and 6, to take stock of 40 years of Vatican II.

That Council is intensely controversial. Some say it saved the Catholic Church, others say it is still devastating the Church, but there are three things that few Catholics deny: firstly, that Vatican II sought to bring the Church up-to-date with modern times; secondly, that that "modernization" has made today's mainstream Church almost unrecognizable from what the Catholic Church was prior to the Council; thirdly, that the highest churchmen now governing the Church in Rome,

Richard N. Williamson

from the Pope downwards, still adamantly believe in that "modernization" wrought by Vatican II. In fact that Council so governs their thinking that if in any dealings with these Romans one wishes to know with whom one is dealing, that Council is the most important thing to know. That is why the Congress in Paris may, however humbly, help the Society to see how it needs to deal with the Romans, for as long as these are in the mental grip of Vatican II.

What, then, was the Council? It was the large-scale penetration within the Catholic Church – or churchmen – of the principles governing the modern world ever since, especially, the French Revolution of 1789. Both friend and foe of the Council (e.g., Cardinal Suenens and Archbishop Lefebvre) said that it was the Church's 1789. Now one may or may not like those principles, but they are what they are, and whether or not one likes them, they will have such and such effects: "liberty," "equality," "fraternity," "the rights of man," "pluralism," are amongst the main ones, and they are objective in their working.

Now from the moment these modern principles began to gain wide acceptance, let us say from the time of the French Revolution onwards, they were clearly, firmly and repeatedly denounced by the Catholic Popes and by the Catholic Church, up until Vatican II, as being principles of godlessness which would destroy the Church and civilization if they had their way. In other words, between the modern world, as such, and the one true God, there is an irreconcilable war.

Not so, said the friends of these principles. They said that the modern world is nice, that God is nice, and so since everybody is nice, there should be an end to the war. They said that the modern principles can and should be taken into the bosom of the Church which can purify them (so says Cardinal Ratzinger) and reconcile them with the still true (?) principles of the good old Catholicism.

And these friends of the modern world, under the decisive leadership of Popes John XXIII and Paul VI, prevailed at Vatican II over the rearguard enemies of those modern principles. Now this rearguard did put up a fight against the admission of the modern principles into the Church, so that <u>the 16 final documents of Vatican II show both the ancient and the modern ideas alongside one another</u>. In fact the ancient ideas are so well represented that even a conservative like Archbishop Lefebvre underwrote 14 (some say 16) of the 16 documents.

However, the modern principles were also there. They had at last gained admission within the Catholic Church, and <u>in accordance with their objective nature</u>, they began to do their work. Their most sensational success, affecting directly or indirectly every Catholic, was the replacement in 1969 of the Tridentine Mass by the Novus Ordo Mass. From that triumph of theirs onwards, they wrought one change after another within the Church to the point that, as said, anyone who knew the Church before the Council could hardly recognize it some time afterwards as being the same Church.

Now a large number of Catholics, layfolk, priests, bishops and cardinals, welcomed these changes. At last the Church was in step with the modern world all around us. That world is not bad, they say, so thank goodness the Church no longer requires us to fight it. Everything in the Church has been renewed, they say, and the signs of the renewal are all around us. For instance, when Italian journalist Vittorio Messori interviewed recently Pope John Paul II for one of his books, it appears that he tried repeatedly to get the Pope to admit that not all the fruits of the Council were good, but the Pope would not once admit it. As an SSPX colleague stationed in Italy says, this Pope has "a mystic belief" in the Second Vatican Council.

On the other hand enemies of modern principles, and therefore of the modern world as such, say that the "renewal" has devastated the Catholic Church and is still devastating what little remains of pre-Conciliar Catholicism. That these modern principles would melt down the Church was as predictable as that heat will melt down ice, they say. Friends of modernity may claim that the modern world is changing, and that there is more and more heat, but therefore to pretend that if ice is put out into this heat, it will not melt, is ridiculous, because ice and heat have not changed their natures. Godless principles are bound by their nature to destroy the true Church of God, yesterday, today or tomorrow.

But the enemies of modernity go further. They will say that the Second Vatican Council, by conserving in its documents the ancient alongside the modern, and by thus seeming to preserve the good old Catholicism, did in fact no such thing. Just as the old elements of validity preserved in the Novus Ordo Mass helped the New Mass to be established by preventing a sane Catholic reaction of rejection of the New Mass, so the old elements of Catholicism preserved in the documents of Vatican II helped the new religion of secular humanism to be established within the Catholic Church by preventing what would otherwise have been a wholesale Catholic rejection of Vatican II and its modernized version of "Catholicism."

Therefore, say those who equate modernity with godlessness (and they have their arguments), the problem lies not in the after-Council (as many "conservatives" pretend) but in the Council itself. The problem is not that the documents have been misapplied following the Council, the problem is that the documents themselves are riddled with contradiction and ambiguity as they try to fit together heat and ice. Of course, then, both friend and foe of the old religion can appeal to the same documents. Of course, then, such documents were tailor-made to produce the civil war and havoc we have seen for 40 years within the Church.

In other words, say the enemies of modernity, whatever may have been the sincerity, good intentions, naivety, etc., of the great majority of cardinals and bishops who at the Council voted for the 16 documents, the 40 years that have passed since the Council have shown by their fruits of devastation what the small minority of Council bishops said from the very beginning, namely that modernity as such is as objectively deadly for Catholicism as heat is for ice. Therefore the Catholic Church, to save souls, must throw out every single paragraph of Vatican II, and have no further truck with, nor mercy upon, the miserable principles of modernity.

Let us hope then that the Paris Congress will help firstly to distil out of the Conciliar fruits, but especially out of the documents, the powerful underlying error. Error, not errors, because a plurality of errors not united by some central idea could never have had the hurricane-force of destruction that Vatican II had upon the Church. If one were to claim that that central idea is the putting of man in the place of God, obviously one would not be pretending that that error of errors is stated in so many words in the Council documents – rather it appears there beneath the disguise of, for instance, the "dignity of the human person."

Secondly, may the Congress show with what skill – consciously or unconsciously – the modern errors are disguised beneath ancient appearances in the Conciliar documents, so that to this day a mass of sincere "conservatives" are still deceived. By insisting on giving to the documents their Catholic interpretation, such conservatives succeed in conserving only the Novus Ordo

Richard N. Williamson

Church, which sweeps them aside! The Revolution eats her own children, says an old saying.

Thirdly, may the SSPX be helped to see that while all due respect must be shown to the churchmen who occupy the seat of Moses (Mt. 23: 2), and while all allowance may be made for their subjective sincerity and even benevolence towards the Society, nevertheless for as long as they have not shaken off the bewitchment of the Council with its reconciling of irreconcilables, they must be treated like madmen, not clinical, but ideological madmen, whose minds are no longer working. And by what sign will we know that they have recovered their non-contradictory Catholic wits? Certainly not by their blanket approval of everything the SSPX nobodies do or say. Certainly by their unconditional approval of the ancient Faith which those nobodies attempt to defend by all they do and say!

All blessings. Let us pray there be no insane onslaught upon Iraq.

Truth Prevails, Times Five

S T. THOMAS AQUINAS says that it is easier for God to create a new galaxy than to move a human being's free will. Since the Second Vatican Council in particular, churchmen have used their free will almost to destroy the Catholic Church. Surely God is now in the process of allowing souls of good will to learn the hard way that His Church cannot be destroyed. Let us give here a few indications of how the new Conciliar religion is slowly but surely grinding to a halt, while the true religion is slowly regaining strength.

Firstly, the Congress held in Paris one month ago by, mostly, SSPX priests and laity, to study the religion coming out of the Second Vatican Council, was an undoubted success. Some 60 priests were in attendance, with some two dozen layfolk, and the large majority contributed a more or less important paper examining some aspect of Vatican II.

It is impossible to pull together in one brief summary the variety of contributions on such a huge subject as, in effect, the wrecking of God's Church by God's own churchmen. What was interesting was the remarkable unity of thinking about Vatican II amongst the variety of contributors. The Society's new French District Superior had been afraid before the Congress that his French priests might all start arguing with one another – where could he have come by such an idea? – but it was the opposite that happened. Everybody agreed that Vatican II was introducing a new humanistic religion, unacceptable to Catholics.

Of course, in a way it was not surprising that priests of that Society which was raised by God in the wake of Vatican II to defend the true Faith, should find themselves all in agreement as to the profound harmfulness of that Council. Nevertheless, the priests' interest and unity in dismantling the Council were reassuring. In particular, the SSPX faithful in France, like, I think, a number of yourselves, were glad to know that their priests were attacking Vatican II, and coming to no soft conclusions about it.

A second indicator of the weakness of the Conciliar churchmen is their on-going interest in talking with the SSPX. For decades now they have been pretending that we are "divisive," "disobedient," "schismatic," and, since 1988, "excommunicated," so one would think that our goose had long been cooked, as the expression goes. However, it must be that the Romans still see the goose waddling around, because here is an instance of their coming back to the attack, but with "plausible deniability," i.e., by such channels as will enable them at any time to deny they ever did any such thing. Here is the approach:

> A crisis is coming in the Church. Things cannot go on like they are now. We want to avoid another long freeze, or war for another 40 years. We want a solution within a very short time. The SSPX has also made its mistakes, but it is in the best situation it has ever been in (!). However, it needs to move a little, from Tradition to transition. Realism requires dialogue, dialogue

requires that the two sides meet. Providence will help, if only the two sides do meet.

Pope John Paul II wants a solution. He can make a deal with the SSPX, as his successor will not be able to do. Perhaps Cardinal Castrillón will be the next Pope, but if he becomes Pope he will no longer be able to make the same offer, of a deal which even Archbishop Lefebvre would not have refused.

Cardinal Castrillón wants to do what is right. He has power, and he has access to Pope John Paul. He can get for the SSPX all it wants, but he cannot change the Newchurch overnight. Let the SSPX visit the new Traditional bishop in Campos, approved by Rome, Bishop Rifan, to see how Tradition can obtain anything it wants from Rome. The offer to the SSPX now is of unconditional approval within weeks.

Now Rome may absolutely – and plausibly – deny that it made any such approach to anyone in the SSPX. However, it seems to me also plausible that such a well-constructed approach is entirely what might have come from Rome. In which case I would reply for my own part to the eminent Cardinal that the one thing which the SSPX wishes for from Rome is the one thing which his channels took care to say he could not provide – an end to the Newchurch cuckoo's occupying the Catholic Church's nest.

Nevertheless, a third indicator suggests that there is perhaps – perhaps – more to this approach by Cardinal Castrillón than meets the eye. It is reported by a Dominican priest from Rome that around the end of last July and the first part of August, the Blessed Virgin Mary appeared some dozen times to Pope John Paul II to warn him that the crisis in the Church is going to grow alarmingly worse. The Pope was hurt. She said nothing about events in the world. All prominent figures in the Curia and the Vatican know about these apparitions, but no-

Richard N. Williamson

body is saying a word. Apparently the apparitions are a serious affair, and not to be shrugged off lightly.

Again, few things are made to seem so plausibly deniable as apparitions of the Blessed Mother of God, but again, an alarming intensification of the crisis in the Church is, in the present situation, all too likely. If then Cardinal Castrillón's apparent desire to re-open dialogue with the SSPX is at all motivated by any such warning from the Blessed Virgin, then we are no longer dealing merely with Roman politics, but we are hearing a stifled call for help.

To which the reply still remains that the SSPX cannot provide the solution by joining in the problem. If anybody thinks – correctly – that the SSPX has its hands on the solution, that is precisely because it has now for decades, without ceasing to belong to the Church, stood away from the Newchurch. As the Newchurch flounders and drowns in midstream of the modern world, the greatest service that the SSPX can render to the many victims which the Newchurch is sweeping away to perdition is to run alongside them on the bank of Tradition, but in no way to jump off that bank into the perilous waters. With all due respect, Your Eminence, you need to move more than a little, from transition to Tradition.

A fourth indicator of the weakness of Conciliarism, or the danger of Vatican II, is the recently appeared book *Animus Delendi II*, by Atila Sinke Guimarães. This is the fifth volume in his eleven-volume series, *Eli, Eli, Lama Sabachtani*, documenting the betrayal of the Catholic Faith by the thinkers, writers and leaders of Vatican II. The first and fourth volumes, *The Murky Waters of Vatican II* and *Animus Delendi I* are the only other volumes of the series so far to have appeared. If Mr. Guimarães after Volume I jumped to Volumes IV and V, it is because he wished to denounce in public as soon as possible the desire to destroy ("animus delendi" in Latin) which truly animated the master spirits of the Council.

Volumes I and IV were briefly presented in this seminary Letter in July of last year. I would like to come back to Volume V in a future letter, because while charity "rejoiceth not in iniquity," it does "rejoice with the truth" (I Cor. 13: 6), and Mr. Guimarães has rendered great service to the truth by piling quotation upon quotation to prove how far from the truth Vatican II was pulled by minds seeking to be modern.

The fifth indicator is more positive, giving us the Catholic answer to the apostasy implicit in the ambiguities of Vatican II. It is the book *Marcel Lefebvre* written in a chaste and noble French by Bishop Tissier de Mallerais, one of the Society's four bishops consecrated by Archbishop Lefebvre in 1988.

Bishop Tissier was an intimate collaborator of the Archbishop from the beginning of the SSPX in the late 1960's through to the Archbishop's death in 1991. It might then be thought that Bishop Tissier was too close to the Archbishop to have been able to write an objective story of his life. However, this monumental book, fruit of ten years' hard labor, seems liable to remain the most complete biography of the Archbishop for some time to come. It certainly presents the Archbishop as I knew him, with those supreme qualities of godliness, selflessness and objectivity which enabled him to stand up to the raging subjectivism of the modernized churchmen. I will certainly return to this noble book, as soon as the English translation appears.

Dear readers, God's Truth will win. Let us only pray that as many free wills as possible allow it to win them over before they are lost for ever.

Newchurch "Canonizations"

THE OCTOBER 6 "canonization" of Msgr. Escrivá de Balaguer, founder of the "Opus Dei," like the September "beatification" of Pope John XXIII, launcher of Vatican II, re-opens an old and hurtful wound – how can the Catholic Church do such things? And if it is not the Catholic Church that is doing them, what is it?

For indeed it is clear beyond any doubt that the Catholic Church prior to Vatican II, when she was still essentially faithful to Catholic Tradition, would never have beatified the Pope who initiated the Council which devastated that Tradition, nor canonized the founder of "Opus Dei," an organization preparing the way for that Council.

There is an abundance of quotes, proudly published by "Opus Dei" itself, to prove that Msgr. Escrivá shared and promoted key ideas of Vatican II. Here are two: Msgr. Escrivá himself said, "Ours is the first organization which, with the authorization of the Holy See, admits non-Catholics, Christian or non-Christian. I have always defended liberty of conscience" ("Conversaciones con Mons. Escrivá", ed. Rialp, p.296). And his successor at the head of "Opus Dei" said about Msgr. Escrivá's book *Camino*, "It prepared millions of people to get in tune with, and to accept in depth, some of the most revolutionary teachings which 30 years later would be solemnly promulgated by the Church at Vatican II" ("Estudios sobre 'Camino'", Msgr. Alvaro del Portillo, ed. Rialp, p.58).

Therefore, for Pope John XXIII to have been truly a Blessed, and for Msgr. Escrivá to have been truly a Saint, the Second Vatican Council would have to have been a true Council, or a Council true to Catholic Tradition. Which is ridiculous, as at least regular readers of this Letter know. Yet are not Catholic canonizations meant to be infallible?

Indeed before Vatican II, Catholic theologians agreed that canonizations (not beatifications) of Saints were virtually infallible, for two main reasons. Firstly, the proposing of model Catholics to be venerated and imitated as Saints is so central to Catholics' practice of their faith, that Mother Church could hardly be mistaken in the matter. This being so, secondly, the pre-Vatican II Popes took such care in examining candidates for canonization, and successful candidates they canonized with such solemnity, that their act of canonizing was as close as could be to a pronouncement of the Popes' solemn and infallible magisterium.

But since Vatican II, firstly the models chosen for imitation are liable, like John XXIII and Msgr. Escrivá, to be chosen for their alignment on Vatican II, i.e., on the destruction of Catholic Tradition, and secondly, the formerly strict process of examination of candidates has been so loosened under the Vatican II popes and there has followed such a flood of canonizations under JP2, that the whole process of canonizing has lost, together with its solemnity, any likelihood of infallibility. Indeed, how can JP2 intend to do anything infallible, or therefore do it, when he often acts and talks, for instance about "living tradition," as though Truth can change?

So this or that Saint "canonized" by JP2 may in fact be in Heaven, even Msgr. Escrivá, God knows, but it is certainly not his "canonization" by this Pope which can make us sure of the fact. Nor need we then feel obliged to venerate any of the post-Vatican II "Saints."

Which leaves us with the problem we began with: the Catholic Church has the divine promise of indefectibility, i.e. it cannot fail ("Behold, I am with you all days, even to the consummation of the world" – Mt. 28: 20). Then how can canonizations, which are meant through infallibility to partake in that indefectibility, fail, by partaking instead in Vatican II? Are we not obliged to admit either that Vatican II was not so bad after all (as the priests of Campos are now doing), or else that the sedevacantists are right after all in saying that John Paul II is not really pope? Sedevacantism would explain any amount of fallibility on his part!

The SSPX, following Archbishop Lefebvre (1905–1991), adopts neither the Conciliar nor the sedevacantist solution. It believes that the Second Vatican Council was amongst the greatest disasters in the history of the Catholic Church, yet it considers that the popes who promoted that Council and its ideas (John XXIII, Paul VI, John Paul I, and John Paul II) were or are true popes. How can that be? How can true popes so act as to destroy the true Church?

Firstly, God creates all of us human beings free, with free will, because He does not want robots in His Heaven. That applies also to the churchmen, to whom He chooses to entrust His Catholic Church. These have therefore an astonishing degree of freedom to build up or to destroy the Church. For instance, when Our Lord asks if He will find the Faith when He comes back on earth (Lk. 18: 8), we know for certain that by men's (not only churchmen's) fault, the Catholic Church will be very small at the Second Coming.

However Our Lord also promised that the gates of Hell would never prevail against His Church (Mt. 16: 18), and so we also know for certain that God will never allow the wickedness of men to go so far as to destroy His Church completely. In this certainty that the Church will never completely fail lies her indefectibility, and since the first function of the Church is to teach Our Lord's doctrine of salvation, then upon indefectibility in existing follows infallibility in teaching. For souls of good will, the Catholic Church and her Truth will always be there.

So the Catholic Church to the end of time will never cease, on however small a scale, to make heard amongst men the doctrine of salvation, the Deposit of the Faith. From eternity this doctrine proceeds from God the Father to God the Son, it was faithfully entrusted by the Incarnate God to His Apostles, and it has been handed down as unchanging Tradition through the successors of the Apostles ever since. "Heaven and earth shall pass away, but my words shall not pass away," says Our Lord (Lk. 21: 33). In fact unchangingness is so essential to this doctrine, that conformity with Tradition is the criterion of the Church's infallible ordinary magisterium. In other words if one wants to know what cannot be false in the day-to-day teaching of the Church's teachers, the way to tell is to measure what is being said against what the Church has said down all the centuries. If it corresponds to Tradition, the teaching is infallible, and if it does not, it is not infallible. Moreover, the Church's infallible extraordinary magisterium is the servant of this ordinary magisterium, insofar as it provides a divinely protected guarantee that such and such a doctrine belongs within the Church's true doctrine, i.e., within ordinary Tradition.

Therefore Tradition, or conformity with what the Church has always taught, is the ultimate yardstick or measure of the Church's infallible teaching, ordinary or extraordinary. Therefore anything outside Tradition is fallible, and anything contradicting Tradition is certainly false, for instance the new Vatican II teaching on religious liberty and ecumenism. But John XXIII was beatified, and Msgr. Escrivá was "canonized," for their sympathy with these Conciliar novelties. Therefore such "canonizations" are certainly to some extent contrary to Catholic Tradition, and to that extent they are automatically not infallible, without my having to examine any further. "If an angel from Heaven preach a gospel to you besides that which we have preached to you, let him be anathema" (Gal. 1: 8).

So if one asks how it can be God's own churchmen who do so much damage to His Church, the answer is that He gives them great freedom, short of letting them completely destroy His Church, and because out of any evil they do he will bring some greater good. For instance, out of dubious canonizations he can bring to "Traditional Catholics" a still better grasp of the primacy of Tradition.

And to the question how canonizations, meant to be infallible, can instead be Conciliar, the answer is that if God allows a pope to believe in Vatican II, He may surely also allow him to take action and to "canonize" in accordance with Vatican II, and to loosen the strict old rules of true canonization which virtually guaranteed the candidate's conformity with Tradition. If Catholics are misled who blindly follow Church authority when it goes astray, that is their own problem, but Catholics who follow Tradition will, on St. Paul's command, with prudence, "anathematize" any clear departure from it.

So we may absolutely refuse Vatican II and all its pomps and all its works and yet not have to become sedevacantists, so long as we understand that Church indefectibility does not mean that large parts of the

Church will never be destroyed, only that the Church will never be completely destroyed. Similarly Church infallibility does not mean that the Church's teachers will never teach untruth by, for instance, dubious "canonizations," only that, amongst other truths, the truth of Christian sanctity will never be totally falsified or silenced.

In conclusion, these more or less Conciliar "canonizations" are correspondingly fallible, and are automatically not infallible. Obviously, Padre Pio was an entirely Traditional Saint, and we need not doubt the worthiness of his canonization. However, it might be advisable not to profit by his Newchurch "canonization" to venerate him officially or in public, insofar as that might be liable to give to other Newchurch "canonizations" a credit which is not due to them.

Dear readers, I must warmly thank all of you whose spiritual and material support has carried the seminary through a remarkably happy calendar year. All September's entrants are still with us, in fact two more have come! Very many thanks.

And let me wish all of you a happy Christmas free of sentimentalism, but forgive me if I again invite you to send me no cards, because I am abroad until early January. Get sentimental about my poor desk!

Is It Just to Attack Iraq?

H APPY NEW YEAR! Alas, as the years spin by the world seems to get no happier, but "we know that to them that love God, all things work together unto good, to such as, according to his purpose, are called to be saints" (Rom. 8: 28). So a soul of good will can use even today's darkening scene as a stepping-stone towards God. However, let us attempt to cast His light upon a major element of darkness today – the impending attack to be led by the United States on Iraq.

For months now the media in the Western nations have been presenting this attack as being just and inevitable, yet it seems that both the US military and the US people still have grave reservations. The time to think about the justice and wisdom of such an attack is certainly now, before it starts. Once war begins, truth is liable to be one of the first casualties, smothered beneath "My country, right or wrong." But God is with truth, not with untruths, however "patriotic" they are made to seem. My own country, England, was ruined by Catholics at the Reformation putting in front of God their "patriotic" King or Queen.

Now when it comes to judging of the justice of a war, the Catholic Church has clear <u>principles</u>, which are basically common sense, at least of a sane mind. Then for the application of those principles to a particular situation, she has further guidelines of prudence, which are also common sense. Often, the confusion of our godless times will make unclear the rightness or wrongness of a particular war, but the wrongness of the attack on Iraq seems to be so clear that apparently not even the Pope and American bishops are confused!

Let us begin with the principles of a just war in general. Classically (cf. St. Thomas Aquinas' *Summa Theologiae*, IIa-IIae q.40 art. 1), three CONDITIONS must be met for a war to be just: it must be declared and waged, firstly, by the lawful authority of a sovereign entity; secondly, for an objectively just cause; and thirdly, with a subjectively right intention (even if the cause is just, I may not fight for it out of greed, cruelty, etc.).

The first condition needs no explanation – the State alone has the right to make war. As to the second condition, there are three MOTIVES for a war that make it just: either *defense* against an unjust attack, or *recovery* of something unjustly taken, or *punishment* of an unjust aggression. As to the third condition, since all men are bound to intend to do good and to shun evil, then war may only be waged with the intention of arriving at a just peace, which is the tranquility of a just order of things – to each his own, to each nation its due.

Then if all three conditions are fulfilled for a particular war, the Church teaches that I must consider the war in the light of practical prudence, according to four guidelines, or CIRCUMSTANCES, which are still common sense: firstly, the good to be gained by restoring justice must more than outweigh the evils that will come with war (especially modern war!); secondly, it must be as certain as can be that there really was an injustice committed; thirdly, this injustice must have harmed major and not just minor interests of the State injured;

and fourthly, war must be the sole means available of re-establishing justice.

Now let us apply these principles and guidelines to the impending attack on Iraq.

First CONDITION: is it the lawful civil authority of the State which is declaring and planning to wage the war? Here in the USA, it would seem so. By the US Constitution, Congress alone has authority to approve a US declaration of war, and it seems that President Bush has obtained that Congressional approval for war upon Iraq. Congressmen may have been under undue pressure, like Pontius Pilate, but like him they made their authoritative decision.

Second CONDITION: is the cause for which the attack on Iraq has been approved either <u>defense</u> against an unjust Iraqi attack, or <u>recovery</u> of something Iraq unjustly took, or <u>punishment</u> of unjust Iraqi aggression? As to the first motive, Iraq has attacked nobody since its attack on Kuwait (green-lighted beforehand by the US ambassador in Baghdad) in 1990. As to the second motive, Iraq has taken nothing since it took Kuwait, which it was forced to restore in the Gulf War of 1991. As to the third motive, there has been no Iraqi aggression since it invaded Kuwait, for which it has been punished by UN sanctions and US and UK bombing ever since. Surely none of the three motives supply just cause for a fresh attack now on Iraq.

Of course things are not always what they appear to be, so what can look like aggression may in fact be self-defense, as when I shoot a criminal just before I know he will shoot me. A classic example is provided by Hitler's June 1941 invasion of Russia. All our history books say Hitler was the aggressor, but historians are now discovering the evidence that Stalin had amassed on the German-Russian frontier a huge army to invade Europe, only "Barbarossa" beat Stalin to the punch by two weeks. Thus what looked like aggression on Hitler's part was – at least in this case – self-defense. Similarly it is now being argued that a "pre-emptive strike" against Iraq may look like aggression, but is in fact self-defense, thus fulfilling the second condition of a just war.

However, again common sense says that the danger of being attacked must be real and imminent to turn aggression into self-defense, otherwise I would have to shoot anybody I saw merely carrying a gun! But where is the evidence today that Iraq is about to attack anyone? Mere possession of weapons does not prove imminent intent to use them. Israel possesses a huge store of ABC (atomic, biological, chemical) weapons, and they are a threat to all Arab states. Yet who talks of the need of a "pre-emptive strike" against Israel, or against North Korea, known to possess such weapons? Why then against Iraq?

We come to the third CONDITION for a just war, namely that it must be waged with an upright INTENTION. Alas, everybody knows that the United States and Great Britain in particular are far from disinterested where Iraq's oil is concerned, from the Bush family and Vice-President Cheney downwards. Oil in the Caspian basin – a large part of our reason for invading Afghanistan – is apparently proving neither so plentiful nor so easy of access as was at first thought, so it is back to the Persian Gulf for our needs, where Iraq's underground supply is second only to Saudi Arabia's. After decades and decades of US and GB intervention in the Persian Gulf, let us just say that the uprightness of their intentions in the project of this latest attack in the area is somewhat less than clear.

To sum up, the attack on Iraq meets in the USA the first condition for a just war, but not the second, and very doubtfully the third. This conclusion is only confirmed when we review in addition the four prudential guidelines or CIRCUMSTANCES.

Richard N. Williamson

Firstly, is it clear that starting a war in the Middle East today will do more good than harm? Nothing is less clear! Attacking Iraq could stir the whole Arab world to fury, and easily start a process leading to World War III. At the least, Arabs now present in the USA could be provoked into acts of that very terrorism which the attack on Iraq is supposed to be preventing!

Second circumstantial consideration: is it <u>certain</u> that Iraq has committed an injustice? As for the Sept. 11 attack on the USA, even assuming that Al-Qaeda was responsible, no evidence has been given us for any connection between that terrorist group and Iraq. As for possessing weapons of mass destruction, why should that be any more of an injustice on Iraq's part than it is on Israel's or North Korea's?

Third circumstance: is it major and not just minor interests of the United States or its allies that have been unjustly harmed or threatened? Certainly the Arabs would take out Israel altogether if they could, which is a major interest for Israel, but is that altogether unjust on the Arabs' part, when we know how Israel treats Palestinians and how it plans to treat all Iraqis, Iranians and Syrians occupying land marked out for "Greater Israel"? And is Israel's survival a major interest for the United States? What has Israel done for the United States in the Middle East besides make it more and more hated by all Arabs?

Fourth circumstance: is an attack on Iraq the only means of re-establishing justice? Clearly not! Even assuming – an astonishing assumption when one comes to think of it – that Iraq has no right to possess weapons of which Israel has an abundance, Iraq has so far submitted to a good deal of UN inspection on this point. The alternatives to war are not yet exhausted.

So neither the conditions nor the circumstances of a just war seem to be present. Then why the fervor and the fever and the escalating preparations for war?

An old saying runs, "Whom the gods wish to destroy, they first make mad." The Western nations are going mad, because they have for centuries now turned away from the true God, and from the one true Church which He instituted for their salvation (Mt. 28: 18).

By a just punishment of God, it is virtually impossible to name the main human agents of the confusion amongst, for instance, the US people and the US military, because the nations have said to God, "We are more enlightened than You are, so Your enemies are no longer our enemies." That the ensuing disorientation is indeed deep down religious is shown by its crusading character. Abandoning God has left a vacuum in the Western nations' lives which cries out to be turned into a crusade against any enemy of Liberalism, Iraq being merely the present one.

Kyrie, eleison. Christe, eleison. Kyrie, eleison. Throughout the New Year, God will remain perfectly in control. It will be a grace of His if events drive us to trust more and more entirely in Him. Mother of God, pray for us!

Nice Rome not Nice Enough

O NE AMONGST A thousand marvelous sayings of St. Augustine is the principle, "In things certain, unity; in things doubtful, liberty; in all things, charity." If there were in the Catholic Church today little confusion, there would be much certainty and we could expect much unity, but since there is much confusion and much doubt, surely we must allow for a corresponding degree of liberty. Speaking for myself, I am sure that the SSPX has the long term solution to the Church's present confusion. The confusion comes from the attempt to mix Catholicism with the principles of the modern world. The solution is to denounce those principles and to refuse even the least mixture. Now one cannot expect all Catholics to understand that, or to accept it, in the twinkling of an eye, but it behooves me to explain patiently why I am so sure the SSPX is right. Let me then gently answer a recent editorial by a – to all appearances – honorable priest in a – to many appearances – honorable monthly Catholic magazine in the United States. I could name both, but in order to stick to the issues, let me leave out names.

"Souls are the only issue," says the editorialist, Fr. J., and because of two recent experiences in which he saw souls being hurt, he made in his editorial a two-edged appeal, to the authorities in Rome on the one side and to the Superior General of the SSPX on the other, to come to an understanding. The first experience was in Rome, where Fr. J. saw a young Fraternity of St. Peter priest being at the last moment forbidden to celebrate in St. Peter's Basilica an early morning Tridentine Mass for a Latin Mass pilgrimage. The second experience was in Ridgefield, Connecticut, where after an SSPX priest in our Retreat House had celebrated the funeral Mass for a devout girl to whom both he and Fr. J. had ministered, Fr. J. found himself being invited by the priest to conduct the burial ritual at the graveside, which he gladly did.

So Fr. J.'s editorial appealed to Rome to grant to traditionally-minded Catholics a canonical structure which would protect them from harassment by diocesan personnel who feel threatened by any manifestation of pre-Conciliar spirituality. And on the other side the ed-itorial appealed to the SSPX's Superior General, Bishop Bernard Fellay, to consider very seriously the Pope's of-fer to the SSPX of a "universal apostolic administration." Fr. J. suggests that Archbishop Lefebvre would have ac-cepted such an offer, because "souls aren't the real issue; they're the only issue."

Dear Fr. J., yours is, if I may say so, a noble appeal. You surely grasp the primacy of souls, and the value of pre-Conciliar – meaning Catholic – spirituality. But have you grasped the full depth of the religious war – no less – raging now for 40 years between Conciliarism and Catholicism? Roman or diocesan Conciliarists are of course perfectly free to present to you their side of the case, and they may persuade you that the SSPX and those who think like it are proud, intransigent, divisive, lacking in charity, etc. But let me here present to you

Richard N. Williamson

the SSPX's understanding of the matter. And let me start with a parable, from arithmetic.

In olden days, everybody used to think that two and two made four, to the point that nobody even doubted it! But then came modern science, engineering, technology and computers, and people began to doubt the old fashioned arithmetic. It was, they came to feel, very narrow and limiting and uncreative to think that two and two could only make four! On the contrary it was broad-minded and progressive and up-to-date and altogether more free to think that they might make five, or six or why not sixty-seven! So one fine day all the arithmeticians woke up to discover that they felt that two and two could make any number they wanted them to make! And since the arithmeticians were all into this New Arithmetic together, then to enjoy their new freedom together, they threw a great party, and they rejoiced exceedingly in their total liberation from two and two making exclusively and only four! What a feeling of freedom!

But then an unpleasant rumor arose amongst them: there was in the boondocks an old arithmetic teacher, named Back Ward, who would not go along with the New Arithmetic. He was apparently still insisting that two and two could only make four! "Hey, he's going to spoil our fun," they said. "He must join in the party!" So they sent a delegation to Back Ward, to bring him around. Whereupon the following conversation ensued:

Del: Hey, Back, what's wrong with you? Join in the fun! The whole world is now arithmetically free, except you! We're enjoying ourselves! We're in tune with the modern world! Why are you raining on our parade?

B.W.: Arithmetic is a question of truth. Two and two can only make four.

Del.: Of course it is a question of truth! We all know that! And we all know that two and two make four. But

— 332 —

now we know that they can make five or fifteen <u>as well as</u> just making four! We have <u>broadened</u> truth!

B.W.: But truth is what it is, independently of all of us arithmeticians. None of us can make two and two equal anything other than what they equal.

Del.: <u>Of course</u> truth is what it is! But what it is is <u>broader</u> now than what it was. We have freedom today!

B.W.: But truth cannot change, nor can it be changed.

Del.: <u>Of course</u> truth can't be changed! But we're not changing it. We are merely discovering an extra dimension of truth that modern times have revealed. After all, we're no longer peasants!

B.W.: But two and two can still only make four!!

Del.: <u>Of course</u> two and two make four! But can't you get it into your head that <u>at the same time</u> they can make six or sixty? Computers today can work wonders!

B.W.: Look, if you say two and two can at one and the same time make four or five or six, then you are completely dissolving arithmetic! No number is then what it is, it can be any other number, you have total confusion!

Del.: You think we're confused? We're liberated! We're H-A-P-P-Y!

B.W.: Oh, go to – Heaven!

Del.: Now, you're not being nice. Be careful. If you're not nice, if you don't join us, then we may make things nasty for you!

B.W.: Be my guest. I would rather think straight on my own than think crooked with the whole world.

At which point the delegates gave up trying to persuade Back Ward. But they were resolved in their own minds that he should not be allowed to continue to rain on their parade, and already on their way home they were planning sticks (and even carrots!) with which to bring, or force, him over. And the sticks and carrots continue to this day!

Richard N. Williamson

Dear Fr. J., between Conciliarism and Catholicism lies the gulf that lies between two totally different ideas of truth. The gulf could not be deeper. And when the Conciliarists – like, surely, our present Pope – sincerely believe that they believe in Catholicism at the same time that they also believe in Conciliarism, that proves that they have no real grasp of Catholicism, just as the arithmetician who believes that he believes that two and two make four, even while he also believes that they can make five or whatever, proves that he is a dissolver of arithmetic with no understanding at all of what makes arithmetic.

Of course, that two and two making four EXCLUDES two and two making anything else is clear to anybody with a grain of common sense. It is, admittedly, less clear that the Nicene Creed excludes Conciliarism. But – one clear example – Pope Pius XI's *Mortalium Animos* excludes today's ecumenism. Yet today's ecumenists do not think so! "'Mortalium Animos' was valid in the 1920's", they will say, "but not from the 1960's onwards." In other words, Truth swings with swinging decades!

Fr. J., are you getting a glimmer of the problem? The Second Vatican Council rests upon principles so opposed to the Catholic Faith that for a Catholic to believe in that Council is like an arithmetician believing that two and two can make both four and five, either at the same time or alternatingly. But to believe such a thing, even alternatingly, is to dissolve arithmetic. Similarly to believe in the Council, even a little bit, is to dissolve the Catholic Faith.

Now all of today's Romans that have any clout believe more or less in Vatican II. Therefore they have all more or less dissolved the Faith in their own heads, and they are – with however good intentions – dissolving it in the heads of all Catholics worldwide who are following and obeying Rome. The problem could not be more grave, because this dissolution of truth, at a supernatural or natural level, rots the mind. Whosoever accepts Vatican II will end up losing his mind, while still persuaded that he is being Catholic, following the Pope, etc. etc. And who loses his mind is well on the way to losing his soul. It is all about souls!

You may ask where all this began, and how it ends. It began, let us say, 700 years ago, in the High Middle Ages, when men began to detach their minds from reality and attach them to fantasy. The process took a giant step forwards with the philosophy of Immanuel Kant (1724–1804). St. Pius X said, "Kantism is the modern heresy." In brief, Kant makes truth no longer objective, but subjective, depending upon man's subjective desires or perceptions.

And where does it end? In my gentle opinion the process is today too far gone to end in anything other than a gigantic reality check, human and/or divine. A human World War III is at our doors, but as WWI and WWII were not enough to make modern man change course, so one may doubt whether even a cataclysmic WWIII would bring 21st century man to his knees. In which case the Lord God Himself may well intervene, because the Triumph of the Immaculate Heart promised by Our Lady at Fatima and still to come suggests we are not yet at the end of the world. But her Heart cannot triumph amongst Kantians. That is why God may intervene. When in the time of Noah He cleaned up mankind with the Flood, He promised He would never use water again for that purpose. I conclude that Kantism will be cleaned out of the Catholic Church by a deluge of fire...

Dear Fr. J., do read the enclosed letter of Bishop Fellay. He does not speak of a deluge of fire, but he does ask the key question: if Rome wants to offer to the SSPX the most magnificent and suitable of "apostolic administrations," would they found it upon the shifting sands of

Vatican II, or upon the Rock of Peter? That says it all, in a nutshell. The SSPX must wait for Romans to climb back onto the Rock of Peter. Until then, we must pray and do penance. Pray especially the true Mass and the Rosary, do penance especially in Lent, coming up.

May God have mercy upon us all! Dear Friends and Benefactors, always, thank you.

Iraq War – In God We Trust

THE BEGINNING OF Lent is always a time to reflect on great truths of God, of life and death, but when war seems imminent as it does now in the Middle East, then there is particular reason to remember that God is in command of events, and that He directs them, strange though that may sometimes seem, for nothing other than for the eternal salvation of the immortal soul of each one of us.

War does seem imminent. The United States (and Great Britain) have over the last several months transported to the Middle East such a mass of troops and weapons that it is hard to imagine them being pulled out again with no action. And since each day hotter at this time of year makes desert warfare more difficult, then an attack soon is all the more likely.

Now it is usual for those who start a war to think they know what they are doing when they start it, but none of them can tell for certain how it will end. That is determined by God. A classic case was World War I, into which the nations of Europe gaily launched, each thinking it would conquer with ease in a matter of weeks. In fact the attack turned into a four-year slugfest, attended by all the horrors of modern trench warfare, which nobody but God had foreseen. Yet anybody with a grain of faith can see how these horrors were a just punishment of the godlessness of those nations, so gifted by God and so misusing their gifts. In brief, especially with war, "Man proposes while God disposes."

For even by the severity of His punishment of those European nations, God was still loving them. Proverbs 3: 11–12 – "My son, neglect not the discipline of the Lord; neither be thou wearied whilst thou art rebuked by him. For whom the Lord loveth, He chastiseth; and He scourgeth every son whom He receiveth." Having quoted which verse, St. Paul adds that a nation – or person – not chastised by God is not loved by Him! – "Persevere under discipline. God dealeth with you as with His sons; for what son is there whom the father doth not correct? But if you be without chastisement, whereof all are made partakers, then are you bastards and not sons" (Hebrews 2: 7, 8). Thus God even chastises out of love.

This is especially clear if one compares the chastisements of this life with the eternal pains of the next. Who with a grain of faith does not cry out with St. Augustine, "O Lord, chastise me how You like on earth, so long as You do not have to chastise me in Hell"? In World War I, the heroic priests in the trenches (on both sides) certainly absolved and sent to Heaven hundreds of thousands of young men of whom God knew that they would have lost their souls in an enervating peace such as we have "enjoyed" since 1945, especially since the 1960's. And in World War II, when a privileged soul able to converse with Our Lord (Sister Consolata Betrone) complained to him of all the young men being killed in the flower of their youth, Our Lord reminded her that by dying young for their country, many more of them were saving their souls for eternity than would otherwise have been the case.

At which point an objector may ask, then why is God not chastising us all the time with uninterrupted horrors? To which objection common sense immediately replies that if God dealt out to men nothing but chastisements, few of us would have enough faith to understand what He was doing and still believe in His goodness, so that, again, few would save their souls. Therefore good things in our life, like peace, God gives us, and evil things in our life, like war, He allows, both minutely calibrated for each of us with a view to our eternal salvation.

For He wishes each one of us to save our souls (I Tim. 2: 4), but He will not take away our free will, because, so to speak, He does not want to fill His Heaven with robots. But just as to move a donkey it takes sometimes the carrot and sometimes the stick, so to move a human being with free will it takes sometimes prosperity to encourage him and sometimes hardship to chasten him. God being goodness itself, He would much rather draw us to Him by His gifts, which is why each of us every day receives from Him a series of blessings, but with our tendency to enjoy the gifts while forgetting the Giver, all too many of these escape our attention, so that we need hardship to bring us back to Him.

Before dying, Moses gave this same warning to Israelites, of how earthly prosperity can make us forget God. In Deuteronomy 8: 7–10, Moses lists a few of the material benefits that God will bestow upon the Israelites in the Promised Land (recalling the benefits bestowed upon the inhabitants of "America the Beautiful"!). Then Moses warns: "Take heed, and beware lest at any time thou forget the Lord thy God, and neglect His commandments and judgments and ceremonies, which I command thee this day: lest after thou hast eaten and art filled, thou hast built goodly houses, and dwelt in them, and shalt have herds of oxen and flocks of sheep, and

Richard N. Williamson

plenty of gold and of silver, and of all things, thy heart be lifted up, and thou remember not the Lord thy God, Who brought thee out of the land of Egypt, out of the house of bondage... lest thou shouldst say in thy heart: My own might and the strength of my own hand have achieved all these things for me" (Deut. 8: 11–17).

Moses concludes: "But remember the Lord thy God, that He hath given thee strength... But if thou forget the Lord thy God, and follow strange gods" (such as idolized democracy or technology!), "and serve and adore them: behold now I foretell thee that thou shalt utterly perish. As the nations, which the Lord destroyed at thy entrance" (of Israel into the Holy Land), "so shall you also perish, if you be disobedient to the voice of the Lord your God" (Deut. 8: 18–20).

It follows that as prosperity can be a punishment if it leads away from God, so hardship can be a blessing if it leads back to God. "In suffering is learning," chanted Aeschylus in ancient Greece. Americans today call it the "school of hard knocks." Therefore God can punish or bless by hardship, just as He can bless or punish by prosperity. Therefore what are truly prosperity and hardship can only be judged in the light of God, which is more or less hidden from us human beings, especially by our sins.

However, that God is all-knowing, all-powerful and all-good, is certain. So, since He knows all that could or will happen to us down to the minutest detail, then we know that He can see the prosperity or hardship best able to bring us to Heaven or stop us falling too deeply into Hell. And since He has all power over every creature (for instance, over the weather on a battlefield), then we know that He can organize the comfort or hardship best suited to the welfare of our souls while still leaving them free. And since He is infinitely good, then we know that He will do so, in accordance with His divine Wisdom so far above our own. Therefore we can and must trust God. In particular we must place our trust in the Sacred Heart, human carrier of the Divine Love.

So we may safely leave in God's hands how events will turn in the Middle East, while we pray fervently for the salvation of souls, God's own desire, whichever way He may dispose events. If no attack takes place, it will certainly look like a mercy of God, but then we must pray for souls not to be internetted by the devil in the on-going materialistic peace. And if an attack does take place and our own armed forces conquer with ease, again it will look like a mercy of God, but it could be a curse, so we would have to pray for our nations not to make an arrogant or unjust use of their victory.

On the other hand if the attack brought great hardship and even defeat upon our military, it might not truly be the curse that it would look like, so we should pray that our nations would humble themselves beneath the mighty hand of God, who would have directed our sufferings. And finally, even if the attack on Iraq were to let loose World War III – also possible – we could and should trust still that it was the goodness of God chastising the entire world, and we should pray more than ever for the salvation of the greatest possible number of souls, all over the world.

For whosoever appear to be our main enemies on earth (they are certainly not those represented as such by the vile media), the real enemies of mankind are the enemies of our eternal salvation, namely "principalities and powers, rulers of the world of this darkness, spirits of wickedness in the high places" (Eph. 6: 12), meaning the fallen angels or devils who do all that God allows them to do to bring our souls down to Hell with them.

That is why with this letter we are enclosing for readers in the USA, besides the usual Retreats flyer and a card to encourage Lenten benefactors, also the card of a prayer revealed to a Catholic soul in the 19th century, a prayer specially designed to appeal to the Mother of God for help in our fight against the devils let loose in modern times: Noble Queen of the Heavens, obtain from your Divine Son mercy for us in our overwhelming distress!

NO. 232 | APRIL 4, 2003

For Ever . . . And Ever . . .

ETERNITY – "THE thought of thoughts," said St. Augustine. The thought that puts this little life on earth in its proper perspective. The thought that will not get into our little heads. The thought that we shall never grasp, yet which helps us to grasp a multitude of other thoughts – the thought of eternity.

Catholics know with certainty that we human beings are composed of body and soul, that at death the soul leaves the body behind, which normally disintegrates without it, that the soul then begins on its own an existence which continues forever. At the end of the world, this soul will be reunited with its body, mysteriously reassembled, and then the two together will either enjoy unimaginable happiness or suffer unspeakable torments, without end . . . without end . . . without end...

Preachers have resorted to a variety of images to represent this endlessness. For instance, they imagine a blackbird flying back and forth the 236,000 miles between the earth and the moon, and each time the bird lands on the moon, it pecks away a lunar fragment, then flies back to earth, and so on. The preachers then ask, how long will it take the blackbird to peck away the whole moon? And when it has done so, will eternity even have started?

— 343 —

Richard N. Williamson

Yet no amount of images can succeed in representing the stretch of eternity. Why? Because all creatures, and images of creatures, are by their nature limited, whereas eternity consists precisely in the lack of limitation. But, it may be objected, if God on the one hand destines us to eternity and on the other hand surrounds us with no creatures capable of adequately representing to us that destiny, is He not being contradictory? How can He expect us to strive for a goal which He gives us no means of knowing?

The first part of the answer is that God wants all of us human beings to get to Heaven (I Tim. 2: 4), because He can have created none of us for any other purpose. This means of course that in some way or other every single human being since Adam and Eve has received grace or graces sufficient to bring that soul to Heaven, if only it chose to co-operate. However, it would be a poor Heaven whose idea could fit inside our little heads, and God means to reward with no small Heaven those who respond freely to His love. That is why St. Paul says, quoting Isaiah (64: 4), "Eye hath not seen, nor ear heard, neither hath it entered into the heart of man, what things God hath prepared for them that love Him" (I Cor. 2: 9).

But the problem remains: how can man be expected to act, in particular to follow the Way of the Cross, for a reward of which he has no idea? Here comes the second part of the answer: man does not have no idea at all of eternity, Heaven and Hell, on the contrary every man has an inkling of them, at least in certain special moments of his life, and this inkling will reach further and further if only he will choose to bend his mind in that direction instead of turning it away. But rather than inkle eternity, most men prefer to short circuit their minds with the pleasures of this life, which is why they fritter their lives away.

And here, following on the thinking of the unthinkable length of eternity, is another huge thought: the <u>value of time</u>. If the whole length of my eternity in the afterworld depends upon my short life in this world, then every moment counts! If whether I spend eternity in Heaven or in Hell depends upon how I spend an average of, say, 70 years on earth, a period which is nothing, but <u>nothing</u>, in comparison, then every single day is a drama of building my Heaven or preparing my Hell!

But how can God let so much depend on, comparatively speaking, so little? How can He make such a limitless and unimaginable consequence depend on so few years of limited images? It is because God knows the innermost secrets of men's hearts, so that even if a man dies in the flower of his youth, he will have lived long enough to make sufficiently, as God knows, his choice between living with God for ever in Heaven or without God for ever in Hell. So at that soul's particular judgment, God will have given to it the eternity it sufficiently chose, and that soul will not be able to deny that the moment of its death was another mercy of God, either to preserve it for Heaven from the dangers of living longer amidst temptations on earth, or to prevent it from falling by a prolonged life of sin much deeper into Hell.

Thus every moment of our brief lives on earth is given to us by God for us either to get out of sin and into the state of grace, or to build up in our souls a higher degree of grace and charity, to which will correspond a higher reward of eternal happiness.

Thus if a soul is living in the grace of God, each new day, every hour of life is a gift of His for us to merit more in eternity. Why else life? We would eat to live, and live to eat? No, we eat on earth to live on earth, and we live on earth to merit for Heaven, and if we make this right use of each moment, who will complain any longer of this life's limitation when it is earning a reward wholly disproportionate by its illimitation? And when Our Lord traces out for us the Way of the Cross as the road to Heaven, who that believes in Him will complain even of a lifetime of suffering? That such suffering should be the way to Heaven is as mysterious as the mystery of sin, but the better I understand Our Lord, the closer I can come to the saints' rejoicing in each moment of pain. War, illness, old age, grief of any kind – it can all be minted into the coinage of Paradise.

Conversely, if a soul is in mortal sin, then without doubt the grace of God is all the time reaching out to it, now very strongly, perhaps most of the time quite faintly, because God will leave the sinful soul free, and He knows that too strong an appeal would merely push the soul into a stronger and more damnable refusal. "Fearful silence of God," said St. Augustine, referring to God's abandoning a soul to its own devices. And again, "Beware of grace passing once, and not twice." Yet, to the very end, God will appeal. Yet how many souls around us only want to drive Him away, and have Him stay away, so that they may sin undisturbed!

This value of time for eternity, for the sinner to repent and for the saint to merit, highlights the length of God's mercy. Knowing how weakened we are by original sin and how much weaker we become by our personal sins, and knowing, as we do not, just what eternity means, God has a boundless compassion on our human frailty. A man may fall again and again and again, but if there is only a spark of true repentance, God can forgive him again and again and again, because this brief life is our only chance, and upon it depends our eternity! "It is appointed to man once to die, and after this the judgment" (Heb. 9: 27). None of us lives or dies twice. Reincarnation is a lie with which the Devil reassures souls wishing to be deceived. But if we live only once, have we not almost a right to God's compassion?

No, compassion should not be defined as something that anyone has a right to on the part of anyone else, least of all on the part of a God continually offended by our sins. Nevertheless in the Old Testament we find an abundance of references to "the mercy of God that endureth for ever," notably Psalm 135, and of course in the New Testament we see Our Lord as the incarnation of compassionate mercy, especially towards sinners: Mary Magdalene, the Prodigal Son, the woman caught in adultery, the good thief on Calvary, etc. It is the same one true God in Old and New Testaments, it is the same mercy, it is the same tireless reaching out of God's Catholic Church towards all souls for their eternal salvation.

And it is the same perversity of men that in most cases responds. A day or two before His crucifixion and death, Our Lord has run into the Temple leaders' deicidal hatred, in which He knows they will be followed by the ordinary people on whom He has lavished so great benefits for the three years of His ministry – "Jerusalem, Jerusalem, thou that killest the prophets, and stonest them that are sent unto thee, how often would I have gathered thy children, as the hen doth gather her chickens under her wings, and thou wouldest not? Behold, your house shall be left to you desolate" (Mt. 23: 37, 38). The Sacred Heart is broken with grief at the thought of souls then and now to whom He made salvation so easy of access, yet who prefer their eternal damnation.

Divine Heart of Jesus, torn with sorrow for the everlasting perdition chosen by so many souls, and, even after death, shedding upon the Cross the last drop of your blood to draw us towards everlasting happiness with you, grant us we beseech you so to ponder on our souls' eternal destiny and so to cling to your Mercy for their eternal salvation, that when our souls are laid bare at death in the unsparing light of your judgment, still we may have full confidence in our sins being forgiven by that divine Mercy that endureth for ever, Amen.

Dear men, there are two five-day Ignatian retreats at the seminary this summer to give a frame to meditation on these and other grand truths (July 7–12, and 14–19), and there is a study session on three encyclicals of John Paul II (*Divini Redemptoris, Dives in Misericordia, Dominum et Vivificantem*), to help study in depth how far the Newchurch is departing from these Catholic truths (July 22–26). But the hand of God is not shortened by the naughtiness of men (Is. 50: 2).

Two Rumors – And More to Come?

A S WAS PREDICTABLE and predicted, Rome is not leaving the SSPX alone. As a Newchurch Cardinal puts it, "We can have no peace, as long as the SSPX is doing its thing." By carrot or stick, the Newchurch must somehow derail the SSPX, however numerically insignificant the SSPX may be, otherwise what the SSPX represents will sooner or later derail the Newchurch, as is already happening.

In the last few weeks two rumors have come flying out of Rome, one to the effect that three of the four SSPX bishops will be "reincommunicated" at a public Tridentine Mass to be celebrated by Cardinal Castrillón in a major Roman basilica on Saturday, May 24; the other to the effect that the Tridentine Mass Indult will be extended to all Catholic priests before the end of this calendar year, 2003. Whether Rome meant these rumors to be true, or whether Rome can make them come true, perhaps only God knows. In any case, both rumors are of a nature to put the SSPX under pressure, and since many more like them could be aimed at rocking the SSPX off its hinges, then we need to keep our Catholic wits about

Richard N. Williamson

us. At the risk of saying once more things I have said already, even many times, let me attempt to explain why, even if Rome is seeming to be extremely generous, the SSPX must be extremely careful.

The root of the problem is the "modernization" of the Catholic Church launched – or at least manifested – in the 1960's by the Second Vatican Council (1962–1965) whose 16 documents revolutionized Catholic <u>teaching</u>, and by the New Order of Mass (1969) which revolutionized the essence of the Church's <u>practice</u>, namely the liturgy of the Mass. Since it is in Catholic principles that the Church cannot change, then the modernizers pretended and still pretend that the updating changed nothing essential. However, modernized "Catholics" bear so little resemblance to old-fashioned Catholics, that the change clearly was essential, and in retrospect Vatican II and the New Mass were clearly laying the foundations of what was meant to be a new religion.

Now the old God-centered Catholic religion and the new man-centered Conciliar religion contradict one another, and as all wars are ultimately religious, so a contradiction of religions can only mean war. The Conciliarists owe it to their new faith to root out and destroy the old Faith, while Catholics are in duty bound to refuse and to condemn the false new religion with all its pomps and all its works. That is why soon after Vatican II, Conciliarists were pretending that it was the most important Council in Church history, while a small number of Catholics were denouncing it as the introduction into the Catholic Church of the anti-Catholic principles of the modern world. Similarly in 1969 the Conciliarist Pope Paul VI pretended that the old Mass was done away with, while a handful of Catholic bishops and priests kept it alive, notably – but not solely – Archbishop Lefebvre and the SSPX which he founded.

Here is the heart of the problem which must never be lost from view. We have a war between two religions which can only come to an end with the death of the one or the other. The Catholics must fight this war with the weapons of Truth. The Conciliarists may fight it by any means available to them. By God's just punishment of many Catholics' lukewarmness, the Conciliarists have been allowed to occupy nearly all positions of power and influence within the structure of the Church. These they have used to the full to establish their new religion.

However, the Catholics had and have on their side the Truth, which "is mighty and will prevail." The Conciliarists were unable to stop Archbishop Lefebvre from denouncing Vatican II and from saving the old Mass. They have so far proved unable to stop his SSPX from continuing to do the same. But the survival of their new religion depends upon the destruction of that old religion which clearly shows Vatican II and the New Mass to be false. Therefore they must destroy, break up, cripple or corrupt the SSPX, which presents for the moment the largest organized resistance to Conciliarism.

One obvious strategy for the Romans is as old as the hills: "Divide and rule." Hence the first rumor, pretending that three of the SSPX's four bishops think one way, while the fourth thinks another way. But first one and then another of the three bishops said it was all nonsense, and the third would no doubt have publicly said so too, but he probably could not be bothered. (As for that fourth, he basked in the publicity!) And if, as the rumor had it, Rome thinks that 70% of the SSPX priests would be happy to be "reincommunicated" with the supposed three bishops, then Rome knows our priests as little as it knows our bishops.

The second rumor represents another strategy, also as old as the hills: "Smother them in kindness," e.g., promise to grant in 2003 the pre-condition demanded

Richard N. Williamson

in 2001 by the SSPX for entering upon negotiations with Rome, namely the permission for all priests freely to use the old rite of Mass. Now whether Rome could follow through on such a promise in the teeth of the opposition of a significant proportion of the world's Conciliar bishops, is less than sure. But if it could, then the SSPX would only rejoice that the free use of the true rite of Mass would mean a steadily increasing flow of grace throughout the Church, as priests realized what a treasure had been put back in their hands. However, even if Rome also "reincommunicated" all four SSPX bishops, the other pre-condition of 2001, still the SSPX engaged itself in 2001 only to enter upon negotiations for its reconciliation with this Rome, and almost certainly the Conciliarists would now insist upon the SSPX in some way recognizing Vatican II, which the SSPX cannot do. The very documents of that Council, not just its aftermath, are shot through with the new religion.

Nevertheless, the strategy of "smothering with kindness" presents real advantages for Rome. Supposing Rome overrode its own bishops and unilaterally declared, "The SSPX is simply reconciled with Rome and readmitted into the Church, including all four bishops, without conditions, without demands"!? What would the SSPX do then? If the SSPX refused, it would really look churlish. But if it accepted, there would be an end to our present protective marginalization, and there would be a mass of contaminating contacts with "Catholics" who, having no grasp of the problem of Conciliarism, have no real grasp on true Catholicism. It could mean the end of the SSPX's defending the Faith.

Such a proposition from Rome might be unlikely, or impossible, but, to cripple the SSPX, it might be the smartest thing that they could do. In any case it highlights the central, central problem. Even if these Romans were to speak exactly the same language as the SSPX, still, by their modernist religion, they would not be meaning the same things. Therefore the "reconciliation" would be verbal, not real, and the SSPX would have lost the protection of its present marginalization.

Then why even think of sitting down to negotiate anything with these Romans? Firstly, "they occupy the chair of Moses" (Mt 23: 2), so they have a huge influence upon the eternal salvation or damnation of millions of souls. Secondly, they have, with these huge responsibilities, souls of their own to be saved, and one or other of them may just be able still to profit from contact with anti-Conciliar Catholics. That is why Archbishop Lefebvre maintained contacts with the Romans all the way down to May of 1988.

However, these contacts came to an end with the Episcopal Consecrations of that June, by when, as the Archbishop said, Rome had demonstrated by its actions such an uncare for souls that the problem had decisively moved out of the domain of diplomacy, into the domain of dogma. So whenever a Cardinal Castrillón Hoyos now insists upon diplomacy, he is from our point of view queering any contacts before they even start. For were the SSPX to negotiate on anything less than dogma, the results would prove deadly for the Faith, as has just been seen once more with the priests of Campos, Brazil.

But can non-elastic dogma be even conceived by elastic minds, for which words have no non-elastic meaning? Personally, I think that the mass of minds today are so far gone in fantasy that only a Chastisement will bring them back to reality, and to do this it will have to take a large number of souls out of this life. Pray meanwhile, dear readers, that the SSPX do what God wants of it.

The special insidiousness of Conciliarism by its apparent resemblance to Catholicism will be a main object of study in the Men's Doctrinal Session to be held at Winona this summer from Tuesday, July 22, to Saturday,

Richard N. Williamson

July 26 (I apologize for a mistake over these dates in the last retreats flyer). The subject will be difficult, three major encyclicals of John Paul II, on God the Father, God the Son and God the Holy Ghost, but the books of Prof. Dörmann will be our clear guide. These books are available from the Angelus Press.

Let us for the month of May especially implore the help and protection of the Mother of God, and let us pray her Rosary to help her obtain the salvation of millions of souls floundering in a world of confusion.

Karl Rahner – Prime Delinquent

SINCE THIS LETTER is set fair to be one of the last monthly letters from the Seminary that I am likely to pen, then let me attempt to give one more overview of the false religion that has been devastating the Catholic Church for the last 40 years in the wake of Vatican II.

For when the Conciliar hurricane struck the Church in the early 1960's, the immediate and pressing need for true Catholics was to protect the true Mass, and the true priesthood that goes with it, from the grave threat of their extinction by the ensuing Novus Ordo Mass (1969). Only when the survival of the Catholic Mass and priesthood was guaranteed some years later were Traditionally-minded Catholics able to look farther, so to speak, and ask themselves where the hurricane came from. They had had to begin by parrying this or that horror of the Novus Ordo. Only now they are starting to fit all the horrors together.

For indeed the diverse horrors of the Conciliar Revolution do fit together. They could never have attained their hurricane-force to almost destroy the Church, had not each horror reinforced the others, providing a united system of errors to replace Catholicism even while resembling it! The new religion of Vatican II and the Novus Ordo is a masterpiece of the Devil!

Two recent analyses of the Conciliar religion as a whole are to be found in Professor Johannes Dörmann's four-volume series on the theological way of Pope John Paul II to the Assisi meeting of religions in 1986, and in the small but dense book on the problem of the liturgical reform, put out by SSPX priests in 2001. These two analyses were made quite independently of one another, but they are remarkably similar in their presentation of Vatican II and the Novus Ordo as the same system of error (both books are available from the Angelus Press in Kansas City, USA).

Now has come another such analysis, this time by an American layman, *A Critical Examination of the Theology of Karl Rahner, S.J.*, by Robert McCarthy. The German Fr. Rahner was one of the very most important "periti" or expert theologians at the Council, on which he had an enormous influence. Mr. McCarthy is a Catholic from Texas in his late 70's who, according to a biographical note in his book, has been puzzling for years over what made Vatican II tick. His little book on Rahner is remarkably readable, makes perfect sense, and presents an analysis wholly corresponding to the two analyses mentioned above. We have three hunters on the trail of the same beast! The beast should be driven from cover before long!

McCarthy's "Critical Examination" is remarkably readable insofar as the writings of Rahner himself are notoriously obscure. Scholars may then dismiss McCarthy's book on the grounds that McCarthy reads no German, so he has had to base his analysis largely on English translations of summaries of Rahner's thinking by two of his German disciples. However Catholics who love their Church know that Vatican II left it in ruins, so if Rahner was one of those responsible, then either English is a surprisingly poor language, or what Rahner said and did must be discernible and describable in English. The question is not just a matter for scholars or a problem of language – it is a question of all-important Truth! So McCarthy's "Examination" may only be a summary of summaries, but if it fits the facts and responds to the ruins, then it is what we need.

Rahner, says McCarthy, started out from a hatred for that old Church and for that old Faith which descended by Revelation from God down to man. He held them to be wholly unfit for modern man, so he set about rediscovering Church and Faith in such a way as would fit modern man. Instead then of working, as Catholics always do, from God down to man to lift up man to God, Rahner set about working from modern man up to God so as to bring God down in a version of God acceptable to modern man. As a disciple of Rahner says, "Rahner himself has said that theology often gives the impression nowadays of providing mythological or at least unscientific answers... The theologian can only overcome this . . . by beginning with man and his experiences."

Notice that this principle of turning to man, as it lies at the heart of Rahner's whole system, so too it is the basis of the novelties of Vatican II which put man in the place of God. Modern man feels that he does not get enough credit from God, so with his <u>feelings</u> he will do an end-run around his Catholic faith.

Thus modern man feels himself to be not a bad guy, in fact he feels he is quite a good guy, so he can no longer believe in the old Catholic dogma of original sin, nor can he any longer believe that God's supernature, or supernatural grace, is so far above his own nature. Based on this feeling, or these "experiences," of modern man, Rahner comes up with his doctrine of the "supernatu-

ral existential," meaning that instead of original sin existing in man's nature, it is the supernatural, or grace,
which exists in, or is built into, man's nature!

Thus Rahner, by starting from modern man's wonderful feeling about himself, has arrived immediately at
those two major heresies of which Donoso Cortés said
that they lie at the root of nearly all modern heresies: the
denial of the supernatural and the denial of original sin.
Now as a Catholic priest and theologian, Rahner could
not come clean with such an overthrow of basic Catholic truth. Here, says McCarthy, is the explanation of
Rahner's almost impenetrable obscurity, and his invention of phrases like "supernatural existential." However,
what is obscure in the master is made clear by the disciples. Similarly Vatican II could not come clean with its
overthrow of the old religion, because it had to pretend
to be still Catholic, but that overthrow, which is ambiguous in the Council's 16 documents, is clear for all to see
in the Council's fruits.

From Rahner's doctrine of the "supernatural existential" whereby grace and not the inclination to sin is
built into man's nature, it necessarily follows that every
human being, whether he knows it or not, or wants it
or not, is in the state of grace, in God's grace! Logically,
Rahner concludes that all non-Christians are "anonymous Christians", i.e., Christians without the name!

From which again it follows that if Jesus Christ's
Church is the society of all Christians, then Christ's
Church includes every human being! Therefore what
Catholics always used to call the Catholic Church is
for Rahner only a part of Christ's full Church, which
is co-terminous with mankind. That is why in "*Lumen
Gentium*" Vatican II decreed that Christ's Church is not
identical with the Catholic Church, but merely "subsists
in" the Catholic Church, in such a way that Christ's full
Church can go way outside the Catholic Church and

include, or be present in, all kinds of other churches – or non-churches – as well! Here is the so-called "ecumenism" which is still ruining true Catholicism. Thus Vatican II followed Rahner in his total revolutionizing of the concept of the Catholic Church.

But if man is so wonderful as to have grace built into his nature, what need does he have of redemption or Redeemer? For Rahner as for modern man, evolution is true, so the wonderfulness of man means that he is always evolving higher, i.e., he is always from within himself rising above and beyond himself. Jesus Christ is simply that person in whom man evolved to the full above himself, i.e., into what men call divinity! And if man had not achieved this total self-transcendence in the person of the carpenter from Galilee, he would have achieved it or would achieve it in some other person at some other point in history! By this doctrine of God no longer coming down into human nature but of man instead evolving up into divine nature, Rahner fits together evolution and his turn to man, but he stands the Incarnation on its head!

Rahner similarly empties out the redemption, or the Cross. If modern man feels he is so wonderful, how can he feel that he sins, or does anything that really offends God? Besides – pardon the blasphemy! – God is a good guy like himself, so would not get upset anyway! Then how can man need to have been rescued from God's wrath by Our Lord dying for him on the Cross? Then what was the Cross for Rahner? McCarthy does not say, but maybe it was what Dörmann says it is for John Paul II (Redemptor Hominis) – a merely back-up demonstration of God's super-luv for man!

Then for Rahner what are the Mass and the Catholic Priesthood? Since man has the "supernatural existential" or the grace of God built into him, then he needs neither atoning sacrifice nor sacrificing priesthood. So priests come, again, not from above but from below; they come not from a divinely instituted anointing or Sacrament of Orders lifting them above their fellow men, but from their fellow-believers around them freely consenting to their position. So for Rahner priests should be ready to hold a worldly job to demonstrate that they are on the level with their fellow men. Hence the Vatican II priests we know, in lay jobs and in lay clothing. Conciliarism is Protestantism.

As for the Mass, McCarthy presents no specifically Rahnerian doctrine, but it stands to Rahnerian reason that sinners supposedly needing, for forgiveness, to partake in offering, through an anointed priest, a sacrifice to placate the anger of an infinite and offended God, no longer makes any sense to modern man. Rather we shall have good guys gathering in fellowship to share in a meal presided over by one of their own number (man or woman!) to express their caring and sharing – the Novus Ordo eucharistic picnic!

Lord, have mercy upon us! McCarthy's book is available from Tradition in Action. Warmly recommended for anyone who wishes to puzzle out today's devastation of the Catholic Church.

This is one of the last Seminary letters your servant will write, because this August he is being appointed to head up the Society's Seminary in the Argentine, South America. Last April he had been for 20 years Rector of the SSPX Seminary in the USA, which is long enough for any priest to stay in one position. From September his successor in Winona, Fr. Yves Le Roux, who may or may not continue this series of monthly letters, but you are begged not to interrupt the flow of your generosity which has made possible the Seminary's work for these 20 years: two new priests this June 21, Saturday, and some each year thereafter.

Thank you all, and God bless you.

Liberalism is a Killer

N EXT MONTH INCLUDES (August 4) the 100ᵗʰ anniversary of the election to the Papacy of Cardinal Giuseppe Sarto, i.e., St. Pius X, patron of
our Priestly Society. Digging out for a colleague a past
Seminary Letter on the true charity of Pius X, I see that
in August of 1996 I told briefly the story of his clash with
Cardinal Ferrari of Milan, but I did not draw out all the
implications. The problem is central to our times. In
honor of St. Pius, let me tell the story again, still more
briefly, with a secular parallel from the post-war United
States.

In 1910, three years after the appearance of Pope
Pius X's great anti-modernist Encyclical letter *Pascendi*, two loyal Italian Monsignors, the Scotton Brothers,
published in their anti-modernist review an article declaring – not without foundation – that the seminary in
Cardinal Ferrari's Archdiocese of Milan was "a seed-bed
of modernism," i.e., of that mother of all heresies which
preserves the appearances of Catholicism but empties
out the substance, in order to adapt the Catholic Church
to the modern world.

The Cardinal was indignant. How could a supposedly
Catholic journal so attack the honor and integrity of the

Seminary Professors and their Superiors, including himself? When Pius X replied through his Cardinal De Lai, amongst other things, that there was not a little modernism in the archdiocese of Milan, the Liberals profited by the controversy to create a media uproar. In early March, both parties appealed to Rome, and Cardinal Ferrari defended the Liberal Catholic paper of Milan, *The Union*, because he sensed it was being called in question.

At the end of March, Pius X wrote himself to the Cardinal, saying that the modernism provoking the Scotton brothers in the archdiocese of Milan might not be doctrinal but it was practical, i.e., good doctrine might be taught, but it was not being applied in practice, for instance when so many of the Milan clergy supported *The Union*, a newspaper leaving much to be desired from a Catholic point of view. Yet less than three weeks after receiving this letter, the Cardinal vigorously defended *The Union* in front of his Milan seminarians, and said that this defense was in accordance with the Pope's will! When Pius X learned of the Cardinal's reaction, he was scandalized and deeply hurt: here was a Cardinal deceiving his future priests as to the will of the Pope, so that they would soon be spreading Liberal ideas throughout the Archdiocese in the name of the Pope! When in turn the Cardinal learned of the Pope's reaction, he replied with a flood of tears, and now I must quote the August 1996 letter in full:

> He was broken-hearted to have offended the Pope. He was humiliated. He would be saddened to the end of his days. He begged forgiveness. He never meant to hurt the Pope. He never said a word disrespectful to the Pope, etc., etc. . . . As for what he said to his seminarians, he never meant it to be copied down or published. All he meant to say was that *The Union* should go on improving. There had been no significant scan-

dal in the Archdiocese. He was ready to take back anything he said, and would come to Rome if necessary. When Pius X read this letter, he replied that there had in fact been great scandal in the Milan Archdiocese because the Cardinal's defense of *The Union* had been clear, and clearly understood. So let the Cardinal correct the scandal by conveying the Pope's real thinking to all concerned, but let him not come to Rome.

This last instruction was intended to calm the agitation, so that the controversy might die a quiet death, but the Liberals turned it into a refusal of the Pope to listen to his Cardinals! Thus when on the death of Pius X Cardinal Ferrari went down to Rome for the conclave to elect his successor, to an Italian senator remarking on the people's emotion and veneration for the deceased Pope, the Cardinal sternly replied: 'Yes, but he will have to give an account to God for the way in which he would abandon his bishops in the face of accusations being made against them'! Truly, as Msgr. Begnini said, Cardinal Ferrari had understood nothing.

Now what are the implications that I did not spell out in 1996? Between Pius X and Cardinal Ferrari we have a clash between two worlds: one of Catholic reality, of man serving God; the other of Liberal dreamery, of God serving man. Pius X is concerned with the issues, the Cardinal is concerned with personal feelings. Pius X worries that the good doctrine is not put into practice in Milan; that the Cardinal's defending *The Union* would spread liberal ideas; that the Cardinal should straighten out the scandal of mistaken thinking. On the contrary the Cardinal takes the Scotton accusation as a personal attack upon his subordinates and himself; when the Pope is scandalized by his defense of *The Union*, he is overcome with personal feelings ("broken-hearted", "humiliated", "saddened") and fanfares his good intentions: when the Pope does not want to see him, he <u>feels</u> <u>personally</u> betrayed ("abandoned") by his Superior.

There is a famous quotation of the arch-Romantic English poet, John Keats (1795–1821):- "I am certain of nothing but the holiness of the heart's affections and the truth of imagination" (Letter to Benjamin Bailey). Now when a young poet in a Revolutionary age allows his feelings and imagination to take over, that is, in a manner of speaking, his prerogative. But when an eminent Prince of the Catholic Church allows questions of doctrine to be overtaken in his mind by the conviction of the holiness of his own heart's affections, then we are in trouble! The Revolution is taking over the Church, and the Catholic Faith is being washed out. Sure enough! The Pius X – Cardinal Ferrari clash was finally resolved in 2001 when Pope John Paul II beatified Cardinal Ferrari! In effect, he was declaring the Cardinal's affections to be Blessed! A Catholic Saint? A saint of the world of Keats!

The secular parallel from the post-war United States is the clash which took place in Washington , D.C., in the late 1940's between Whittaker Chambers and Alger Hiss. Whittaker Chambers' book *Witness* is a classic of US history, culture and literature, which should be studied in every American school, but because it refuses the modern dream, it is disappearing down the memory hole. Chambers was not a Catholic, but he had real and deep insight into the soul of modern man.

Born in Philadelphia, PA, in 1901, and reared in a more or less unhappy middle-class home on Long Island, NY, Chambers had a serious and searching mind which led him as a university student in the 1920's to tour Europe's centers of culture in pursuit of an answer to what seemed to him a grave crisis of Western Civilization. But post-WWI Europe had no answer either, which is why in the 1930's, like many another desperate young man, he joined the Communist Party. Within the Communist underground which he served with distinction for several years, he met and befriended an equally brilliant rising D.C. bureaucrat, by name Alger Hiss. The two worked together, until Stalin's Great Purge in 1937 and 1938 opened Chambers' eyes and drove him out of the Communist Party and out of Communism. He went to ground until the Communists no longer risked killing him, and had quietly resurfaced in the late 1940's as a journalist with *Time* in New York. Meanwhile Alger Hiss had gone on to make a brilliant wartime and postwar career in Washington, partaking for instance at the highest level in the Conference of Yalta and in the constituting of the United Nations.

Chambers and Hiss met again in August of 1948 when Chambers stepped forward out of his obscurity into blazing publicity in D.C. to give witness that Hiss, while in the US Department of State, had helped to transmit confidential government documents to the Russians. Hiss denied that he had ever even met Chambers! But Hiss was finally convicted of perjury in January of 1950, and sentenced to a five-year prison term. He died only a few years ago, still protesting his innocence, remaining no doubt still convinced of the holiness of his heart's affections! Chambers died a sad man in 1961, sure that his cause was doomed to perish.

The Chambers-Hiss clash was again a clash between two worlds, between two Americas. As Pius X represented the centuries-old true Church while Cardinal Ferrari represented in effect the looming Church of Vatican II, so the dumpy little Chambers represented all the decent little folk across the United States while Hiss, darling of the DC and NY Establishment, represented the Liberal-Communist march towards the New World Order. When Chambers quit Communism, without the Catholic Faith, he clearly saw that he was joining the losing side. His agonizing decision to testify against Hiss was a

Richard N. Williamson

noble but desperate gesture, made in the hope of obtaining for civilization no more than a slight reprieve. In this Chambers succeeded when we think of US anti-communism in the 1950's, but, of course, anti-communism without the Catholic Faith has no long future, so by the 1960's the Liberal-Communist march to the Brave New World was more irreversible than ever.

Insights abound in Chambers' *Witness* but here are two that could come straight out of pre-Vatican II Papal Encyclicals: communism is a religious problem, and all liberals are virtual communists. That is why, regardless of the truth or facts of the case, the DC-NY Establishment of liberals rallied to a man behind Hiss, because they knew that if he was condemned, so were they, and with them their substitute-religion of liberalism. That is why, to this day, they will maintain that Hiss was innocent, just as Pope John Paul II innocented Cardinal Ferrari.

Dear readers, the whole world can go the way of Alger Hiss, and nearly all the churchmen can go the way of Cardinal Ferrari, but God remains God and He is neither deceived nor mocked. We may for the moment be like crushed beneath the juggernaut-dream of Alger Hiss and Vatican II, but it will come to an end, whereas God will not come to an end. Patience. Prayer. Tradition is gently stirring again in many a Catholic breast.

Let us pray that the Precious Blood of Jesus descend in July as a laver of regeneration upon more and more souls.

Persevere in Truth

M ANY OF YOU, bless you, have been asking whether on the eve of leaving the United States I plan still to write a monthly letter. If I do, it will certainly not be this letter, which belongs to the seminary and will therefore go to the new Seminary Rector, to do with as he wishes. Nor should anyone interfere with a successor in a post of command by "hanging around." Nor would any letter written for an Argentinian readership be quite the same. But time may have me pick up the pen again – I could even be driven onto the Internet ! But not willingly !

Meanwhile enclosed you have the promised poem of farewell. Brother Marcel did the cartoons. I hope he and it suggest how much I have enjoyed my 21 years in the United States, and I thank all of you for your support and friendship. When I get to the Argentine, I shall need a hole-in-the-heart operation – the hole left by all of you! Lest however the light-hearted poem give anyone to think that this time I have really lost my marbles, let me sketch out one last time the serious danger represented by today's Rome.

I can remember Malcolm Muggeridge saying that just when the modern world had proved itself a busted flush in the aftermath of WWII, and just when the Catholic Church could and should have accepted the world's unconditional surrender to her Truth, just then the Catholic churchmen themselves surrendered at the Second Vatican Council, and went over to those modern principles which are the dissolution of Catholicism. Similarly today, Vatican II is proving for steadily more souls of good will to be a busted flush, and the SSPX's stand for the Catholic truth is coming closer to being widely recognized as such. This is just not the moment for the Society to lay down its arms and go over to the Conciliar enemy! Yet that is just what the Devil has in mind!

For as in a tug-of-war between two teams of eight men, the anchorman with the end of the rope wrapped around his midriff is usually big, fat and correspondingly ugly, but he is still the most important man on the rope, so in the tug-of-war between Vatican II's Conciliarism and (Traditional) Catholicism, the SSPX acts as Tradition's anchorman, so that it may in the eyes of all kinds of people – especially "conservative" Catholics – appear to be fat and "disobedient" and ugly and "schismatic," but the fact remains that those "conservatives" would have no rope on which to pull against Conciliarism unless the SSPX were acting as Tradition's anchor-man.

Which means that the Romans tugging the Church away from Tradition must at all costs undo the SSPX. In 1988 they pretended to use the biggest stick available to them as churchmen: a declaration (false) that the SSPX leadership was "excommunicated." Alas, the SSPX failed to disintegrate, even when its great Founder died in 1991, so Rome resorted to a policy of smothering the Society in silence and neglect. Alas, the SSPX would still not wither away, so when its perseverance generated for the Jubilee Year of 2000 what was surely the largest integrally Catholic pilgrimage to Rome of the whole Jubilee, even the Romans could neglect the Society no longer, so they switched from stick to carrot.

Accordingly, since 2000 the SSPX has been subjected to wave upon wave of what the French call "a charm offensive," or assault by charm. The Big Bad Wolf began to coo like a dove! – "Dear SSPX, we love you, we need you, do come in from the cold!" But the SSPX in its little red riding hood has not budged so far. Why not? To explain this crucial point I have before resorted to a comparison with arithmetic. Let me now extend and expand that comparison. I imagine a dialogue between an updated Roman and a true Catholic:

Catholic: If I am to follow you in arithmetic, I need to know you are a true arithmetician. Please make a profession of your two-times table, up to 20.

Roman: 2x2=4; 2x3=6; 2x4=9; 2x5=10; 2x6=13; 2x7=14; 2x8=19; 2x9=18; 2x10=20.

Catholic: I am afraid you have made three mistakes. Kindly repeat.

Roman: (He corrects all except 2x8=19).

Catholic: (Respectfully) I fear you have still made a mistake. 2x8 are not 19.

Roman: (Gently) No, 2x8=19. That is not a mistake.

Catholic: (Still respectfully) But how can you say such a thing? If 2x8 were 19, they would be more than 2x9!

Roman: (As if inspired) Ah, but I FEEL that 2x8 are 19. That is my inward EXPERIENCE and my personal NEED!

Catholic: (Puzzled) But then what makes you say that 2x2=4?

Roman: (Enthusiastically) Just the same, my inward EXPERIENCE and my personal NEED!

Catholic: (Shocked) But the two-times table, like every other part of the multiplication table, rests upon objective reality!

Roman: (A little exasperated) Of course its does, but objective reality must still be <u>assimilated</u> by me, i.e. it must become my personal EXPERIENCE.

Catholic: (Slowly) So if today you "assimilate" that 2x2 are 4, but tomorrow "assimilated" that they were 5, then to-morrow they would be 5?

Roman: (Triumphantly) Exactly! What value would any arithmetical table have if it was not assimilated by me in accordance with my present needs?

Catholic: (Jumping up, and jamming on his base-ball-cap sideways!) Get me outa' here! You're CRAZY! (Exit, as fast as his legs can carry him.)

Notice three things. Firstly, the comparison between arithmetic and Catholic dogma is apposite, insofar as both are a <u>connected</u> body of <u>objective</u> truths. Thus as the single error that 2x8=19 is enough, if applied enough, to destroy all arithmetic (then 2x8 is greater than 2x9, so 8 is greater than 9, etc., etc.), so the denial of a single Catholic dogma is enough to destroy the entire Catholic Faith (dogmas also interlock), and he who denies a single dogma is a heretic.

Secondly – worse – notice in our comparison how close our Roman seemed to come to objective reality. Had he corrected all three errors and not just two, or had he from the outset recited correctly the whole two-times table, then our Catholic might have thought he was dealing with a Roman Catholic and not with a Roman modernist. Only our Roman's insistence upon 2x8=19 drove our Catholic to discover that our Roman rested his <u>entire</u> multiplication table not upon objective reality but upon his personal inward experience and needs! Similarly today's Rome could come closer and closer to resembling outwardly the true Rome, yet if the very basis upon which it seemed to be the true Rome was, for instance, ecumenical need or modern experience, then the Society would still have to not budge an inch!

But how then will we ever know that the Romans are back to professing the true Faith upon its true basis? Archbishop Lefebvre used to reply: when they subscribe to Pius IX's *Quanta Cura* (against liberalism in politics), to Pius X's *Anti-Modernist Oath* (against modernism in religion) and to Pius XI's *Quas Primas* (against secularism in society). And the sure sign of the Romans' subscribing sincerely to these papal documents will be when they have no more problem with the SSPX, assuming always that the latter will not have budged. In other words, until the Romans subscribe as above, any Rome-SSPX agreement is impossible, and once they subscribe, it will no longer be necessary! Meanwhile, as the Romans tug towards Conciliar perdition, the one thing that the "schismatic" anchorman must do is not budge one inch from his "schism"!

Notice thirdly from the comparison with arithmetic another tremendous element of deception in our present situation – our Roman as presented above <u>need not be of ill will</u>. He can be a rabid modernist and still a "very nice guy." Of course the ring leaders of modernism who know exactly what they are doing to detach souls from objective reality, supernatural and natural, are of a diabolical pride and malice, but if our Roman learned from his mother's knee onwards that the multiplication table has an inward basis, how can he think any differently? How can he not be sincere? And if he is sincere, he can be very convincing in defense of his error, as, for instance, Pope John Paul II, Cardinal Ratzinger and Cardinal Castrillón all seem to be (God alone knows for sure what is in the human heart – Jer. 17: 9, 10).

Now no amount of sincerity or niceness can turn objective error into objective truth. For if a man wants to preserve ice, what does it matter how sincere he is in thinking that the best way to do so is to expose it to warm sunshine? It will still melt. However, while subjective sincerity cannot change objective reality, it can be deceiving, highly deceiving. Thus the more innocent or ignorant – "sincere" – these Romans are in what is objectively their deluded fight against Catholic reality, the more dangerous any contacts or negotiations with them can be. The SSPX, like any other defender of the objective Catholic Faith, must today and tomorrow beware like the plague of "nice guys" in Rome. As St. Teresa of Avila said, "I do not need my confessor to be a Saint, I <u>do</u> need him to know his <u>Catholic doctrine</u>."

Should then the SSPX have no contact at all with the Romans? No. Even if a man's mother is a leper, he stays by her bedside, while taking care not to catch the illness which would put an end to his being able to look after her. In May I said that the Romans, as holding authority over the Church, have huge influence and responsibility for millions of souls, and they are not necessarily impervious to the Truth – while there is life, there is hope. To which one can add that if by the grace of God the SSPX possesses the Truth, it is the SSPX's duty to make that Truth – prudently – available and accessible to the churchmen who so need it. Also, that Truth will have the effect of discerning the spirits in Rome, and of dividing the Romans who are truly in good faith from those who are not. But how can the little stone of Truth bring down the giant of error (Dan. 2: 34, 35) if there is no contact?

My dear friends, let us all persevere in the Truth, however much more difficult yet that may become in the next several years. For if we do persevere, our reward in Heaven will go far beyond anything we can imagine. Let us pray for one another. I will not forget the United States. I send you all my blessing as a bishop. Please support my successor in Winona.

So, dear friends, after one and twenty years
I leave the United States, with many tears –

At sixty-three, I've given what I can,
It's time to yield my place to a younger man.
When I came here, I came with heavy heart,
And now with equal sadness I depart.
For when I came, I did not want to leave
Where I had been before. So now I grieve
To quit the scene of one third of my life,
Laden with priestly toil and happy strife.
Yet clearly I remember, when I came,
To three companions on the aeroplane
I said, "I shall in the U.S.A. have fun!"
And that proved true. So now my time is done,
I might expect the same fun where I go,
Except – America's unique, and so
The fun-ny third of my career must end,
As to a serious land my way I wend.
My friends may shed a tear, but not my foes
Who think my leaving terminates their woes.
But let them not exult! "I SHALL RETURN"
As bishop, to ordain and to confirm!
So if the Liberals dare to rise again
I'll thunder, growl, and strike with might and main!
Nor let me hear of women growing S-L-A-C-K,
Or instantaneously I will be back!!
And if they're S-L-A-C-K- ING off when I am dead,
My ghost will come to haunt them, fierce and dread!
Meanwhile, dear U.S. ladies, girls, God bless
Your being so docile with your feminine dress!
Never have men so needed women true!
In Europe they would learn a thing or two
From Yankee gals, in gracious dresses dressed!
Well done! – by your own children you'll be blessed
Who learn what is a mother – NOT A MAN!
Alas, it's difficult to make a plan
For future newsletters. They hardly fit
In countries lacking ripe old Yankee . . . wit!
But trust that I support you from afar.
Men, be good fathers. In the home you are
By God's design the head. Do not wimp out!

Richard N. Williamson

Not only women are meant to be devout!
Be full of God, and lead against the world –
By Catholic men the Devil must be hurled
Back into Hell! Pray hard! Pain's on the way
With shrieks and howls of grief, nor is that day
Far off. Then gird your loins, be strong, stand tall –
Tomorrow has no room for spirits small.
Flee electronics. Stay with real life.
Give time, love and attention to your wife.
Forget "The Sound of Music", silly stuff
Of which the world has had more than enough
So ends the last Newsletter I shall write.
Soon I must fly far South into the night.
Ah, my dear friends! – I feel like I could cry! –
SO LONG! FAREWELL! AUF WIEDERSEHEN!
GOOD BYE!

INDEX

A

Richard N. Williamson

COMBINED INDEX TO THE

LETTERS FROM THE RECTOR SERIES

A

Letters from the Rector Series Index

Americanization, 3:64
American National Conference of Catholic Bishops, 2:104
American Patriot's Catechism, 2:278–284
American priests, 3:259
Amerika, 1:199
Amerio, Romano, 3:113, 3:169, 3:185
Andy Warhol Museum, 4:261, 4:262–263, 4:265
The Angelus, 1:3–4, 1:18, 1:34–35, 1:70, 1:105, 1:185, 2:1, 2:7, 2:42, 2:44, 2:84, 2:166, 2:170, 2:180, 2:183, 2:260, 2:280, 2:331, 3:112, 3:166, 3:290, 4:20, 4:131, 4:187
Anglicanism, 1:134, 3:162, 3:303
Anglicans, 1:157
Anglo-Saxons, 2:280, 3:287
Animus Delendi (Desire to Destroy), 4:202
Animus Delendi I, 4:316
Animus Delendi II, 4:316
anonymous Christians, 2:311, 2:316, 3:112, 4:358
Anthony, Mark, 2:114
anti-abortionists, 2:130
anti-Americanism, 3:96, 3:197
Antichrist, 1:129, 1:176, 1:194, 1:196, 1:197, 1:212, 2:54, 2:95, 2:119, 2:135, 2:150, 2:194, 2:203, 2:204, 2:343, 3:51, 3:133, 3:151, 3:158, 3:172, 3:269, 3:335, 3:336, 4:84
The Antichrist (Fr. Miceli), 1:25
anti-culture, 3:4, 3:5, 4:284
"Antidote to Oklahoma," 3:53
anti-family, 2:271
Anti-Lefebvrists, 2:250, 2:252
anti-liberalism, 2:2, 2:80, 3:48, 3:123, 3:197, 3:289, 4:43, 4:44–45, 4:131, 4:251
anti-modernism, 1:16, 1:56, 1:57, 2:2, 2:11, 2:76, 3:147, 4:279, 4:361
Anti-Modernist Oath, 2:2, 4:279, 4:371
anti-religion, 2:93, 3:47, 4:196, 4:199
anti-Semitism, 3:96, 4:88, 4:99–100
anti-Vietnam War parades, 3:108
apartheid, 2:30
Apologia pro Marcel Lefebvre (Davies), 1:256
apostasy, 2:8, 2:83, 2:124, 2:150, 2:157, 2:227, 2:305, 2:317, 2:394, 2:400, 3:67, 3:101, 3:138, 3:139, 3:172, 3:197, 3:225–226, 3:247, 3:302, 4.25, 4:101, 4:113, 4:115, 4:139, 4:207, 4:276, 4:277, 4:278, 4:304, 4:317
Apostle James, 4:22
apostolic administration, 4:251–252, 4:331, 4:335
Apostolic authority, of Pope, 2:220, 3:44
Apostolic Delegation, in Lisbon, 2:119
Apostolic Penitentiary, 4:76
Apostolic See, 2:107
Approaches, 2:250
Arabs, 4:226
Archbishop of Lyons, 2:3

Letters from the Rector Series Index

Letters from the Rector Series Index

marriages, 1:134–135, 1:188, 1:247, 2:186, 2:208, 2:229, 2:271, 3:235, 4:282, 4:284, *see also* children; families; husbands; wives
  destruction of, 1:30, 1:31, 1:32, 1:135
  mixed marriages, 1:134
  sacramentality of, 2:271
  Swiss marriage law, revision of, 1:135
Marriage Tribunal, 3:273–278
Martinez, Fr., 2:155
Martin, Malachi, 1:223, 1:257, 1:272, 2:190, 3:151, 3:152, 3:153, 3:154, 3:155, 3:156, 3:170, 3:175, 4:255, 4:258
martyrs, 2:373, 3:185
Martyrs of the Coliseum, 1:150
Marxism, 1:164, 2:78
Marx, karl, 2:97
Mary, 1:200, 1:261, 1:268
  experience of birth of Jesus, 1:178–182
Mary Magdalene, 4:256
Masonic Treaty of Versailles, 4:300
Mater Ecclesiae, 2:4
materialism, materialists, 2:30, 2:31, 2:69, 2:88, 2:93, 2:294, 3:71, 3:160, 3:189, 3:215, 4:122–123, 4:240
Matt, Michael, 4:196, 4:198
Mattress Factory, 4:261, 4:263–266
Mayer, Archbishop Augustin, 1:62, 1:65, 1:119
May Ordinations (videotapes), 1:107
McAlvany Intelligence Advisor, 2:92–93
McCarthy, Robert, 4:356–358, 4:360
McGlynn, Judge, 1:152–153
McLuhan, Marshall, 2:261
McMahon, Denis, 1:26
McNabb, Fr. Vincent, 3:243–244
McVeigh, Timothy, 4:224
Measure for Measure (play), 3:224
media, 4:11, 4:22, 4:80, 4:324, *see also* television
  Catholic media, 2:34
  mass media in the US, 4:268
  power of, 1:165
Medina, Cardinal, 4:60, 4:64, 4:178
Melbourne, 2:32
Men's Three-Day Retreat, 1:101
mentevacantists, 2:253
Merton, Fr. Thomas, 3:35
Messori, Vittorio, 4:309
Mexico, 2:158
  earthquake in, 1:121
Miceli, Fr. Vincent, 1:25
Michael, Brother, 2:84, 2:288, 4:105, 4:116, 4:119
Middle Ages, 3:280, 4:24, 4:161, 4:166, 4:214, 4:225
middle-class liberalism, 3:40

Letters from the Rector Series Index

architects of, 2:305-317
executives of, 2:323-234
neo-Nazism, 3:96
neo-paganism, 2:363
The New American Man, A Call to Arms, 2:78
New Arithmetic, 4:332
Newchurch, 3:62, 3:63, 3:64, 3:93, 3:100, 3:112, 3:236, 3:240, 3:247, 3:251,
    3:258, 3:259, 3:264, 3:276, 3:277, 3:294, 3:309, 3:311, 4:48, 4:77, 4:92, 4:94,
    4:119, 4:133, 4:141, 4:197, 4:250, 4:251, 4:255-260, 4:259, 4:273, 4:276,
    4:315, 4:316, 4:348, 4:349
    canonizations, 4:318-323
    against nature, 4:268-274
Newchurchmen, 4:76, 4:78, 4:258
New Deal, 2:99
Newfaith, 3:100
New Frontiers, 2:99
Newman, Cardinal, 4:214, 4:218
New Mass, *see* Novus Ordo Mass (NOM)
Newsday, 1:73
New Testament priesthood, 2:318-322
"New Theology," 2:310, 2:323, 2:324, 2:325, 2:330, 2:331, 2:333
Newthink, 3:102
New World Order, 2:291, 2:366, 3:52, 3:62, 3:64, 3:105, 3:153, 3:155, 3:160,
    3:175, 3:180, 3:201, 3:202, 3:210, 3:294, 4:23, 4:24, 4:225, 4:258, 4:365
New World Religion, 2:56
New Year 1990, message, 2:87-91
New York, 2:151
New York Archdiocese, 2:41
New York City, 3:61
New York Stock Exchange, 4:9
New York stock market, 3:327
New York Times, 1:49, 1:174-175
New Zealand, 2:32
Ngo-dinh-Thuc, Archbishop, 3:95
Nicaragua, Communist Revolution, 1:154, 1:164
Nicene Creed, 4:334
Nick (a teenager's story), 3:1-7
NIF (nice internal feeling), 3:310
Nimes, 2:58-62
1984 (novel), 3:52
Nixon (film), 3:104
Nixon, Richard, 3:117, 4:9
    career of, 3:104-109
Noè, Archbishop Virgilio, 1:56, 1:65, 1:157
Noebel, David, 4:29, 4:33
Nominalism, 2:123
non-Catholic religions, 2:332
non-Catholics, 1:156-157, 3:140
non-Christian religions, 3:112

— 426 —

original sin, 2:186, 2:227, 2:314, 3:23, 3:79, 3:80, 3:100, 3:166, 3:315, 3:316, 4:156, 4:346
Orthodoxy, 4:94, 4:97
Orwell, George, 2:31, 3:52, 4:123
Osaka, 2:68
Ossuary of Douaumont, 2:243, 2:245
Oswald, Lee Harvey, 4:224
Ottaviani, Cardinal, 4:117, 4:118
Ottaviani Intervention, 1:100, 1:114
Our Lady, message from, 3:48–54
Our Lady of Akita, 2:101–105
Our Lady of Fatima, 1:200, 2:98, 2:102, 2:119, 2:150, 2:229, 2:230, 2:231, 2:299, 2:337, 4:103–108
Our Lady of Guadalupe, 2:158
Our Lady of La Salette, 1:100
Our Lady of Lujan, 1:125, 2:262
Our Lady of the Rosary Home School, 2:223
Our Lady of Victory Home School, 2:223

P

Pablo, Fr., 4:188
pacifism, 1:158
paganism, 2:350, 2:362, 2:363, 2:373, 3:201
Palazzini, Cardinal, 1:91, 1:174
Palestine, 2:150
papacy, 1:16, 1:110, 1:268, 4:180
    dissolution of, 3:176
Papal Encyclicals, 3:134
papal infallibility, 1:128–129, 3:173
Papists, 2:130
parents, 3:1, 3:4, 3:83, 3:156, 3:190, 3:202, 4:72, *see also* children; families; young mothers
    responsibilities of, 1:249–250, 3:80
    role in disciplining their children, 3:190
    young parents, 4:280–285
Paris, 4:136
Pascendi, 2:56, 3:145, 4:44, 4:46, 4:361
Pasqualacci, Professor[AQ: Please verify spelling.], 3:99
Pasqualucci, Professor[AQ: Please verify spelling.], 3:100
Passion, 4:255–256
patriotism, 2:246, 2:338, 3:21, 3:64, 4:21, 4:22
Paul, an African Catholic (letter on Consecrations at SSPX), 2:42–45
Paul II, Pope John, 4:356
Paul VI Mass, 3:321
Paul VI, Pope, 1:43, 1:55, 1:56, 1:57–58, 1:65, 1:68, 1:99, 1:114, 2:107, 2:108, 2:109, 2:112, 2:128, 2:220, 2:258, 2:324, 2:325, 2:330, 2:394, 3:85, 3:98, 3:110, 3:111, 3:123, 3:259, 3:293, 3:322, 4:2, 4:15, 4:38, 4:44, 4:57, 4:58, 4:76, 4:164, 4:250, 4:276, 4:309, 4:350

R

Letters from the Rector Series Index